THE
HIDDEN PLACES

of

The South East

Surrey, Sussex and Kent

Edited by
Shane Scott
Front Cover: Bosham Harbour
by Les Darlow

ACKNOWLEDGEMENTS

This book would not have been compiled without the dedicated help of the following:
Elaine, Adele - Administration. Albert, Les & Graham Sarah - Artists. Bob, Jody,
Simon, Lou, Jim, Clare, Adele & Debbie - Research. Leon & Chris- DTP.

All have contributed to what we hope is an interesting, useful and enjoyable publication.

OTHER TITLES IN THIS SERIES

Printed and bound by Guernsey Press, Channel Islands
© M & M PUBLISHING LTD
Tryfan House, Warwick Drive, Hale, Altrincham, Cheshire. WA15 9EA

Introduction

THE HIDDEN PLACES is designed to be an easily used book, taking you, in this instance, on a gentle meander through the beautiful countryside of the South East. However, our books cover many counties and will eventually encompass the whole of the United Kingdom. We have combined descriptions of the well-known and enduring tourist attractions with those more secluded and as yet little known venues, easy to miss unless you know exactly where you are going.

We include hotels, inns, restaurants, various types of accomodation, historic houses, museums, gardens and general attractions throughout this fascinating area, together with our research on the local history. For each attraction there is a line drawing and a brief description of the services offered. A map at the beginning of each chapter shows you each area, with many charming line drawings of the places we found on our journey.

We do not include firm prices or award merits. We merely wish to point out *The Hidden Places* that hopefully will improve your holiday or business trip and tempt you to return. The places featured in this book will we are sure, be pleased if you mention that it was The Hidden Places which prompted you to visit.

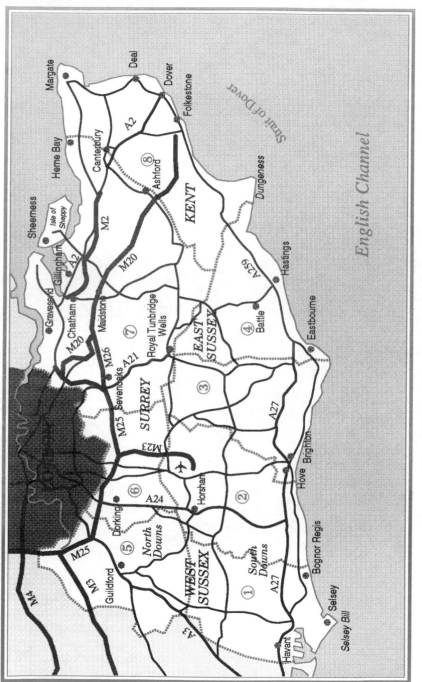

The Hidden Places of the South East.

THE HIDDEN PLACES

OF THE

South East

CONTENTS

West Sussex .

From The Hampshire Border to the River Arun.

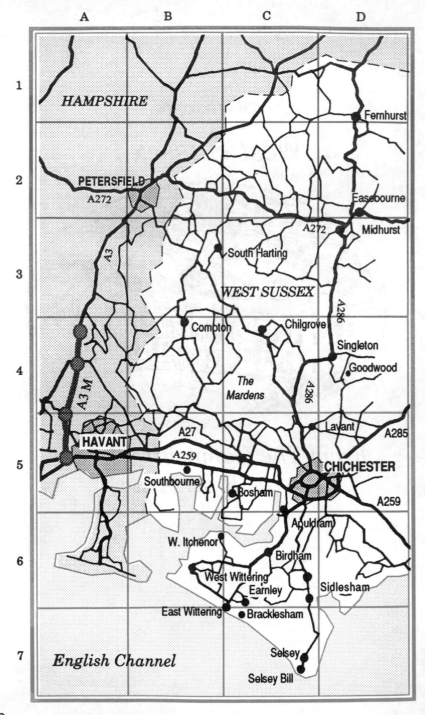

A   B   C   D

HAMPSHIRE

Fernhurst

PETERSFIELD
A272

Easebourne

A272

Midhurst

South Harting

WEST SUSSEX

A286

Compton

Chilgrove

Singleton

Goodwood

The Mardens

A286

Lavant

A285

A27

HAVANT

A259

CHICHESTER

A259

Southbourne

Bosham

Apuldram

W. Itchenor

Birdham

West Wittering

Earnley

Sidlesham

East Wittering

Bracklesham

Selsey

Selsey Bill

English Channel

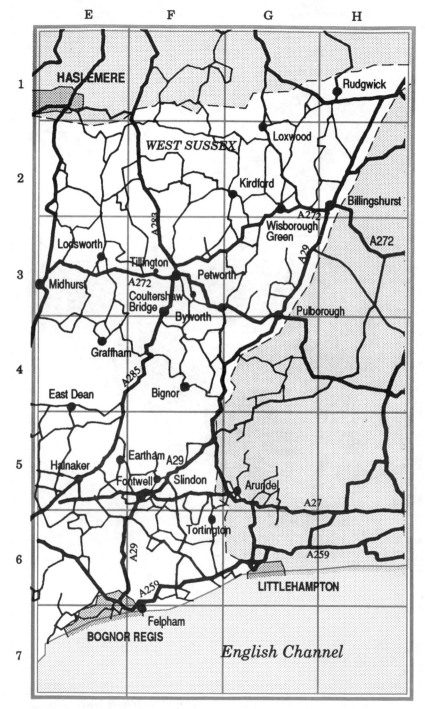

E   F   G   H

HASLEMERE

Rudgwick

WEST SUSSEX

Loxwood

Kirdford

Billingshurst

A272

Wisborough
Green

A29

A272

Lodsworth

Tillington

Petworth

Midhurst

A272

Coultershaw
Bridge

Byworth

Pulborough

Graffham

A285

East Dean

Bignor

Eartham

A29

Halnaker

Fontwell

Slindon

Arundel

A27

Tortington

A29

A259

LITTLEHAMPTON

A259

Felpham

BOGNOR REGIS

English Channel

View from Blackdown towards Telegraph Hill.

West Sussex.
From The Hampshire Border to the River Arun.

Our journey through Sussex, the ancient kingdom of the South Saxons, began along the **A286** Haslemere to Chichester road. A good place to stretch the legs lies just over the Surrey/Sussex border on **Marley Common**, a broad stretch of National Trust-owned sandstone heathland which affords some fine views over the Weald to the South Downs. **Shottermill Ponds**, a pair of interesting hammer ponds, can be found at the foot of nearby Marley Lane.

A couple of miles further south along the A286 we came to **Fernhurst,** a pleasant community with an attractive village green which is surrounded by an assortment of tile-hung cottages. Here, we discovered the first-rate **Red Lion** inn. The Red Lion, resembles a quaint country cottage and indeed, on entering you will find the atmosphere old-fashioned and homely. Overlooking the village green, with plenty of parking at the front, this is the oldest pub in Fernhurst and has been there for some 400 years. In former times, the landlord had his own horse and cart which he used to collect the beer, but today The Red Lion is much more than just an alehouse, and landlady Brenda Heath provides first class food in the pub's restaurant. Braised Pigeon and Sticky Toffee Pudding are just two of the mouthwatering options available, but whatever your choice, you won't leave The Red Lion feeling hungry! And you'll enjoy the warm welcome.

To the east of Fernhurst, **Black Down** (or Blackdown Hill) rises abruptly from the Sussex Weald. The slopes of this 919ft National Trust-owned sandstone hill are covered in heather, gorse, silver birch and Scots pine, creating an ideal environment for a variety of upland birdlife. The summit of Black Down is the highest point in Sussex and from here, there are spectacular views over the Weald and South Downs all the way to the English Channel. A particularly good viewpoint is the group of firs on the southern crest known as the **Temple of the Winds**. One of the paths leading to the top of Black

Down is known as Tennyson's Lane after the famous poet who lived for twenty years at Aldworth House on hill's the eastern slope.

The Red Lion, The Green, Fernhurst, West Sussex 0428 643112
Map Ref: 1D

At one time a Royal Navy signal tower stood on **Tally Knob**, a prominent outcrop which lies to the southeast of the Temple of the Winds. As a development of their tried and tested system of fire beacons, in 1796 the Admiralty introduced the Shutter Telegraph as a more sophisticated means of passing messages between Portsmouth and London. Though ingenious, the system was found to be impractical and was soon abandoned.

From Black Down, we made our way towards **Midhurst**, a quiet and prosperous country town which stands on a sandstone rise five miles to the south. The town possesses a number of noteworthy buildings, including the tall timber-framed Elizabeth House, the 15th-century Spread Eagle coaching inn, and the 19th-century cottage library in Knockhundred Row. This delightfully-named thoroughfare is believed to have been the focal point for the ancient custom of knocking for 100 militia men when there was a call to defend the town. Midhurst's renowned Grammar School was founded in the 1670s in the Old Market Hall. Over two centuries later, it was attended by the young H G Wells when his mother was a housekeeper at nearby Uppark House.

A good place to stop for a drink and bite to eat in Midhurst is the **Crown Inn**. Just off the market Square in the pretty Sussex town of Midhurst stands the charming Crown Inn. This is a warm, friendly establishment run by Paul and Daria Stevens, who ensure The Crown lives up to the name 'freehouse', a place to meet friends and enjoy fine food and drink. The attractive restaurant provides extensive, imaginative menus and a selection of daily specials, whilst for the beer drinker Paul serves a wide range of traditional hand-pulled ales.

Half Timbered House at Easebourne.

There is a games room and large function room and the spit roast lamb on the first Sunday of the month always proves popular. Visitors staying here will love the beautifully decorated guest rooms which are situated in the oldest part of the building, dating back to 1580.

The Crown Inn, Edinburgh Square, Midhurst, West Sussex
0730 813462 Map Ref: 3D

The delightful estate village of **Easebourne** lies a mile along the **A272** to the northeast of Midhurst. This is the site of a former Augustinian nunnery which was founded in the 13th-century and prospered until 1478 when the prioress and two of her nuns were accused of 'gross immorality' and of squandering the income of the priory on 'hunting and extravagant entertaining'. Parts of the mediaeval institution have survived as the parish church, vicarage and garden. Along with its picturesque collection of yellow-painted estate cottages, Easebourne contains another building with a unusual history, **Budgenor Lodge**. This was built in 1793 as a model workhouse for the Easebourne union of parishes and in its day, was much admired by groups of visiting dignitaries.

Returning to the A272 Petworth road, we continued eastwards and soon passed the ruins of **Cowdray House**. This once-magnificent courtyard mansion was built of local sandstone around 1530 by the Earl of Southampton on the site of an earlier 13th-century manor house. Henry VIII stayed at Cowdray in 1538, and later in the century, Elizabeth I was a regular visitor. On one occasion, the queen and her entourage were said to have consumed three oxen and 140 geese during a week-long stay, no doubt making her departure something of a relief for her overstretched host, Viscount Montague.

In 1793, Cowdray House was gutted by fire and a week later, its owner, the last Lord Montague, was drowned whilst on a visit to Germany. This fulfilled a legendary curse placed on the owners of

Cowdray House.

Cowdray House by a monk evicted from Battle Abbey by the first owner during Henry VIII's Dissolution of the Monasteries. Today, visitors can view the roofless remains of the east side of the quadrangle court, along with parts of the west side where the turreted three-storey gatehouse remains largely intact. The 17000-acre Cowdray Park is one of the largest private estates in Sussex and is a well-established for venue for summer polo tournaments.

From Cowdray Park, we continued eastwards along the A272 for a couple of miles before turning north to reach **Lodsworth**, a pleasant community which lies beside the River Lod, a small tributary of the River Rother. The village contains some attractive buildings, including a manor house dating from the 13th-century, an early 18th-century Dower House, and a more recent country residence known as the Great House. Despite occupying a wonderful site with views across the valley, the village church of St Peter is rather disappointing.

The Hollist Arms, Lodsworth, Near Petworth, West Sussex
GU28 9BZ 07985 310 Map Ref: 3E

The picturesque village of Lodsworth provides the perfect setting for **The Hollist Arms**, a delightful country pub named after a local 13th century family. The small green opposite has seating around the base of a large tree where you can relax with a drink on warm summer days, whilst for those chillier evenings, the bar and restaurant has a lovely feature inglenook fireplace which enhances the warm welcoming atmosphere of this charming establishment. Here you can choose from a wide selection of ales, including occasional guest beers, whilst the restaurant is ideal for a family meal out where, in addition to a fine Sunday roast, you can savour an excellent a la carte menu which includes the speciality Rainbow Trout, and award-winning Chiddingfold Sausages.

After returning to Midhurst, we decided to explore the western fringe of the county and set off along the A272 Petersfield road. The

10

broad valley of the River Rother to the west of Midhurst was once a densely-wooded area known for its timber and charcoal production. At Trotton, three miles to the west, we crossed an impressive five-arched bridge, the money for which was provided by Thomas, the first Lord Camoys, who accompanied Henry V on the Agincourt campaign. Completed in the early 1400s, it still carries the busy main road.

Most of the older buildings in Trotton, including the bridge, are constructed of local honey-coloured sandstone. The ancient church of St George stands beside Trotton Bridge; built around 1300, its west wall contains an exceptional wall painting of the Last Judgment dating from the 14th-century. There is also a monumental brass of the first Lord Camoys, as well as one of Margaret, Lady Camoys; dating from around 1310, this is believed to be the earliest such memorial to be dedicated to a woman. The door jambs of the west door are pitted with curious indentations which are thought to have been made by local bowmen honing their arrows before Sunday archery practice. The church also contains a memorial to Thomas Otway, the 17th-century dramatist who was born in the rectory and died at the age of 33, reputedly of a broken heart after being turned down by the actress, Mrs Barry.

The site of the now-demolished **Durford Abbey** lies close to the country border. This isolated monastery was founded in the 12th-century by a community of Premonstratensian monks, a strict vegetarian order which was founded in 1120 by St Norbert at Prémontré in France. Unlike other institutions which grew hugely wealthy on income from their monastic estates, life at Durford seemed more a matter of survival. In fact, so harsh was the monk's existence that on dissolving the monastery in 1539, Thomas Cromwell's commissioner described Durford as 'the poorest abbey I have seen, far in debt and in decay'.

Although little of the original abbey now remains, the canons of Durford succeeded in leaving an important legacy in the form of three 15th-century bridges over the River Rother. (During the mediaeval period, it was a duty of religious houses to provide and maintain such bridges.) Both Maidenmarsh Bridge near the site of the abbey and Habin Bridge to the south of Rogate are worth a visit; the latter still carries the road to South Harting and consists of four semi-circular arches interspersed with massive stone cutwaters.

A twisting three-mile journey from Habin Bridge led us to **South Harting**, the largest of the three settlements known collectively as the Hartings. South Harting, with its ancient thatched cottages, flint walls and unusually wide main street of fine Georgian (and earlier) houses, must be one of the most attractive village in the South

Downs. Writer Anthony Trollope spent the last two years of his life here, during which time he penned four novels. A pen and paper-knife belonging to the acclaimed 19th-century novelist, creator of *Barchester*, can be seen in the village church of St Mary and St Gabriel.

South Harting's famous church spire is faced with copper shingles, creating a bright verdigris hue which can be seen for miles. Memorials in the church include several to the former owners of the nearby downland estate, Uppark, including one to Sir Henry Fetherstonhaugh. The distinctive war memorial in the churchyard was carved in Portland stone by the renowned modern sculptor and typographer, Eric Gill. Near the entrance to the churchyard, an ancient set of parish stocks can also be found, along with a whipping post complete with three pairs of wrist irons.

South Harting stands at the foot of **Harting Down** beneath the steep scarp slope of the South Downs ridge. The ridge is traversed by the **South Downs Way**, the spectacular long-distance footpath which stretches for over eighty miles from Winchester and Buriton in the west to Beachy Head in the east. Here, the path skirts around **Beacon Hill**, which at 793 feet above sea level is one of the highest points in the Downs. A 2500 year-old rectangular Iron Age hill fort surrounds the summit and from the surviving ramparts, there are spectacular views over the Weald to the north and as far as Chichester's Harbour and Cathedral to the south.

On Treyford Hill, a short distance to the southeast, a line of rounded mounds known as the **Devil's Jumps** can be seen. The name is derived from the superstitious habit of attributing unusual features in the landscape to the work of Satan. In fact, the five larger and two smaller mounds are bell-barrows, Bronze Age burial sites containing the remains of dead tribal leaders who, having been cremated, were then interred in pottery urns.

The **B2146** to the south of South Harting climbs sharply onto the South Downs escarpment. Just beyond the crest, the road passes **Uppark**, a fine late-17th-century country mansion which is now owned by the National Trust. In August 1989, the upper floors were almost completely destroyed by fire, ironically just as a programme of restoration was nearing completion. Most of the largely 18th-century contents were, however, saved and are now in safe storage. At the time of writing, major reconstruction work was being carried at the house which was closed to visitors. However, the gardens, which were landscaped in the early-19th-century by Humphry Repton, are open from early-April to end-September, along with an exhibition and small shop; small admission charge payable (free to National Trust members). During the 1880s, H G Wells spent several years at Uppark where his mother was employed as a housekeeper.

A couple of miles to the south, the B2146 led us to **Compton**, a tranquil settlement of brick and flint buildings which include a church, shop and pub. An exceptional Neolithic long barrow known as **Bevis' Thumb** stands on nearby Telegraph Hill. This mysterious burial site was named by more recent inhabitants of the area after the legendary giant, Bevis, who, according to folklore, crossed the Solent from the Isle of Wight in a single stride and whose weekly diet consisted of an ox washed down with two hogsheads (150 gallons) of beer.

The quiet lanes crisscrossing this section of the west Downs connect four settlements known collectively as **The Mardens**. North Marden's church of St Mary is one of the smallest in Sussex, having only a nave and apse. St Michael's at Up Marden stands on the ancient Pilgrims' Way between Winchester and Chichester; approached through a farmyard, this remotest of churches possesses a delightfully simple 13th-century interior. From East Marden, there is a lovely circular walk through the Forestry Commission's **Wildham Wood**, one of the finest areas of beech and broad-leaved woodlands on the Downs.

On the **B2141**, a mile-and-a-half east of East Marden, we passed through **Chilgrove**, another charming small community with a village green and pub. A pleasant walk to the south of here leads up onto **Bow Hill**, the site of the Iron Age hill fort known as Goosehill Camp whose ancient ramparts can still be made out in the form of two raised earthwork circles.

The narrow country lanes to the east of Chilgrove led us towards **Singleton**, a closely packed community of attractive flint and brick buildings standing on the old Chichester to London road in the valley of the River Lavant. Prior to the Norman invasion, the local manor, one of the largest and wealthiest in England, was owned by Earl Godwin of Wessex, father of the ill-fated King Harold. The village church of St Mary's was built in the 13th-century on the foundations of a Saxon predecessor. Inside, there are a number of interesting monuments, including a pair in Purbeck marble erected in memory of two successive Earls of Arundel who died within two years of each other in the 1540s. Singleton also possesses two fine inns and a characteristic village green with a cricket pitch whose pavilion, an ancient Sussex barn, was moved to its present position from a nearby field.

Singleton is also the home of the famous **Weald and Downland Open Air Museum**, a fascinating collection of rescued historic rural buildings which is situated in a delightful forty-acre parkland setting on the southern edge of the village. Founded in 1971 by J R Armstrong, the museum consists of over thirty structures which were previously under threat of demolition. The exhibits were transported here from a variety of locations throughout southern England and include agricultural buildings from the 15th- and 16th-centuries, Titchfield's old Tudor market hall, a village school, a working water mill, an 18th-century granary and a working blacksmith's workshop. The museum also arranges special demonstrations of rural skills, such as thatching, shearing and charcoal burning. There is also a lovely woodland nature trail and picnic area beside the millpond. Open daily, 11am to 5pm between March and October; Sundays and Wednesdays, 11am to 4pm between November and February; admission charge payable.

A mile or so to the south of Singleton, the land rises towards the ancient hilltop site known as **The Trundle**, one of the four main Neolithic settlements in the county. The twelve-acre site was later fortified during the Iron Age between 300 and 100 BC when massive circular earthwork ramparts and a dry ditch were constructed. The hill fort has two entrances, arranged in such a way as to expose attackers to defensive fire from above. Named after the Old English word for *wheel*, the Trundle enjoys fine views over Chichester, Singleton and nearby Goodwood Racecourse.

The **A286** to the west of Singleton passes the 35-acre **West Dean Gardens**. Here, visitors can enjoy a two-mile circular stroll through St Roche's Arboretum and Park with its fine collection of rare trees and shrubs. There is also an interesting exhibition of antique lawn mowers dating from 1850, including pony-powered mowers and early mechanically-driven garden machinery. Open daily, 11am to 6pm between March and October; admission charge payable.

A couple of miles to the southwest, the B2141 Petersfield to Chichester road passes along the eastern edge of **Kingley Vale National Nature Reserve**. This unique 350-acre forest lies in a shallow valley on the southern slopes of Bow Hill and contains some of the largest and oldest yew trees in Europe. Some examples growing on the valley floor are believed to be over 500 years old and have a girth of up to sixteen feet. The younger trees - a mere 50 to 100 years old - have seeded themselves on the higher slopes, creating a wonderful mile-and-a-half long nature trail through dark and densely-packed woodland. The original yew trees were probably planted for making longbows and arrows, and because of their military significance, they remained under royal protection until the reign of Elizabeth I. Towards the summit of Bow Hill, the trees give way to heather and open heathland; here, a group of four Bronze Age burial mounds (two bell- and two bowl-barrows) can be found which together are known as the King's Graves or **Devil's Humps**.

Just south of the junction of the B2141 and A286 we came to the **Lavants**, two attractive villages which are named after the small river which flows southwards from Singleton to Chichester Harbour. The church of St Nicholas in Mid Lavant contains an interesting 17th-century monument to Lady Mary May by the sculptor John Bushnell. Whilst here, we took the opportunity of calling in at the first-rate pub and eating place, the **Earl of March**.

The Earl of March in Lavant is a charming inn that is at least 300 years old. The spectacular view from here across the Downs is said to be the inspiration for those immortal words 'England's Green and Pleasant Land' which appear in Blake's hymn 'Jerusalem'. The Earl of March has a great deal to offer inside as well, with a magnificent wood panelled bar and a delightful restaurant with a large inglenook fireplace. The beer drinker is definitely spoilt for choice with a selection of over 21 draught beers to choose from and landlord Andrew Laurin also specialises in malt whiskies. Outside there is a pleasant beer garden where parents can enjoy a drink while the children play.

Earl of March, Lavant, Nr. Chichester, West Sussex 0243 774751
Map Ref: 5C

From Lavant, it was only a short drive south along the A286 to **Chichester**, the ancient county town of West Sussex. Founded by the Romans in the first century AD, Chichester still retains its original street plan, its four major thoroughfares - North, East, South and West Streets - intersecting at the point where the **Market Cross** now stands. This ornate fifty-foot octagonal structure was built around 1500 by Bishop Edward Story to provide shelter for traders who came to ply their wares at the city's busy market.

Chichester was used as a base camp by the invading Roman

15

legions who named it *Noviomagus*, the 'new city of the plain'. The Romans were also responsible for constructing Chichester's city walls around 200 AD. These originally consisted of raised earthwork embankments which were built in an irregular eleven-sided polygon. The following centuries, however, saw a series of alterations and improvements and today, large sections of the mainly mediaeval stone walls can be seen on the boundary of the old city. The city's modern name is derived from Cissa's *ceaster* (or castle) after the Saxon King Cissa who ruled this part of Sussex around 500 AD.

In the post-Roman era, Chichester remained an important administrative centre and market town. Between the 14th- and 18th-centuries, it was a major trading and exporting centre for the Sussex wool industry, and many handsome merchants' houses remain, especially around St Martin's Square and the elegant Georgian enclave known as **The Pallants**. Pallant House is a fine example of a redbrick town house built in 1713 by the local wine merchant Henry 'Lisbon' Peckham. The building is guarded by a wonderful pair of carved stone dodos and has an unusual observation tower where the owner would look out for his merchant vessels returning laden with goods from the Iberian Peninsula.

Now restored and refurbished as a gallery, **Pallant House** houses a collection of modern British art based around the impressive collection bequeathed to the city by the late Dean Hussey, an acknowledged patron of the arts. Exhibits include Bow porcelain and work by Graham Sutherland and John Piper, as well as regular special exhibitions. Open Tuesdays to Saturdays, 10am to 5.30pm, all year round; admission charge payable.

Just past the RMP Barracks on your right as you leave Chichester, you will find The Avenue. Number 12 is a large house with gable windows, the home of Neil and Joan Mackintosh. Joan takes great delight in sharing her comfortable home with her guests and has been doing so for the past 12 years. Wheelchair users are welcome here, as some guest rooms are on the ground floor. There is a resident's lounge with a welcoming log fire on those chillier evenings and an attractive dining room where the full English breakfast is served at a time to suit you, within reason. Built in 1906, the house stands in its own beautifully laid out gardens, with a pond complete with ducks forming an added attraction.

Chichester also has a long and colourful ecclesiastical history. Although St Wilfrid chose nearby Selsey as the site for the area's first cathedral in the 8th-century, the conquering Normans decided to build a new cathedral in its present location at the end of the 11th-century. (This turned out to be a wise decision as the site of the original building has been washed away and now lies in the sea somewhere off Selsey Bill.) Construction work began in 1091 and the new cathedral was finally consecrated in 1184. Three years later, however, it was reduced to a shell by fire, requiring a rebuilding programme which was carried out in the 13th-century by Richard of Chichester, a venerated bishop who was canonised in 1262 and subsequently adopted as the town's saint.

12, The Avenue, Chichester, West Sussex PO19 4PU 0243 527135
Map Ref: 5C

Chichester Cathedral is unique on two counts: it is the only mediaeval English cathedral which can be seen from the sea, and it has a detached bell tower. This was built because it was feared the existing tower was insufficiently sturdy to hold the cathedral bells, a justifiable concern as it turned out for in 1861, the spire blew down in storm, demolishing a large section of the nave. The present 277-foot spire was designed by Sir Gilbert Scott in sympathy with the original style and can been seen for miles around in every direction.

Inside, the cathedral contains some fine Norman arches, a double aisle, a set of 14th-century choir stalls and some excellent modern works of art, including an altar tapestry by John Piper, a paining of Christ appearing to Mary Magdalene by Graham Sutherland, and a stained glass window by Marc Chagall. Guided tours of the cathedral are available Mondays to Saturdays, 11am to 2.15pm between Easter and end-October.

The Prebendal School, the cathedral choir school and the oldest school in Sussex, stands alongside the main building. A little further south, the Bishop's Palace has a delightful garden and a 12th-century chapel containing a unique wall painting. (Permission to view this can be obtained from the bishop's office.) Other early buildings in Chichester include **St Olave's Church** in North Street, now a bookshop, the **Guildhall** in Priory Park with its collection of Roman relics, and **St Mary's Almshouses** off Priory Road, which are still used to house 'the deserving elderly of the city'. The lady warden is pleased to show visitors around the chapel and certain parts of the residents' quarters.

One of Chichester's most distinctive modern buildings can be found at Oaklands Park, just north of the city walls. Since the hexagonally shaped **Festival Theatre** was opened in 1962, it has built up an international reputation for staging the finest classical and contemporary drama, opera and ballet. The theatre is one of the focal points of the annual **Chichester Festival**, a two-week programme of cultural events which takes place each July. Festivities include classical concerts in the cathedral and fireworks displays at Goodwood Racecourse. Along with Salisbury and Winchester, Chichester also plays its part in the summer **Southern Cathedrals Festival**.

Tucked away on North Street in the bustling Sussex town of Chichester, you will find the delightful **Orchard Tea Rooms**. Housed in a 13th century former inn this is the perfect stopping-off point whether you just want a refreshing cup of tea or something more substantial. Run by Alison Ellis, this attractively decorated establishment has a warm, friendly atmosphere. There is an eyecatching mural on the wall and the beamed room downstairs has a lovely horseshoe oven. This is a true tearoom, with an extensive range of speciality teas including herbal, which make an excellent accompaniment to the freshly baked bread and home-cooked food on offer.

Orchard Tea Rooms, 47 North Street, Chichester, West Sussex
PO19 1NF 0234-536896 Map Ref: 5C

The acclaimed **Chichester District Museum** is located in the area of the city known as Little London. This interesting and well laid out museum creates a vivid picture of life in this part of West Sussex

18

Market Cross, Chichester.

from the Stone Age to the present day. There is a particularly good collection of artefacts from the Roman period, along with a recently opened exhibition illustrating the many changes which have affected Chichester during the last 100 years. The museum also contains a special section dedicated to the history of the Royal Sussex Regiment from its foundation in 1701 to the present day. Open Tuesdays to Saturdays, 10am to 5.30pm, all year round; admission free.

Those keen on military history will also be interested in the **Redcap Museum** which can be found at the Royal Military Police barracks on the A286 Broyle Road. This unique museum chronicles the history of the British military police from its Tudor origins to the Gulf War. Open Tuesdays to Fridays, 10.30am to 4.30pm (closed 12.30pm to 1.30pm), all year round, plus Saturdays and Sundays, 2pm to 6pm between April and September; admission free.

11/2 miles North West of historic Chichester on the **B2178** road, stands Primrose Cottage, a delightful guest house run by Ann Brooks. Built circa 1870, it was originally an Estate cow-man's cottage: visitors can enjoy first class bed and breakfast service, which starts with a welcoming cup of tea on arrival. The three guest rooms are beautifully decorated, designed by Ann; each with its own individual theme. When you awake refreshed, you can look forward to a wholesome fresh breakfast which includes:- free range eggs straight from the farm, bacon and sausages from the local butcher. Selection of cereals, fruit juice, delicious fruit compote. Convenient for Festival Theatre - Goodwood - local walks - facing South, 'Primrose Cottage' makes the perfect touring base.

Primrose Cottage, Old Broyle Road, Chichester, West Sussex
PO19 3PR 0243 788873 Map Ref: 5C

At Portfield, just off the **A27** one mile east of Chichester, we called in at the **Mechanical Music and Doll Collection**, a fascinating museum of barrel organs, Pianolas, fairground organs and music boxes. The curators offer regular demonstrations of these rare and historic instruments which are all fully restored and in working order. There is also a collection of over 100 late-Victorian china-headed dolls, along with phonographs, stereoscopes, magic lanterns and a number of related artefacts from the Victorian and Edwardian eras. Open daily, 10am to 5pm between Easter and September, and Saturdays and Sundays only during the winter months (closed December); admission charge payable.

Two miles west of the city centre on the other side of Chichester (and well signposted off the A27 and A259) stands the site of the largest non-military Roman building yet to be uncovered in Britain. **Fishbourne Roman Palace** was only rediscovered in 1960 when a new water main was being laid for a proposed housing scheme. Instead, the site was acquired by the Sussex Archeological Society who conducted a series of excavations under the leadership of Professor Barry Cunliffe of Southampton University. The work revealed the remains of a grand and luxuriously fitted Roman villa set around a 250ft square courtyard. The structure is believed have been built between 75 and 100 AD for King Cogidubnus of the Atrebates, a leader of the ancient Britons who cooperated with the Romans and took on the role of viceroy. His reward for collaborating was a palace containing an underfloor heating system, hot baths, a colonnade, an ornamental courtyard garden, and a series of elaborate floor mosaics, wall paintings and Purbeck marble carvings. The building is thought to have been largely destroyed by fire around 320 AD and then abandoned.

Present day visitors to Fishbourne can see the layout of the Roman Palace, including sections of the walls, plumbing and heating systems. They can also admire the remains of some superb floor mosaics, the most outstanding of which is a 17ft-square panel with a central medallion depicting the winged Cupid sitting astride a dolphin. A recently constructed building protects the remains of the north wing allowing visitors to view the original rooms and corridors from above. There is also an interesting museum on the site describing the history of the palace and its role in the local economy of the day, along with a reconstruction of 2nd-century dining room and an informative audio-visual presentation. Open daily, 10am to 6pm (or dusk if earlier) between March and November; Sundays only between December and February; admission charge payable.

A couple of miles to the southwest of Fishbourne, the picturesque village of **Bosham** stands beside Chichester Harbour on its own small peninsula. An important settlement since the days of the Romans, the Irish monk Dicul established a church here in the 7th-century on the foundations of a Roman basilica, predating St Wilfrid's community at Selsey by several years. The village has strong associations with King Canute whose youngest daughter is thought to have been buried here in the 11th-century. (Indeed, a stone coffin containing a child's skeleton was discovered in the floor of the church in 1865). Bosham's Quay Meadow may even have been the site of Canute's infamous confrontation with nature when the dauntless monarch, believing his power and influence to be absolute, ordered the incoming tide to roll back. (Predictably, he and his courtiers ended up with very wet feet.)

Bosham.

Quay Meadow features again a few decades later when King Harold embarked here in 1064 on his abortive journey to appease his rival for the English crown, William, Duke of Normandy. However, Harold's plans went awry when he was taken captive and made to swear to assist William in *his* claim to the throne, a promise which Harold failed to keep. This forced William into making a return visit and a couple of years later, he landed on the beaches near Hastings with decidedly more successful results. (Harold's Sussex estates were among the first to be seized by the conquering Normans.) Bosham's characteristic Saxon church spire, one of the finest of its kind in the country, is featured alongside Harold's ship on the Bayeux Tapestry.

Today, Bosham is a must for those keen on yachting, bird watching or just relaxing in delightful mellow surroundings. The streets are filled with elegant 17th- and 18th-century flint and redbrick shops, pubs and residential buildings, those on the sea front having short flights of steps to prevent the occasional invasion of the sea through the front door. An interesting place to visit is the Bosham Walk craft centre and art gallery in Bosham Lane, but be warned, visitors are often tempted to park beside the harbour-side road, only to discover their car half-submerged when they return some hours later at high tide.

From Bosham, we returned to the outskirts of Chichester before heading southwest onto the Selsey peninsula along the **A286**. Our journey took us close to **Apuldram**, an attractive village on the Chichester Channel with a 13th-century church, a 15th-century manor house, Rymans, and an unusual museum of D-Day aviation which is open daily 10.30am to 5pm between Easter and October; admission charge payable. Two miles further on, we came to **Birdham**, the setting for Turner's famous painting of Chichester Harbour which is now on view at Petworth House. The village also has a 16th-century parish church with an unusually small door which, according to local legend, was partially blocked to prevent Satan from returning after he had been forcibly thrown out. At nearby **Itchenor**, water-borne tours of Chichester Harbour are available throughout the year.

Visitors to the pretty village of Birdham will find **The Bell Inn**, a warm and welcoming establishment. Families are made very welcome here, with a special children's menu provided and an attractive garden outside where there is a play area with an adventure climbing frame. The comfortable bar serves a wide selection of traditional hand-pulled ales and there is an extensive choice of bar food available, with a blackboard listing the daily specials. After savouring a tasty homecooked main course, for those with any room left, there is a very tempting sweet and pudding menu.

The Bell Inn, Birdham 0234-670541 Map Ref : 7C

The charming seaside village of **West Wittering** stands at the western tip of the Selsey peninsula, close to the narrow entrance to Chichester Harbour. This former fishing village has been carefully developed as a small up-market residential community and holiday resort. There are excellent sandy beaches here, along with some noteworthy buildings, including the parish church of St Peter and St Paul and **Cakeham Manor House** with its distinctive early-16th-century brick tower. This splendid part-mediaeval, part-Tudor, part-Georgian country residence was originally built as a summer palace for the bishops of Chichester.

Situated on the **B2179** between East and West Wittering, close to Cakeham Tower, you will find Cakeham Stables. This fairly small riding stables is run by Tessa Bayley who provides full tuition plus beach rides for anyone over the age of three, with hats, tack and all equipment provided. Open 7 days a week for riding in the Summer, Tessa is also very proud of the useful holiday livery service she provides. Whatever your experience and ability, a trip to Cakeham Stables is definitely a treat for all horse lovers.

Cakeham Stables, Cakeham Road, West Wittering, Sussex
PO20 8LP 0243 672194 Map Ref: 6B

The sandy stretch of land jutting out into the eastern approaches to Chichester Harbour is known as **East Head**. Now under the ownership of the National Trust, this 110-acre sand and shingle spit supports a variety of bird, plant and marine life. In recent years, marram grass has been introduced to the sand dunes to reduce the ravages of the sea, wind and visitors' footsteps. A walk around the headland is well worth doing and takes about an hour.

An entirely different atmosphere can be found a couple of miles to the east at **East Wittering** where the beaches are bordered by fast food outlets and shops selling brightly-coloured seaside paraphernalia.

24

To the north of the village in Church Farm Lane there is a unusual museum in a 12th-century church known as 'Rejectamenta'. Describing itself as a 'nostalgia centre', the thousands of everyday items on display reflect the changes in lifestyle which have occurred throughout the centuries. Open Sundays to Fridays, 11am to 6pm between Easter and October; Sundays only, 12 noon to 4pm during winter; admission charge payable.

A little further to the east at **Bracklesham**. Here, you will find the Lively Lady. The Lively Lady is a modern pub whose exterior looks do not represent the warmth and comfort of the interior. It is situated at Bracklesham near Chichester and was named after the round the world yachtsman Sir Alec Rose's boat. The pub serves a fine selection of beers, wines and spirits. It boasts a large restaurant area where you can sample food of the highest quality. You can choose from bar snacks to house specials or from a very fine a la carte menu, a variety which covers everybody's appetite. In the second bar, pool tables and amusements are situated to keep the family happy. To complete your evening, the pub regularly hosts 'themed' evenings", dinner dances and quiz nights.

The Lively Lady, Bracklesham Lane, Bracklesham, West Sussex
PO20 8A 0243 670541 Map Ref: 7C

The Old House at Home is a charming and traditional pub situated on the B2174 road in West Wittering. The pub was originally a simple thatched cottage that served as an ale house. It is now a very popular pub with visitors and locals alike. You can sample a very good selection of wines, spirits, beers and Real Ales, some of the Real Ales are brewed locally. Food is a speciality at The Old House, from the extensive range of bar food, to the excellent menus of the restaurant. Parents can relax while children play in safety in the rear, which also houses an aviary and large fish pond.

From Bracklesham, we turned inland and followed a winding

route along narrow country lanes in the direction of Selsey Bill, a journey which took us through **Earnley**, a charming small village with an interesting 14th-century church. **Selsey Bill**, the southeastern tip of the Selsey peninsula, is the southernmost point in Sussex; from here, there are some fine views along the coast and across to the Isle of Wight. Over the centuries, this part of the coastline has been gradually eroded and many of the area's most important historic remains have been lost beneath the encroaching tides.

The Old House at Home, Near East Wittering 0234-670541
Map Ref: 6C

The popular resort of **Selsey** lies to the north and east of Selsey Bill. There is an interesting **Lifeboat Museum** here at Selsey Lifeboat Station which is open on Tuesdays to Fridays and Sundays, 10.30am to 12.30pm and 2.30pm to 4.30pm between Easter and October; admission free. In the 1860s, the decision was made to move the mediaeval parish church of St Peter to Selsey from its lonely position at **Church Norton**, one-and-a-half miles to the north. According to ecclesiastical law, however, a church chancel cannot be moved, and so this remains in its original location as a chapel dedicated to St Wilfrid, the Northumbrian missionary who brought Christianity to the South Saxons in the 7th-century.

St Wilfrid founded a monastery near Selsey which subsequently became a cathedral; however, in the 11th-century, the Normans relocated the centre of the diocese at Chichester and the original cathedral site was left to the mercy of the encroaching waves; it now lies some distance offshore. St Wilfrid's chapel at Church Norton stands beside the remains of a Norman motte and bailey castle on the edge of Pagham Harbour and is well worth a visit.

The 1000-acre **Pagham Harbour** is managed by the West Sussex County Council as a nature reserve. Its tidal mud flats attract an abundance of animal and marine life and the site is an important

26

breeding ground for a number of bird species, including the little tern. An interesting information and interpretation centre is located beside the B2145 at **Sidlesham Ferry**. Guided walks around this important conservation area can also be joined here.

Our journey inland from here took us through the pleasant community of **Sidlesham**. Tucked down Mill Lane in the harbour area of Sidlesham is the appropriately named Crab and Lobster. One of only two such named pubs in the country, this family-run freehouse is over 400 years old, although there has been an alehouse on this site since the 10th century. This is very much a traditional pub full of character, with pictures of boats adorning the bar walls merely adding to the seafaring atmosphere. Calling in here you can choose from a selection of traditional Gales and Ballards bitter and will find yourself tempted by a varied lunchtime and evening menu, which in addition to the traditional Bangers and Mash or Steak and Kidney Pie includes the pub speciality, Crab or Lobster Salad.

The Crab and Lobster, Mill Lane, Sidlesham, Near Chichester, West Sussex PO20 7NB 0243 641233 Map Ref: 6C

From Sidlesham, we continued north along the **B2145**, before turning east onto the **B2166** to reach **Bognor Regis**, a pleasant south coast resort town with some elegant Regency features. At the end of the 18th-century, Bognor was transformed from a quiet fishing village by Sir Richard Hotham, a wealthy London milliner who had ambitions of creating a rival for Brighton, Eastbourne and Bournemouth. Hotham was responsible for constructing some imposing residences, including the Dome in Upper Bognor Road, and even planned to have his creation renamed *Hothampton*. However, the fashionable set of the day stayed away in droves and Hotham's dream was never realised, at least not until 1929 when George V convalesced in the town following a serious illness. On the strength of this royal patronage, Bognor was granted the title *Regis (of the king)*.

Today, Bognor Regis is a quiet seaside town with traditional public gardens, a children's fun park, a long sandy beach, a pier and a 'subtropical waterworld' at Butlin's South Coast World. The resort hosts the World Clowns Convention every March, as well as the annual Birdman Rally; this international competition involves a variety of winged contestants launching themselves off the pier in an attempt to make the longest unpowered flight. There is also an informative local history museum at Hotham Park Lodge in the High Street which is open from 1pm to 5pm on Wednesdays, Fridays and Sundays between May and September; admission free.

On the eastern side of Bognor, the village of **Felpham** is a pleasant sailing centre with a lovely church. The artist and writer William Blake lived here between 1800 and 1803 and in describing the location wrote 'Heaven opens here on all sides her golden gates'.

Visitors to the delightful coastal town of Bognor will find a real gem at The Old Priory, an above average, licensed guest house run by Deborah and Nigel Collinson, which combines a friendly family atmosphere with a quiet taste of luxury. There are three tastefully decorated guest rooms, one with four poster, another with a water bed, but all with individual character and charm. The imposing dining room provides an elegant setting in which to enjoy the hearty breakfasts and mouthwatering evening meals that Deborah provides. A Cordon Bleu chef, Deborah offers varied and imaginative menus to choose from which can be complemented by a bottle of fine wine.

The Old Priory, 80 North Bersted Street, Bognor PO22 9AQ
0243 863580 Map Ref: 7E

From Bognor, we drove north along the **A29** London road towards **Fontwell**, home of the pleasantly situated **Fontwell Park** National Hunt racecourse. The delightful three-and-a-half-acre **Denman's Garden** can be found close by; this beautifully sheltered semi-wild garden welcomes visitors and has a section offering a good range of homegrown plants.

The picturesque village of **Slindon** stands on a shelf of the South Downs one mile to the northeast of Fontwell. In a nearby beech wood, which sadly was much damaged in the storm of 1987, there is a shingle beach, evidence that the seashore once was situated here instead of five miles away to the south. With its views across the coastal plain to the English Channel, this excellent observation point has been occupied since Neolithic times and many fine examples of early flint tools having been found in the locality.

Today, Slindon is an exceptionally attractive settlement of redbrick and flint cottages which forms part of the 3500-acre Slindon Estate, the largest National Trust-owned estate in Sussex. The village, whose name is derived from the Saxon word for *sloping hill*, is arranged as a loose square of narrow lanes, the focal point of which is a crossroads at the northwestern corner where a tree stands in small open area near the church. Dating from the 12th-century, this charming flint-built church contains an unusual reclining effigy of a Tudor knight, Sir Anthony St Leger, the only wooden carving of its kind in Sussex.

Slindon House was founded as a residence for the Archbishops of Canterbury. (Archbishop Stephen Langton, a negotiator and signatory of the Magna Carta, spent the last weeks of his life here in 1228.) Rebuilt in the 1560s and extensively remodelled during the 1920s, the house is now a private boys' school. Slindon's wonderful post office is an amalgamation of two 400 year-old cottages and is the village's only remaining thatched building. Just to the north of the village, there is a cricket field where Sir Richard Newland is said to have refined the modern game over 200 years ago.

Mill Lane House, Slindon, Arundel, West Sussex BN18 0RP
0243 65440 Map Ref: 5F

Slindon near Arundel is a picturesque, old-fashioned village where daily life continues at a gentle pace, preserved and protected by the National Trust from the stresses of modern life. A little way past the pub on the right hand side you will come to Mill Lane House which has extensive views to the coast. Here Peter and Sarah Fuente provide first class accommodation in seven very attractive, well-equipped guest rooms, all en-suite and two of which are located in the converted stables and have full facilities for the disabled. Dogs are welcome by prior arrangement and Sarah is happy to provide an evening meal if required. The public footpath that runs nearby offers lovely views across Littlehampton to the sea and makes a pleasant stroll to the local pub.

From Slindon village, there is a marvellous circular walk around the Slindon Estate which takes in **Slindon Folly**, a lonely flint archway built in 1817, and the village of **Eartham**, the former home of the 19th-century MP William Suskisson. Suskisson was knocked down by Stevenson's Rocket during its inaugural run in 1830, earning himself the doubtful honour of being the world's first recorded victim of a railway accident. Within a mile of the South Downs Way at the northern end of the estate, the National Trust has recently opened **Gumber Bothy**, a traditional farm building which has been converted to provide basic accommodation and cooking facilities for up to 27 people.

To the north, the Slindon Estate is bordered by **Stane Street**, the remarkably straight Roman road which once connected the important administrative centre of Londinium with the port of Chichester, 57 miles away. The remains of the Roman pavement which was constructed, complete with sophisticated drainage ditches, almost 2000 years ago lie a foot beneath the surface of the present-day bridleway. The three-and-a-half mile stretch through Eartham Wood and on to Bignor Hill is unusually well preserved, perhaps because for centuries the local community knew it as the 'Devil's Road' and left it well alone.

At **Tangmere Airfield**, on the southern side of the A27 four miles to the west, there is an interesting museum dedicated to Britain's military flying personnel. The **Tangmere Military Aviation Museum** houses a fascinating collection of airmen's personal effects, maps, photographs and aircraft relics from the earliest days of the Flying Corps to the present day. Also on display is a Spitfire cockpit simulator, along with a number of full-sized aircraft, including a Gloucester Meteor and a Hawker Hunter. Open daily, 10am to 5.30pm between February and November; admission charge payable.

The site of **Boxgrove Priory** lies on the opposite side of the A27, a mile to the north of Tangmere. Now a collection of ruins surrounding the still complete parish church of St Mary and St Blaise, this once-glorious Benedictine priory began life around 1115 as an outpost of Lessay Abbey in France. Initially a community of only three monks, over the centuries Boxgrove grew to become one of the most influential monastic houses in Sussex. The sumptuous interior of the sturdily-built great church reflects the institution's former importance; the roof is supported by Purbeck marble columns and there is a wonderful series of 15th-century ceiling paintings by Lambert Barnard. Perhaps most lavish, however, is the **De La Warr Chantry**

Chapel, a miniature church-within-a-church which was built by the local lord of the manor as a proposed resting place for himself and his wife. His plans, however, were upset by the Henry VIII's Dissolution of the Monasteries, and despite taking ownership of the priory for a time, he was subsequently forced to dispose of the building. De La Warr was eventually buried at Broadwater, near Worthing, the extravagant marble chapel at Boxgrove remaining empty. Elsewhere in the village, the 17th-century Nightingale Cottages and 18th-century Derby Almshouses are worth making the effort to find.

The village of **Halnaker** (pronounced *Hannacker*), a mile-or-so to the north, was the De La Warr family's seat. This contains a fine modern country residence, Halnaker House, which was designed by Edwin Lutyens in 1938. An earlier Halnaker House was built in mediaeval times by the De Haye family, founders of Boxgrove Priory; situated to the north of its modern counterpart, it fell into ruin around 1800. Above the village on Halnaker Hill stands a mid-18th-century tower windmill which remained in use until the end of the 19th-century. The exterior was restored in 1934 enabling the structure to used as an observation tower during World War II; the internal workings, however, have been removed. Hilaire Belloc wrote a famous poem about **Halnaker Windmill** in 1912 when it was still in ruins.

One of the reasons the original Halnaker House was allowed to decay was that it was overshadowed by **Goodwood House**, the spectacular country home of the Dukes of Richmond which lies a mile-and-a-half to the northwest of Halnaker village. Although Goodwood started out in 1720 as an unexceptional brick residence, it was rebuilt on a grand scale in the late 18th-century for the third Duke of Richmond by the architect James Wyatt. Several rooms in the house, including the state apartments, are now open to visitors; items on show include paintings by Canaletto and Stubbs, fine Sévres porcelain, relics from the Napoleonic Wars, an assortment of royal gifts and many fine pieces of English and French furniture. Open 2pm to 5pm on Sundays and Mondays between May and end-September, plus Tuesdays to Thursdays in August (closed event days); admission charge payable.

Goodwood House is the focal point of the **Goodwood Estate**, 12000 acres of downland which incorporate the home of the famous 'Glorious Goodwood' horse racing meeting each July, the Trundle Iron Age hill fort, a sixty-acre country park, a motor racing circuit, golf course, airfield and children's adventure play area.

On leaving Goodwood House, we retraced our steps eastwards for a short distance before turning north onto the minor country road

Goodwood House.

which leads to the attractive village of **East Dean**. Here, we called in at the excellent village pub and eating place, **The Hurdlemakers**. The Hurdlemakers, which gets its unusual name from the once thriving rural craft which employed several men from the village. Built from the traditional flint and brick which is such a prominent feature of Sussex, this delightful establishment makes a popular stopping-off point for walkers on the South Downs Way. Your friendly host Roger Waller serves a selection of traditional local ales and provides a wide range of first class bar meals, available at lunchtime and in the evening. Children are welcome and on fine days you can enjoy your food and drink outside in the lovely beer garden.

The Hurdlemakers, East Dean, Chichester, West Sussex PO18 0SU
024363 318 Map Ref: 4E

From East Dean, we made our way back onto the **A285** Petworth road and climbed onto the crest of the Downs ridge near the 837ft **Duncton Hill**. Continuing northeastwards, we descended sharply into the Weald and after a couple of miles, turned east onto the minor road leading to **Bignor**, a pleasant community whose central thoroughfares are arranged in an uneven square. The village contains some wonderful domestic buildings, including the photogenic 15th-century **Old Shop**, a two-storey thatched house whose ramshackle timber-framed walls are infilled with brick, flint and plaster.

Bignor is perhaps best known for having been the administrative centre of a large Roman agricultural estate, the focus of which was a sizable villa which was accidentally uncovered by a farmer's plough in 1811. Excavations revealed the foundations of **Bignor Roman Villa**, a grand courtyard residence covering four-and-a-half acres which was inhabited between the 1st- and 4th-centuries. The most striking feature of the building is its floor mosaics; these include depictions of Diana, Venus, Ganymede and Medusa, and in the north corridor, there is an 82ft mosaic pavement which is the longest of its type in the British Isles. Open daily, 10am to 6pm between June and September; 10am to 5pm Tuesdays to Sundays (and Bank Holiday Mondays) in March, April, May and October; admission charge payable.

From Bignor, we retraced our steps back onto the A285 and continued northwards for a mile-and-a-half before turning west into the country lanes. Our next destination was **Graffham**, a pleasant community spread out along the foot of the Downs escarpment which is the home of the famous Lavington Stud. Here, we discovered an excellent bed and breakfast establishment, the **White House**, a splendid 17th century pub. Here you can choose from a wide selection of fine hand drawn ales and there are excellent bar meals available every lunchtime and evening with a menu that combines traditional pub fare with daily specials such as Oxtail Casserole or Stilton and Cauliflower Flan, all served with fresh vegetables. The lovely conservatory provides the perfect setting in which to relax with your drink and admire the outstanding views across to the Sussex Downs, whilst for those who prefer a livelier environment, the pub hosts monthly jazz evenings.

The White Horse, Graffham, West Sussex 07986 331 Map Ref: 4E

We found our way back onto the A285 and crossed the River Rother at **Coultershaw Bridge**. One of the earliest pumped water systems was installed here in 1790 to pipe water the two-mile distance to Petworth. The **Coultershaw Water Wheel and Beam Pump** is now a scheduled ancient monument which has been restored to working condition by the Sussex Industrial Archeology Society. The beam pump can be seen in operation on the first and third Sundays in the month between April and September, and there is also an exhibition giving some interesting background information on water supply, pumps and local natural history; small admission charge payable.

From Coultershaw, we made our way into the centre of **Petworth**, a densely-packed small country town which stands on the crest of a sandstone ridge. Between the 14th- and 16th-centuries, Petworth was an important cloth-weaving centre and a number of fine merchants' and landowners' residences, including Daintrey House, North House and Tudor House, can be seen in its narrow streets. The cramped Market Place contains a fine late-18th-century arcaded town hall and a striking bank building, the National Westminster, built in baroque style in 1901. Other noteworthy buildings include the Somerset Almshouses (or Upper Hospital), built in 1746 for twelve widows, each of whom received a pension of £10 per year.

However, the most dominant feature of Petworth is the grand house and park which together make up the National Trust-owned Petworth Estate. Surrounded by a wall over thirteen miles long, the 700-acre **Petworth Park** was landscaped by Lancelot 'Capability' Brown in the 1750s. The sweeping grounds contain a lake and a deer park, and are a fine example of 18th-century emparking.

Petworth House was built between 1688 and 1696 on the site of a 13th-century manor house, the present building incorporating the original mediaeval chapel and hall undercroft. The house, with its magnificent 320 foot west front, was built in French style on the instructions of Charles, Sixth Duke of Somerset. The design has been attributed to the architect Daniel Marot, except for the south front which was added in 1869-72 to a design by Anthony Salvin. The galleries and state rooms house one of the finest art collections in the country. Paintings on show include work by Turner, who was a regular visitor to Petworth, Rembrandt, Van Dyck, Holbein and Gainsborough. There are also some outstanding examples of the work of the master carver, Grinling Gibbons. House open daily (except Mondays and Fridays), 1pm to 5.30pm between 1st April and end-October; admission charge payable (free to National Trust members). Park open daily, 8am to dusk, all year round; admission free.

Just south of Petworth you will find the village of **Byworth**, off the **A283.** Here also, you will find a traditional English pub called **The Blackhorse Inn.** Built in the 16th Century, on the site of a monastery, it has always been a restng place for the weary traveller. The atmosphere is warm and friendly with open log fires, scrubbed floors and pine tables to give it a delightful olde world feel. There is a large and secluded garden to enjoy as well.

Run by owners Jenny Reynolds and Paul Wheeler-Kingshott the inn has a fine restaurant, with a non-smoking area, and an imaginative menu, featuring a good vegetarian selection, as well as rabbit and swordfish.

The Blackhorse Inn, Byworth, Petworth, West Sussex GU28 OHN
0798-42424 Map Ref: 3F

The pleasant community of **Tillington** lies a mile upstream on the western side of Petworth. Bordered by the famous wall around Petworth Park, this charming estate village contains a fine parish church with an imposing Scots Crown tower and a first-rate inn, the **Horseguards**. The Horseguards Inn is a beautiful 17th century Grade II listed building run by a friendly couple Rex and Janet Colman. This warm, welcoming family pub is full of character with exposed oak beams, stone flagged floors and open log fires. Here you will find a combination of fine ales including specially brewed Horseguards Bitter plus first class menus that provide more than just "pub" food. All the food is freshly prepared from the finest ingredients and includes game, fresh fish and a selection of delicious homemade desserts. The Horseguards Inn offers a lovely comfortable atmosphere for that special family meal out or a quiet drink with friends.

The Horseguards Inn, Upperton Road, Tillington, Petworth, West
Sussex GU28 9AF 0798 42332 Map Ref: 3F

A little further to the southeast, **Fittleworth** is a village of charming sandstone buildings stretching down to the River Rother. The historic Swan Inn has a wonderful wood-panelled dining room hung with paintings by some of the many acknowledged artists who have stayed here over the centuries, and the isolated church of St Mary at Hallelujah Corner has two mediaeval bells dating from the 14th- and 15th-centuries. A little further on, **Stopham** is family home of the Barttelot family, an old Norman family who still reside in Stopham House. The Barttelots are strongly associated with the building of the early-15th-century **Stopham Bridge**, an impressive stone structure which is widely regarded as the finest mediaeval bridge in Sussex. The tall central arch was rebuilt in 1822 to allow masted vessels to pass upstream towards the Wey and Arun Canal.

After returning to Fittleworth, we turned north off the **A283** and followed a minor country road along the Arun valley, rejoining the **A272** a mile to the west of **Wisborough Green**. This wonderfully open village has a huge rectangular tree-lined green covering nine acres, making it one of the largest in the country. The village church of St Peter Ad Vincula (St Peter in chains) stands near the circular village pond. This handsome building contains a fine mediaeval wall painting which was covered over in the 13th-century during the rebuilding of the chancel arch and was only rediscovered by accident in 1867.

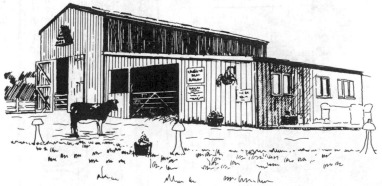

Fishers Farm Park, Newpound Lane, Wisborough Green, West Sussex RH14 0EG 0403 700063 Map Ref: 2G

For a fascinating and fun day out, look no further than **Fishers Farm Park** which can be found by heading West on the A272, to Wisborough Green, then following the brown tourist board signs. This is a clean, well-run establishment where the animals are very tame and all individually named with a character to match. Try talking to Corrie the Shetland pony or Horace the pot-bellied pig! The woodland

Stopham Bridge.

walks are beautiful and the secluded picnic area provides a peaceful setting for lunch, while the children run off energy in the exciting adventure playground.There are even two self-catering cottages available, ideal as a holiday base. There is so much here it would be impossible to list everything, so take a trip out and see for yourself.

To the west of Wisborough Green, there are two areas of preserved woods, together amounting to 400 acres, which are in the care of the Sussex Wildlife Trust. These ancient Wealden woodlands provide an indication of how most of Sussex north of the Downs would have looked before the arrival of modern humankind.

Present-day visitors to this peaceful rural landscape may find it hard to imagine that in the 16th- and 17th-centuries, this area was an important industrial centre. Thanks to the seemingly limitless supply of trees for fuel, iron foundries and forges prospered throughout the area right up until the Industrial Revolution. A plentiful local supply of high quality sand also led to a number of early glassworks being set up at Kirdford, Wisborough Green and Loxwood. During the 16th-century, Huguenot settlers from France and the Low Countries introduced new and improved methods of glass manufacture, and the industry flourished until 1616 when lobbying by rival shipbuilding and iron-smelting interests led to government legislation banning glass-makers from using timber to fuel their furnaces.

The country lanes to the north of Wisborough Green connect a number of interesting rural communities. As well as being a former glass-making and iron-founding centre, **Kirdford** has a 12th-century church and some fine tile-fronted cottages set along a green-and-pleasant tree-lined avenue. Three miles to the northeast, **Loxwood** once had an extremely rare timber-framed church, some of the original wooden pews from which were transferred to its late-19th-century replacement. The nearby Onslow Arms stands beside the Wey and Arun Junction Canal, the inland waterway which was opened in 1816 to link London with the south coast at Littlehampton. In common with most British canals, the coming of the railways sounded its death knell and in 1871, it was closed. Certain stretches are now being renovated for recreational use by the Canal Restoration Trust, an organisation which also publishes a useful guide to the canal-side footpath.

Loxwood is the former base of the 'Society of Dependents', a puritanical sect founded in 1850 by the former-London evangelist, John Sirgood. The group became known as the *Cokelers* because of their preference for cocoa instead of alcohol (*not* cocaine as it was once suggested!). The sect established a meeting house and a series of cooperative enterprises, including a bakery, butchery and even a taxi service. Despite their austere code which banned sport, theatre and music, the Cokelers were known for their charitable work. However, the group gradually went into decline; the store survived until 1980 and the few remaining sect members now live in retirement cottages near the chapel.

From Loxwood, we followed country lane northeastwards to our final stopping place in this part of West Sussex, the characteristic Wealden settlement of **Rudgwick**. This charming village of attractive tile-fronted cottages stands on high ground surrounded by woodland. The 14th-century village church has some delicate carved tracery and there are some fine views southwards to Chanctonbury Ring. From here, we set off eastwards along the wooded valley of the Upper Arun and crossed into the area covered in our next chapter.

West Sussex.

From the River Arun to the East Sussex Border

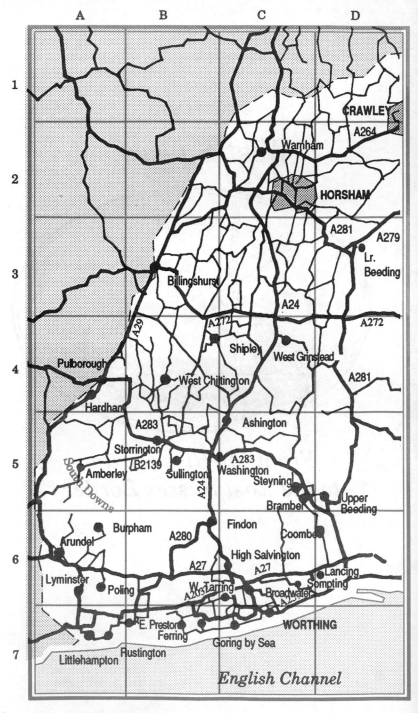

	A	B	C	D
1				CRAWLEY A264
2			Warnham	HORSHAM A281
3		Billingshurst	A24	A279 Lr. Beeding A272
4	Pulborough Hardham	A272 West Chiltington	Shipley	West Grinstead A281
5	Amberley	Storrington B2139 Sullington	A283 Ashington A24	Washington Steyning
6	Arundel Burpham Lyminster Poling	A280 A27 W. Tarring A203	Findon High Salvington A27 Broadwater	Bramber Coombe Upper Beeding Lancing Sompting
7	Littlehampton Rustington	E. Preston Ferring	Goring by Sea	WORTHING

South Downs

English Channel

42

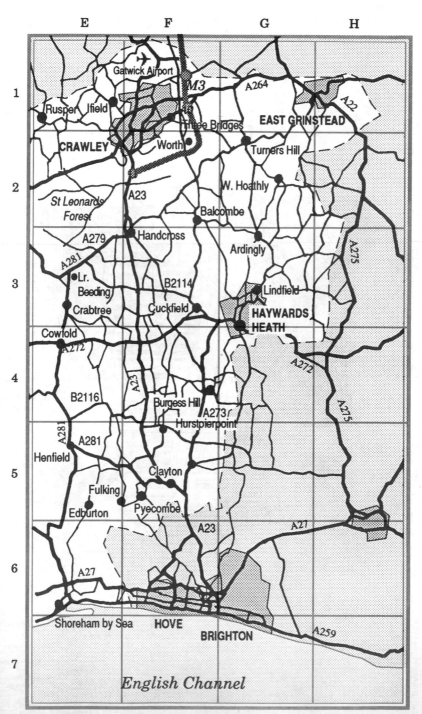

Horsham.

CHAPTER TWO

West Sussex.
From the River Arun
to the East Sussex Border

We began our tour of the eastern part of West Sussex along the A281 Bucks Green to Horsham road. Our first port of call was the village of **Warnham**, a diverse community which lies scattered between the A29 and A24 trunk routes. The buildings here vary from a modern brickworks to some fine old residences, including Warnham Court, the home of the Lucas family. Field Place on the edge of Warnham was the birthplace of the poet Percy Bysshe Shelley in 1792. After a reasonably happy childhood which included boating on Warnham's millpond (now part of a nature reserve), Shelley was cast out of his family home by his father who didn't approve of his son's chosen profession. Horsham museum now has a gallery devoted to his life and work, and the gardens of Field Place are open to visitors for a few days each year. Less anguished was the life of local shoemaker and amateur musician, Michael Turner, who served for fifty years as Warnham's church sexton; some of his personal effects are on display in the church, and the inscription on his gravestone gives an account of his life in verse.

Those with a desire to venture closer to the sprawling new town of Crawley will find a good country house hotel, Ghyll Manor, in the old monastic village of **Rusper**, and an interesting museum, the Ifield Water Mill, at **Ifield** on Crawley's western outskirts. Open Sundays, 2.30pm to 5pm, (2pm to 4pm in winter), all year round; admission free.

Despite lying only seven miles to the southwest of Crawley, the historic country town of **Horsham** has a very different atmosphere. Founded in the mid-10th-century, the town takes its name from the Saxon term meaning *horse pasture*; along with Oxford and Exeter, it one of only three towns in England whose central crossroads is known as the *Carfax*. By the 13th century, Horsham had grown into a prosperous borough and market town which was considered sufficiently important to send two members to the new Parliament which was established in 1295.

Between 1306 and 1830, Horsham took it in turns with Lewes and Chichester to hold the county assizes. During the weeks the court was in session, large numbers of outsiders were attracted into the town which would take on something of a carnival atmosphere. Public executions were sometimes carried out on Horsham Common or in front of the country gaol, including one in 1844 of a man who refused to plead to a charge of robbery and murder and was subjected to 'death by compression', the last such execution of its kind in England. During the 17th-century, Horsham's county gaol was also used to accommodate members of the much-persecuted Society of Friends.

The old part of Horsham consists of a long wedge-shape, formerly a green, with the Carfax at one end and the part-Norman church of St Mary at the other. Stretching between the two is a unique walkway known as the Causeway and many of the town's finest buildings are located here, including the town hall with its façade built by the Duke of Norfolk in 1812, the Manor House, headquarters of the RSPCA, and the 15th-century King's Head Hotel. One of the finest examples of a timber-framed Sussex town house can be seen at 30 The Causeway, whilst at No. 9, the Tudor-built Causeway House is the location of the impressive **Horsham Museum**, with its delightful walled garden, recently-opened Shelley gallery, and interesting collection of historic artefacts from the surrounding area. Open Tuesdays to Saturdays, 10am to 5pm, all year round; admission free.

The famous **Bluecoat School** (or Religious, Royal and Ancient Foundation of **Christ's Hospital**) lies in the heart of the Sussex countryside, two miles to the southwest of Horsham. The school is named after the traditional long dark blue cloak and girdle which is still worn by the 800 or so pupils, both boys and girls. Originally founded by Edward VI in 1552, Bluecoats moved from the City of London to its present stark, purpose-built, brick and Bath stone home in 1902. The school has a strong academic and artistic reputation, and incorporates an arts complex and a refectory where a famous painting by Antonio Verrio is on permanent display. Visitors' guided tours are available by arrangement.

From Christ's Hospital, we made our way southwestwards along the country lanes to **Billingshurst**, an attractive small town which stands at the junction of the **A272** and the **A29** London to Bognor Regis road. In the days prior to the coming of the railways, Billingshurst was an important coaching town and several good former coaching inns, including the 16th-century Olde Six Bells, can still be found in the old streets. The Norman church of St Mary's suffered the same fate as many of its contemporaries and was heavily 'restored' during the Victorian era; however, it still retains its original

120ft eight-sided spire which since 1884, has featured a clock whose mechanism is a half-sized replica of Big Ben.

Following the A272 towards Billingshurst, if you turn right down the lane 400 yards after passing over the hump-backed bridge, you will find **Wooddale Cottage**, a secluded and peaceful base from which to explore this beautiful part of West Sussex. The original 16th century farmhouse here burnt down and was replaced by a 19th century workman's cottage which was extended to form the present farmhouse. This is a working organic farm run by Tim and Susie Sherlock who have free-range chickens, sheep and cattle and provide comfortable overnight accommodation in three traditionally furnished guest rooms. The house enjoys a woodland setting and is ideally situated for observing wildlife, with a patio adjacent to two ponds, well-stocked with trout and carp.

Wooddale Cottage, Wooddale Lane, Billingshurst, West Sussex
RH14 9DU 0403 782996 Map Ref : 3B

Just south of the A272 four miles to the east of Billingshurst, the parish church at **Shipley** contains some fine 12th-century features and a wonderful alabaster memorial to Sir Thomas Caryll and his family. The village also features a small disused toll house and a distinctive hammer pond which in the 16th-century would have supplied water to drive the bellows and mechanical hammers in an adjacent iron foundry. Shipley is perhaps best known, however, for being the former home of the celebrated Sussex writer Hilaire Belloc, who lived at King's Land from 1906 until his death in 1953. In the grounds stands the famous **Shipley Windmill**, a great five-storey 'smock' windmill which is open to the public on a limited number of days each year; now restored, a memorial plaque to its former owner hangs above the entrance.

The ancient settlement of **Pulborough** stands a mile or so from the confluence of the Rivers Arun and Rother, five miles to the southwest of Billingshurst. This scattered community was founded by the Romans as a staging post, or *mansio*, on Stane Street, the arterial road which once connected London with Chichester. Despite its strategically important location beside the Arun river crossing, Pulborough failed to grow like some of its rivals, and today it remains a sizable village which is perhaps best known for its excellent freshwater fishing.

Appropriately named, The Water's Edge in Pulborough enjoys a beautiful location beside a lagoon which connects with the River Arun, making it possible to travel by boat as far as Littlehampton. This delightful pub and restaurant is a popular haven for walkers and birdwatchers, lying only 2 miles from the South Downs Way and surrounded by a variety of birdlife. A popular stopping-off point for visitors and locals alike, it provides a delightful setting whether for a family lunch or an intimate dinner for two. There is an extensive and varied selection of tasty hot and cold specials, as well as a salad bar in the summer, all freshly prepared using local produce,but popularity makes it advisable to book for Saturday evening and Sunday lunchtime.

The Water's Edge, Station Road, Pulborough, West Sussex
0798 872451 Map Ref : 4A

One mile south of Pulborough on the A29, the village of **Hardham** is well worth a visit for its Saxon church of St Botolph (one of the few churches in the area, it seems, *not* dedicated to St Mary). This exceptional little building contains a near complete series of wall paintings dating from the early 12th-century which are believed to be the earliest examples of their kind in Britain. The murals are thought to have been painted by a team of artists based at St Pancras Priory in Lewes who were also responsible for those at Coombes and Clayton, further to the southeast. The site of Hardham Priory, a small Augustinian monastic house, lies close by and from here it is possible to join a footpath leading to the disused Hardham Tunnel, a channel which was built to provide a short cut for river barges wishing to avoid the broad eastern loop of the Arun.

Having made our way back onto the eastern side of the River Arun, our next port of call was **West Chiltington**, a pleasant village which lies on a low hill three miles due east of Pulborough. The Norman church of St Mary has a shingled spire and like Hardham, contains some fine wall paintings which were painted between the 12th- and 14th-centuries and were only rediscovered in 1882. The church also possesses an unusually long squint, or *hagioscope*, a narrow angled opening in the wall which allows a view of the main altar from the south aisle. A former glass-making and iron-smelting centre, the village has an interesting industrial and social history, further details of which can be obtained at the **West Chiltington Museum** in Church Street. Opening times displayed on site; admission free.

From West Chiltington, we retraced our steps onto the **A283** Pulborough to Shoreham road and continued southwards for a couple of miles before turning west onto the B2139 to reach the famous house and gardens at **Parham Park**. Probably the finest Elizabethan country house in Sussex, Parham stands in the heart of a great deer park on an open plateau at the foot of the South Downs ridge. Designed in the classic 'E' shape, the mansion was built in the 1570s for Sir Thomas Palmer, a wealthy cloth merchant, on the site of a smaller monastic house which once belonged to Westminster Abbey.

Parham contains one of the finest Elizabethan interiors in the country. The magnificent state rooms, including the 160ft Long Gallery, Great Hall and Great Parlour, feature mullioned windows and wood panelled walls, and are furnished with an exceptional collection of period furniture, oriental carpets, rare needlework and fine paintings. The house is surrounded by seven acres of wooded parkland containing a statue garden, lake, picnic enclosure and a beautiful four-acre walled garden with traditional herb beds.

The diminutive church of St Peter stands close to the main house; rebuilt early in the 19th-century, its interior features carved ceilings, an unusual lead font and a set of high box pews. The squire's pew had its own fireplace which he was reputed to stoke loudly when the vicar's sermon was becoming tiresome. House and garden open Sundays, Wednesdays, Thursdays and Bank Holidays, 2pm to 6pm between Easter and early-October; admission charge payable.

Two miles to the west of Parham, the village of **Amberley** consists of a delightful assortment of flint, brick, stone, timber and thatched cottages spread out below the steep scarp slope of the South

Downs ridge. The ancient village church of St Michael is thought to have been founded by St Wilfrid, the missionary who converted the South Saxons to Christianity. Rebuilt in the 12th-century by Bishop Luffa of Chichester at around the same time as Chichester Cathedral, the church interior contains some strong Norman features. The murals to the right of the chancel arch date from the time of a further remodelling in the 13th-century.

Nearby **Amberley Castle** began life in the 12th-century as a fortified summer palace for the bishops of Chichester. More a manor house than a castle, alterations over the centuries include the construction of a great curtain wall to enclose the entire manorial site. Charles II is believed to have stayed here whilst en route to a safe haven in France following his defeat at the Battle of Worcester in 1651. The building now operates as a privately-run hotel and restaurant, the Amberley Castle Hotel.

The series of water meadows to the north of the village are known as the **Amberley Wild Brooks**. Often flooded and inaccessible by car, this thirty-acre conservation area is a haven for bird, animal and plantlife. Trains on the Arun Valley line cross the marshes along specially constructed embankments which were considered engineering marvels of their day when the line was opened in 1863. Amberley railway station lies a mile to the southwest of the village at **Houghton Bridge**, the point where the South Downs way crosses the River Arun.

Houghton Bridge is also the location of the renowned **Amberley Chalk Pits Museum**, a working museum of industrial history featuring a narrow gauge industrial railway, a collection of vintage motor buses, and a range of workshops which offer live demonstrations of traditional rural trades, including blacksmithing, pottery making, printing, boat building and ironmongery. This fascinating 36-acre open-air museum is a must of all those with an interest in industrial archeology or transport history. Open Wednesdays to Sundays (and Bank Holiday Mondays), 10am to 5pm between 1st April and end-October; daily mid-June to mid-September; admission charge payable.

During the 18th- and 19th-centuries, chalk was quarried at Amberley for shipping to the many lime kilns which at one time could be found throughout the lime-deficient farming areas of southern England. Later, large quantities of chalk were needed to supply a new industrial process which involved the high-temperature firing of chalk with small amounts of clay. The revolutionary product resulting from this process was named 'Portland Cement', and the Amberley Chalk Pits Museum includes an exhibition on the background and history of this invaluable building material.

From Amberley, we made our way eastwards along the **B2139**, a scenic road which follows the base of the South Downs ridge. We paused for a few minutes in **Storrington**, a sprawling village which provides good access to the South Downs Way near **Kithurst Hill**. The nearby dry chalk valley known as **Chantry Bottom** is a deserted settlement which was populated by Iron Age, Roman and mediaeval people.

Just to the east of Storrington lies **Sullington Warren**, a sandy area of National Trust-owned heathland which once was used for the farming of rabbits. On the other side of the main road a mile to the south, the hamlet of **Sullington** contains a barn which at 115ft long, rivals many of the tithe barns which were a feature of mediaeval monastic estates. This exceptional building has a braced tie-beam roof and, although privately-owned, can be viewed by appointment.

A couple of miles further east, the village of **Washington** stands at the northern end of the Findon Gap, the ancient pass through the Downs now carries the A24 London to Worthing road. Despite its American-sounding connotations, the name of this peaceful village is derived from the Saxon term for *settlement of the family of Wassa*. Thankfully now bypassed by the main road, Washington's varied assortment of buildings reflect its location between the chalk Downs and sandstone Weald. Standing in a picturesque position at one end of the village street, the castellated 15th-century parish church still retains a mediaeval air despite being heavily 'restored' during the 19th-century.

The picturesque village of Washington is the delightful location of **The Frankland Arms**, a traditional, family inn. Dating back to 1820, when it was known as The Washington Inn, it was renamed in 1927 after Sir William Frankland. This is the only pub in the village and consequently provides everything you could wish for. It is very popular with walkers, tourists and locals alike, who all come to enjoy the mouthwatering food which is available lunchtime and evening, plus the wide selection of real ales, wines and spirits to wash it down. There is a toilet for the disabled and children are well catered for with the play area and large beer garden, where you can enjoy the Summer barbecues.

Did You Know...

There is a full list of

Tourist Information Centres

at the back of the book?

The Frankland Arms, Old London Road, Washington, West Sussex
RH20 4AL 0903 892220 Map Ref : 5C

Lying two miles along the A24 to the north of Washington, the village of **Ashington** contains an unexpected attraction, the **Holly Gate Cactus Garden**. This unusual collection of over 20,000 cacti and succulents from the hot and arid regions of the world has been built up over thirty years by a private enthusiast whose hobby has turned into a living museum. The cacti, many of which can be seen in flower, are laid out in a 'natural' landscaped setting in a series of glasshouses covering a total area of over 10,000 square feet. Holly Gate is located beside the B2133 Billingshurst Road half-a-mile north of the village and is open daily, 9am to 5pm, all year round; admission charge payable.

Peter and Jan Bench run **The Mill House Hotel** at Ashington, which is just south of Dial Post on the A24. What a pretty place it is, and well deserving of its credits by Egon Ronay, the AA, the Michelin Guide and the Logis of Great Britain. The house is about 300 years old and has all the charm that a well-preserved house gathers over the years. There are eleven bedrooms, two of which have four-poster beds. Seven of the eight double rooms and two of the three singles are en-suite, but whichever room you have you will find it furnished elegantly, in keeping with the age of the house. All the rooms have direct dial telephones and facilities for making tea or coffee, together with colour TV, hair dryers and trouser presses. In fact everything possible is done for your comfort. We stayed there for one of their "Breakaway" weekends; ours was from Friday to Sunday inclusive. We enjoyed every minute of it. Apart from being excellent hoteliers, Peter and Jan Bench are fine restaurateurs, which is something that is not always recognised. It is one thing to run a good hotel, and most efficient people could achieve this, but you need a special flair to run a good restaurant. This is reflected in the the high standard and charm of the Miller's Room candlelit restaurant. Local residents use the Miller's Room regularly for intimate lunches and dinners, and not surprisingly, for the food is first class and the atmosphere relaxing. We noted with interest that the hotel offers full service for conference and private parties of up to forty people. We could imagine a very successful small business seminar being held there, especially if it was an occasion when the partners were brought as well. For them there is so much worth seeing every day quite nearby. Golfers have a choice of around eight courses, all within easy distance; Goodwood is not too far, and Parham Park is very close. If you want the theatre, Brighton, Guildford, Chichester and Worthing are all close enough to make it a simple evening out. Horse racing enthusiasts can choose between Goodwood, Fontwell, Plumpton or Brighton. The Mill House Hotel is in such a lovely setting, and the garden just adds to the sense of well-being that you have when you wake up in the morning after a good night's sleep in this super place.

Mill House Hotel, Mill Lane, Ashington, West Sussex RH20 3BZ
0903 892426 Map Ref : 5C

One of the most striking landmarks in Sussex is located within a few yards of the South Downs Way on the southeastern side of Washington. The copse of beech trees on **Chanctonbury Ring** can be seen from miles around in every direction. These were planted in 1760 by Charles Goring when he was still a boy; in later years, Sir Charles, as he became, inherited Chanctonbury Hill along with Wiston Park, the part 16th-, part 19th-century mansion lying at the foot of the hill to the northeast which is now run as a conference centre by the Foreign Office. The four-acre hilltop site was first occupied by Iron Age people who surrounded it with a ditch and fortified earthen bank. Several centuries later, the Romans built a temple and shrine near its centre, some new remains of which were discovered after several trees had sadly been uprooted during the devastating storm of October 1987.

A characteristic downland dew pond lies within a few yards of the South Downs Way just to the west of Chanctonbury Ring. Now restored and maintained by the Society of Sussex Downsmen, the pond is lined with a layer of impervious clay and relies on water condensing from the cool night air to keep it topped up with water.

The much larger Iron Age hill fort of **Cissbury Ring** lies two-and-a-half miles to the south of Chanctonbury and is accessible via the village of **Findon**. Overshadowed only by Dorset's Maiden Castle, this impressive hilltop site covers an area of 65 acres and is surrounded by a double rampart almost a mile in circumference. It has been estimated that over 50,000 tons of chalk soil and boulders would have had to be moved in its construction, a feat which was carried out in the 3rd-century BC and would have required a sizable Iron Age community. Cissbury was occupied for around two centuries before it was allowed to revert to pastureland; however, the threat of a Saxon invasion following the departure of the Romans led to reoccupation and a major strengthening of the earthwork ramparts.

The brisk uphill walk to the summit of this natural defensive position is rewarded with some breathtaking views along the Sussex coast to Beachy Head in the east, and Selsey Bill and the Isle of Wight in the west. Closer are the Iron Age hill forts of Chanctonbury Ring to the north and Highdown Hill to the southwest. Visitors will also notice a series of shallow depressions in the scrub-covered area at the southwestern edge of the fortifications. These are the remnants of flint mines which were worked during the New Stone Age, over 4000 years ago. At that time, an extensive series of pits and radiating shafts, some up to 40ft long, were dug in order to extract much-prized flint nodules; these were then fashioned into tools and weapons on the spot, an activity which would have made this a Neolithic industrial site of some significance. Today, Cissbury Ring is owned by the National Trust and is open to the public free of charge.

Standing at the foot of Cissbury Ring on the eastern side of the **A24**, this pleasant community of Findon is centred around an elegant square containing a 17th-century inn and some fine 18th-century residential buildings. The flint-built village church of St John the Baptist stands on the opposite side of the main road; despite having been heavily restored by Sir George Gilbert Scott in the 1870s, this contains some interesting early features, including a 13th-century oak screen and a mediaeval font fashioned from Sussex marble which is shaped like a cattle trough (a more dainty 19th-century replacement stands nearby). Set within attractive wooded grounds a few yards from the church is **Findon Place**, an early-18th-century mansion which was enlarged later in the century.

Findon is perhaps most famous for being the venue for one of the two great Sussex sheep fairs (the other is at Lewes), an annual event which takes place on the second Saturday in September. A market on Nepcote Green has been held since the 13th-century; each year, the village takes on a festival atmosphere, and as well as around 20,000 sheep changing hands, there are a great many additional activities and attractions which people come from miles around to enjoy. At one time, there were three farriers' workshops in the village, reflecting Findon's other long tradition as a horse-training centre.

From Findon, we followed the A24 southwards for a couple of miles before turning west onto the main **A27** at Salvington. Nearby **High Salvington** is the site of a recently-restored post mill, a type of windmill which was in common use from the late-mediaeval period and consists of a heavy cross-shaped base with a strong central upright around which the windmill's sails and timber superstructure were able to pivot.

A couple of miles further west, the A27 passes to the north of the cone-shaped **Highdown Hill** which, although only 266ft high, stands out above the surrounding coastal plain. Its prominent nature has led to a long history of occupation and in its time, it has been an Iron Age hill fort, a Roman bathhouse and a Saxon graveyard. (Relics from these different eras are on view in Worthing Museum.) During the 18th-century, an unconventional local miller, John Olliver, built a tomb on Highdown Hill and insisted that, when he died, he should be buried head downwards so that he would be the right way up when the world turned upside down on Judgment Day. The white-painted country house known as **Castle Goring** stands on the northern side of Highdown Hill; this exception residence was built in Italian style for the grandfather of the poet, Percy Shelley.

From Highdown Hill, we decided to make a five-mile westward dash along the A27 to spend some time in the historic town of **Arundel**. A settlement since pre-Roman times, Arundel stands at the strategically important point where the major east-west land route through Sussex crosses the River Arun. One of William the Conqueror's most favoured knights, Roger de Montgomery, first built a castle on the high ground above the river. This was similar to the castle at Windsor in that it consisted of a motte and double bailey, a plan which, despite several alterations to the fabric of the building, remains largely unaltered to this day.

The period of stability the castle brought to the town in the late

River Arun and Arundel Castle.

mediaeval period made Arundel into an important port and market town. It was during this era that the 14th-century parish church of St Nicholas was built, a unique building in that it is now divided into separate Catholic and Anglican areas by a Sussex iron screen. The Fitzalan Chapel in the choir houses the tombs of the Catholic Earls of Arundel and Dukes of Norfolk, in whose family the castle has remained for the past 500 years; entry to this section can normally only be made through the castle grounds.

During the English Civil War, Parliamentarian forces bombarded the castle using cannons fired from the church tower. This bombardment led to the destruction of most of the Norman fortifications, the only parts to survive being the 12th-century shell keep on the central mound and parts of the 13th-century barbican and curtain wall. The rest of the structure remained in ruins until a programme of restoration during the 1790s made the castle habitable once again. (One of the finest rooms in Arundel Castle, the mahogany-lined library, dates from this period.) A second restoration, amounting to a virtual rebuilding, was carried out about 100 years later by the 15th Duke, funded by profits from the family's ownership of the newly-prosperous steel town of Sheffield.

Most of the colossal structure which can be seen today is therefore a 19th-century Gothic reproduction. However, the state apartments and main rooms contain some fine period furniture dating from the 16th-century and paintings by such artists as Reynolds, Van Dyck, Gainsborough, Holbein and Constable. Castle open Sundays to Fridays (closed Saturdays), 12 noon to 5pm between 1st April and 30th October; admission charge payable. Members of the public also have unrestricted access to the nearby 1000-acre Arundel Castle grounds; dogs, however, are not allowed.

Despite religious persecution, particularly during the 16th-century, the Fitzalan family and the successive Dukes of Norfolk remained staunchly Roman Catholic. The 15th Duke who was responsible for the 19th-century rebuilding of the castle also commissioned the substantial Catholic church of St Philip Neri which was designed in French Gothic style by Joseph Hansom, the inventor of the Hansom cab. In 1965, this impressive building became the seat of the Catholic bishopric of Brighton and Arundel and was renamed the **Cathedral of Our Lady and St Philip Howard**. (St Philip Howard was the 13th Earl of Arundel who died in prison after being sentenced to death by Elizabeth I for his Catholic beliefs; his remains are now in the cathedral, along with an impressive memorial shrine.) Each June, the cathedral hosts the two-day **Corpus Christ Festival** during which the entire length of the aisle is laid out with a carpet of fresh flowers.

Other historic sites in Arundel include the **Maison Dieu**, a mediaeval hospital which can be found outside the Mill Road lodge of Arundel Castle. Founded around 1380 and dissolved in 1546, this semi-monastic institution combined the roles of clinic, hotel and almshouse. The heart of the old town contains some fine Georgian and Victorian houses and inns, most notably in Maltravers and Tarrant Streets. The Norfolk Arms in the High Street is a pleasant 18th-century coaching inn; however, for a warm welcome and some first-rate food and drink we suggest trying the **Arundel Park Inn** in Station Road.

Close to the magnificent Arundel Castle and within easy reach of the Wildfowl and Wetlands Trust, the inn makes an ideal touring base for this beautiful part of West Sussex. A real family concern, the inn is run by the Pooles whose long experience in the hotel and catering world is immediately apparent, in the beautifully furnished en-suite accommodation, the comfortable well-stocked bar which serves 'Real Ales', and the spacious informal restaurant where you can sample a wide range of excellent home-cooked fare that caters to all tastes.

Arundel Park Inn, Station Approach, Arundel, West Sussex
BN18 9L 0903 882588 Map Ref : 6A

Arundel also contains a couple of interesting museums; the privately-owned **Arundel Toy and Military Museum** is located in a charming Georgian cottage in the High Street known as the Doll's House. Inside, visitors can see a unique collection of antique dolls, teddy bears, puppets, games, boats, tin toys and around 3000 toy soldiers. Open daily, 10.45am to 5pm between Easter and October; admission charge payable. Further along the High Street, the **Arundel Museum and Heritage Centre** gives an fascinating insight into the people and activities of the town through imaginative use of models, old photographs and historic artefacts. Open Tuesdays to Sundays, 11am to 1pm (not Sundays) and 2pm to 5pm between Easter and October; small admission charge payable.

Another good place to visit lies just to the north of Arundel on the road to Offham and South Stoke. The sixty-acre woodland site run by the **Wildfowl and Wetlands Trust** contains a wide variety of ducks, geese, swans and other wildfowl from all over the world. Many of the birds can be viewed at close quarters, with Arundel Castle providing a dramatic backdrop. There is also an award-winning visitor centre with a viewing gallery, gift shop and restaurant. Open daily, 9.30am to 6.30pm (5pm in winter), all year round; admission charge payable.

Another impressive view of Arundel Castle can be enjoyed from the picturesque village of **Burpham**. This small and peaceful settlement lies across the river from the Wildfowl Trust, but can only be reached along a narrow three-mile cul-de-sac which leads up from the A27 along the eastern bank of the Arun. Burpham consists of an attractive collection of flint and brick-built thatched cottages, with a pleasant 18th-century inn and a sizable village church. This was built in the 12th- and 13th-centuries, mainly of flint but with the occasional inclusion of rubble from a Roman structure which once stood on the site (sections of a Roman pavement have since been discovered in the north transept). During the Middle Ages, a remote farm on nearby Wepham Down was the site of a leper colony and the track leading down to the village from the Downs is still known as Lepers' Way.

Poling, a small settlement on the other side of the A27 three miles to the south, was once the regional headquarters of the Knights Hospitallers. This holy order of the Hospital of St John of Jerusalem (a present-day descendant of which is the St John's Ambulance Brigade) was founded around 1070 as a sanctuary for Christian travellers making the pilgrimage to the Holy Land. However, during the Crusades the order took on a more military role and became hugely wealthy as a result of some clever manoeuvring; they later established themselves throughout the eastern Mediterranean and then across the whole of western Europe. The Knights founded an important preceptory in Poling, and some of its remains, including the chapel, now form part of a private residence which still goes by the name of St John's Priory.

From Poling we returned to the A27 and drove westwards for a mile before turning south onto the A284 Littlehampton road. Our next stop was **Lyminster**, an ancient settlement of flint-built cottages and protective walls which appears (as *Lullyngminster*) in Alfred the

Great's will of 901. Another marvellous view of Arundel Castle can be enjoyed from here, this time looking northwest across the water meadows of the lower Arun. Local legend has it that the deep pool known as the Knucker Hole which lies 100 yards northwest of Lyminster church was once inhabited by a savage sea dragon. The monster terrorised the local population to such an extent that the King of Wessex offered half his kingdom and his daughter's hand in marriage to the man who killed the beast. The dragon was finally done away with after a terrible fight, either by a gallant young farm boy known as Jim Pulk or a handsome knight, depending on which version of the legend you choose to read. Both versions agree, however, that the ancient tombstone in the north transept of the church is where the conquering hero was finally laid to rest; it is still known today as the Slayer's Stone.

At the mouth of the River Arun two miles to the south, **Littlehampton** is a pleasant coastal town which has all the ingredients for a traditional seaside holiday. As well as safe sandy beaches and a harbour, there is a promenade, a funfair, a swimming and sports centre, a boating lake, an amusement park, a cinema, a theatre, and an eighteen-hole golf course on the western side of the river; Littlehampton is also a popular yachting centre and pleasure boat trips are available for trips up the river to Arundel and Amberley.

Despite appearing to have been specially made for holidaymakers, the modern face of Littlehampton only developed after 1860 when the railway first connected it with London. Prior to that, the town had a rich past, though sadly there is little visible evidence of this today. Signs of Roman occupation have been discovered here, and the local manor is mentioned in the Domesday Book; after the Norman Invasion, Littlehampton became an important cross-Channel port, importing stone from Caen and exporting timber from the Sussex Weald. In 1139, Queen Matilda landed here from France to launch her abortive campaign to claim the English throne from her cousin, Stephen.

Further information on the history of the town can be found at the informative **Littlehampton Museum** which is located in the old Manor House in Church Street. Open Tuesdays to Saturdays, 10.30am to 4.30pm, all year round; admission free. Another interesting museum on the social and cultural history of the district is situated in the parish council offices in **Rustington**, the town bordering Littlehampton to the east. The **Rustington Heritage Centre** is open on Tuesdays, Thursdays and Saturdays, 10am to 12 noon between April and October; admission free.

The coastal communities of **Rustington, East Preston,**

Angmering-on-Sea, Ferring and **Goring-by-Sea** have that pleasant suburban air much loved by those in search of a peaceful retirement or a holiday without any surprises. The towns grew rapidly from small fishing villages following the arrival of the railways in the mid-19th-century. Relics from this almost forgotten past include the church of St Peter and St Paul in Rustington which has a 12th-century tower, St Mary's church in East Preston, and a sprinkling of old cottages dating from pre-Victorian times. Modern Angmering-on-Sea has a couple of good restaurants and hotels, and East Preston a locally-renowned eating place, the Old Forge Restaurant. An impressive avenue of mature ilex oaks connects Ferring with Goring-by-Sea, and the English Martyrs Catholic church in Goring contains an astonishing two-thirds replica of Michelangelo's Sistine Chapel ceiling which was completed in 1992 by local sign-writer, Gary Bevans.

Continuing eastwards along the coast, our next port of call was the sizable resort of **Worthing**. Despite having been inhabited since the stone age, Worthing remained a small and isolated fishing community until the end of the 18th-century when the combined effects of a new northern road link through the Findon Gap and the sudden popularity of sea-bathing amongst the rich and fashionable set led to a period of rapid development. This reached its peak after 1798 when George III sent his sixteen year-old daughter, Princess Amelia, to Worthing to recuperate from an ill-chosen affair with one of his royal equerries. During this period, several fine Regency thoroughfares were constructed, most notably Warwick Road, Montague Place, Liverpool Terrace and Park Terrace, all of which survive today.

By 1830, however, Worthing's Golden Age had come to an end. Further expansion was interrupted by the cholera and typhoid outbreaks of the 1850s and 1890s, and it was not until the inter-war years of the 20th-century that the town once again saw a period of development, albeit of a less grandiose kind. Today, Worthing is a bustling seaside town with a pier, theatre and cinemas which offers some excellent shopping and entertainment facilities in an atmosphere of dignified Regency charm.

Visitors interested in finding out more about the town's history from Neolithic times to the present day should make a point of finding the award-winning **Worthing Museum and Art Gallery** in Chapel Road. Exhibits here include a model of a Neolithic flint mine, Anglo-Saxon glass and jewellery, a fascinating collection of antique toys and dolls, and a display of English paintings, glassware and china from

61

Worthing Pier.

the Regency period onwards. Open Mondays to Saturdays, 10am to 5pm (6pm in summer), all year round; admission free.

As Worthing expanded during the 19th-century, it swallowed up a number of ancient nearby settlements: **Broadwater** still contains some fine old cottages and a Norman church with two ornate carved arches and a number of fine monuments, and **West Tarring** contains the remains of a 13th-century palace belonging to the Archbishops of Canterbury, the central building of which now doubles as a village hall and primary school annexe. West Tarring's High Street features a group of exceptional timber-framed houses dating from the 15th-century known as Parsonage Row; now restored by the Sussex Archeological Society, the row features an interesting folk museum and a charming restaurant, the Parsonage.

Lying just to the north of the A27, two-and-a-half miles northeast of Worthing, the parish church of St Mary the Virgin at **Sompting** is built to a design which is unique in Britain. The distinctive spire consists of four diamond-shaped faces which taper to a point; known as a *Rhenish helm*, the form was popular in Rhineland Germany but is unknown elsewhere in the U.K. This largely Saxon structure dates from well before the Norman Conquest; however in 1154, it was acquired by the Knights Templars who carried out a number of major alterations. Growing unease about the Templars' unbridled military power led to their disbandment in 1312 and the church then passed into the hands of their great rivals, the Knights Hospitallers, who decided to 'restore' the spire and settled upon the present design which they considered was in keeping with original Saxon structure.

The towns along this narrow stretch of the Sussex coastal plain converge into one sprawling urban area, the next part of which is **Lancing**. South Lancing is an undistinguished residential area which was built to house the workforce of the Lancing railway carriage works which relocated here in 1910 and continued to operate until the 1960s. By contrast, the most distinctive feature in North Lancing is its famous public school, **Lancing College**, whose lofty chapel stands out above the valley of the River Adur. The school was founded 1848 by Nathaniel Woodard, a curate at nearby New Shoreham whose ambition was to establish a group of 'classless' schools. (By the time of his death in 1891, fifteen schools had joined his federation.) Despite its French Gothic style, the great chapel was only completed in recent years; its towering floodlit walls and hilltop location make it a striking feature on the nighttime horizon.

The minor road which runs up the western side of the Adur to the north of Lancing College led us to a truly hidden place, the tiny settlement of **Coombes**. Apart from a few houses and a farmyard, the

St Mary the Virgin at Sompting.

only other building in the hamlet is a modest church; however, it is worth taking a look inside, for this unassuming building contains some exceptional 12th-century murals which are believed to have been painted by the group from St Pancras Priory, Lewes who were also responsible for those at Clayton and Hardham. Coombes churchyard is entered through a rare *tapsel* gate, an unusual design characteristic of Sussex in which the frame revolves around a central upright (another example can be seen at Pyecombe). Nearby Church Farm is an open farm set in a wonderful downland setting which welcomes pre-booked groups of visitors.

The ancient port of **Shoreham-by-Sea** stands at the mouth of the River Adur, two miles to the south. There is evidence of both Roman and Saxon occupation here, although it was not until the Norman period that the town became an important river- and seaport. At that time, the Adur was navigable as far as Bramber (and for small craft, on up to Shipley) and the main port stood a mile-or-so upstream from its present position at Old Shoreham. Here, the Normans built a church, St Nicholas', on the foundations of a Saxon predecessor which was later to be sympathetically restored by the Victorians.

After 1100, however, the river estuary began to silt up and the old port and toll bridge were abandoned in favour of a new purpose-built site at New Shoreham. The great church of St Mary de Haura (meaning *of the harbour*) was built here with huge Caen stone walls and an 80ft tower. It was one of the largest non-monastic churches of its day, although sadly the nave collapsed in 1720 and was never replaced. The new port then flourished until the 16th-century when the growth of a shingle spit diverted the course of the river with economically disastrous results. Shoreham then declined for two centuries until the rise of nearby Brighton and the excavation of a new river course in 1818 led to a revival in the town's fortunes.

To reflect this new-found importance, **Shoreham Fort** was constructed at the eastern end of Shoreham Beach as part of Palmerston's coastal defence system. Built around 1854, this half-moon shaped *lunette* was capable of accommodating six muzzle-loading guns which each could fire 80lbs of shot; in recent years the structure has been restored and is open to visitors free of charge. Today, Shoreham handles three million tons of cargo a year and is well-established as the nearest south coast port to London.

Further information on the history of Shoreham can be found at the **Marlipins Museum**, a fascinating establishment which is housed in one of the oldest surviving non-religious buildings in the country. This former Norman customs warehouse was refaced during the 14th-century with an unusual knapped-flint and Caen stone chequerwork façade and has a single 42ft beam supporting the first floor. The building, whose galleries have recently been comprehensively rearranged, has been owned by the Sussex Archeological Society since 1929. Along with special maritime and topographical displays, there are good general exhibits on local geology, history and archeology. Open Tuesdays to Sundays, 10am to 1pm (not Sundays) and 2pm to 4.30pm between May and September; admission free.

From Shoreham, we joined the A283 and after crossing the A27, headed north along the Adur valley to the old mediaeval towns of Steyning and Bramber. Now a prosperous small country town, **Steyning** was founded in the 8th-century by St Cuthman who, according to local legend, settled here as a boy after the cart in which he was pushing his invalid mother broke down on a journey from the West Country. St Cuthman went on to build a timber church in which Ethelwulf, father of King Alfred, is believed to have been buried. In the 12th-century, the Saxon structure was replaced by the fine Romanesque church of St Andrew which at one time was part of a larger monastic house belonging to the abbey at Fécamp in Normandy. Despite its unexceptional outward appearance, the building has a striking interior with towering Norman columns, a 12th-century marble font and some impressive carved stonework.

By the late-Saxon period, Steyning had grown to become an important port on the then-navigable estuary of the River Adur, but around 1100, the silting up of the river forced the quay to close. However, the community had become sufficiently established by then to sustain itself as a small market town and many of the fine late-mediaeval buildings which survive in High and Church Streets were constructed in a variety of styles and materials in the centuries which followed.

Indeed, Steyning is filled with exceptional examples of early domestic buildings, including several 14th- and 15th-century 'hall' type houses, such as the Post Office and Penfold Cottage, and Wealden cottages, such as Workhouse Cottage in Mouse Lane. Another outstanding structure is Steyning's famous Old Grammar School which was founded in 1614 in a long timber-framed building in Church Street; this has a characteristic overhanging upper storey and a roof covered with thin slabs of Horsham stone, and is now used as a school library. A good place to discover more about the town's long and eventful history is the **Steyning Museum** in Church Street; copies of an informative walking tour guide published by the Steyning Society are also on sale here. Open Tuesdays, Wednesdays, Fridays and Saturdays, 10.30am to 12.30pm and 2.30pm to 4.30pm, all year round; admission free.

At one end of the High Street in the country town of Steyning, you will find **The White Horse Inn**. Although the original inn had its frontage on the High Street in Victiorian times, it actually dates back to 1441 and it is said that Charles I resided here on occasions. The present inn building used to be the stables which were converted into an extension over 100 years ago. At one stage, the place was badly burned and the occupant died, along with his dog who had gone in to help his master. On entering this first class establishment, you are met by a warm, welcoming pub atmosphere. This is obviously a popular meeting place for visitors and locals alike. The bars are long which makes serving easier, and here you can choose from a wide selection of wines, spirits and 'Real Ales'. The excellent food menu is extensive and reasonably priced with something to suit every taste, including such delights as Peppered Smoked Mackerel, Lamb Rump Steaks, or Tuna and Pasta Bake. Alternatively you can choose from the list of 'specials' on the blackboard, which change daily.

Please Don't Forget...

To tell people that you read about them in

The Hidden Places

The White Horse Inn, 23 High Street, Steyning, Sussex BN4 3YE
0903 812347 Map Ref : 5C

Its close proximity to the South Downs Way and the Downs Link, the long-distance bridleway which follows the course of the old railway line to Christ's Hospital near Horsham and on to Guildford, makes Steyning an excellent base for walking and riding holidays. The same can be said of **Bramber**, the former Norman administrative centre and garrison town which lies beside the Adur, one mile to the east.

Following the Norman Invasion, William the Conqueror granted the land at Bramber to his trusted lieutenant, William de Braose, who erected a wooden keep on top of a prominent chalky outcrop beside the river. In due course, the timber structure was replaced by stone fortifications which included a gatehouse and a number domestic buildings surrounded by a curtain wall. During the Middle Ages,

Bramber Castle became an important stronghold which was visited, among others, by King John and Edward I; however, the town's subsequent decline and the effects of Parliamentarian cannon-fire reduced most of the castle to rubble except for the conspicuous 75ft high section of the gatehouse keep which can be seen today. William de Braose was also responsible for building the chapel at the foot of the castle mound which is now the parish church of St Nicholas. Despite a number of major alterations throughout the centuries, the original nave and church tower remain.

In the 15th-century, the lands of the de Braose family were transferred to Magdalen College, Oxford whose founder, William Waynflete, the then Bishop of Winchester, once owned the mediaeval residence in Bramber known as **St Mary's**. This unique half-timbered structure was originally built as a monastic hospital to serve pilgrims en route to Canterbury; it was remodelled around 1470 and has recently been restored. At one time, it was lived in by the monastic wardens of the adjacent bridge over the Adur, a structure which until the 1470s, had an unusual chapel at its centre. In October 1651, Charles II is alleged to have rode across Bramber Bridge on his flight from the Battle of Worcester to the ship waiting to take him from Shoreham to safe exile in France. Today, visitors to St Mary's can view the magnificent Painted Room which was specially decorated for a visit by Elizabeth I, before enjoying a homemade tea in the music room.

Before the Reform Act of 1832 swept away the so-called rotten boroughs, the tiny constituencies of Bramber, Steyning and Shoreham each returned two MPs to Westminster. This was in spite of the fact that at one time Bramber had only 32 eligible voters. One MP who benefited from the unreformed system was William Wilberforce who was more or less 'awarded' one of the Bramber seats in recognition for his campaigning work against slavery and social injustice; he is said to have made only one fleeting visit to his constituency during the whole of his twelve-year tenure.

Lying between the castle and the bridge, Bramber High Street contains some interesting shops and businesses including the unusual **House of Pipes**, a museum with a collection of 38,000 cigarette cards, tobacco tins and other items relating to the smoking of tobacco.

A delightful stopping-off point for visitors to the picturesque village of Bramber is **The Old Tollgate Restaurant and Hotel**. This charming hostelry stands on the site of the original Toll-House and is a perfect blending of the old with the new. In the older part of the hotel, the Cubby Hole and Tack Room provide cosy intimate surroundings for a romantic dinner, whilst the carvery-style restaurant offers a magnificent visual a la carte display which leaves you spoilt for choice. In the more recent extension the accommodation comprises 31 beautifully furnished and excellently equipped en-suite bedrooms. With the ruins of Bramber Castle on the hill behind and outstanding views all around, The Old Tollgate is ideal for that relaxing break away from it all.

The Old Tollgate Restaurant and Hotel, The Street, Bramber,
Steyning, West Sussex BN44 3WE 0903 879494 Map Ref : 5C

Continuing eastwards across the bridge from Bramber, our next stopping place was **Upper Beeding**, a sprawling village with a pleasant main street. The now-demolished Benedictine priory of Sele was founded here around 1075 by William de Braose; now occupied by a private residence, its former site lies to the north of the present parish church, a building which in turn suffered a brutal remodelling at the hands of the Victorians. During the early 19th-century, an important turnpike road passed through Upper Beeding and the old village toll cottage, one of the last in the county to remain in service, is now an exhibit at the Weald and Downland Museum at Singleton (see chapter one).

To the east of Upper Beeding, the narrow road running along the spring-line at the foot the South Downs ridge connects a series of attractive villages. At **Edburton** there is a small 13th-century church, and at **Fulking**, a spring gushes out across the road near the ancient village pub. At no other place are the Downs more dramatic than above the village of **Poynings**; this is the location of the famous local landmark, **Devil's Dyke**, a steep-sided dry ravine which, according to folklore, was dug by Satan in an unsuccessful attempt to flood the Christian churches of the Weald with the sea. At almost 700ft above sea level, the fifteen-acre promontory above Devil's Dyke forms an easily defendable site on which the Iron Age people built a formidable hill fort. A high earthwork wall was built to defend the

Devil's Dyke.

gently sloping southwestern approaches of the fortifications, the remains of which can still be seen today (indeed, the course of the present-day road passes through the original fort entrance).

During Victorian times, the Devil's Dyke viewpoint became a popular attraction. Not only was a railway built to connect it with Brighton, but a cable car system was installed across the ravine and down to the villages at the foot of the steep Downs escarpment. Evidence of these has long since disappeared and today, Devil's Dyke is the domain of motorists, walkers and hang-gliding enthusiasts. A little further along the South Downs Way, and inaccessible by road, lie two delightful areas of National Trust-owned downland which are worth making the effort to reach, **Fulking Escarpment** and **Newtimber Hill**.

After returning to the valley floor, we crossed the **A23** near **Pyecombe**, a former coaching village with a good inn and a Norman church with a tapsel gate similar to the one we encountered at Coombes. Our next destination was **Clayton**, one mile to the northeast, an unusual village whose parish church contains a series of 12th-century wall-paintings which are thought to be by the same group of artists from the St Pancras Priory in Lewes who were responsible for those at Hardham and Coombes. Rediscovered in the 1890s, the murals depict some salutary scenes of eternal damnation from the *Last Judgment*.

The village stands at the northern end of the one-and-a-quarter-mile long **Clayton Tunnel**, an engineering wonder of its day which opened in 1846 and still carries the busy London to Brighton rail link. A towering Victorian folly known as Tunnel House stands at the tunnel's northern portal. Built to house the resident tunnel-keeper, this castellated mock-Tudor fortress is still in occupation today.

A unique pair of windmills known as **Jack and Jill** stands above the village on Clayton Hill. Jack is a black-painted tower mill which fell into disuse in the 1920s and has since been converted into an unusual private home; Jill is a smaller timber-built post mill which was built in 1821 and was removed from its original site in Dyke Road, Brighton by a team of oxen around 1850. Now restored, it is still capable of grinding corn and is occasionally open to visitors.

A couple of interesting country houses lie within easy reach of Clayton; **Danny**, a characteristic E-shaped manor house with an impressive great hall, lies one mile to the northwest, and **Newtimber Place**, a moated flint and brick-built residence, lies on the western side of the A23 a couple of miles to the west.

Henfield, three miles west of Albourne, was once an important

71

Jack and Jill Windmills.

staging post on the busy London to Brighton coaching route. The village contains a couple of good former coaching inns, a much-restored church built on Saxon foundations, and an eccentric 16th-century cottage known as the **Cat House** which is decorated with a collection of highly unusual iron cats. These were made by local joiner Bob Ward to scare off the vicar's cat after it had crept in and eaten his pet canary. The Henfield Village Museum in the village hall contains an interesting collection of historic artefacts from the area. Open 10am to 12 noon on Mondays, Tuesdays, Thursdays and Saturdays; 2.30pm to 4.30pm on Wednesdays; admission free.

The impressive headquarters of the Sussex Wildlife Trust are situated a mile to the south of Henfield at **Woods Mill.** Set within a fifteen-acre nature reserve, this three-storey 18th-century water mill contains a fascinating exhibition on the natural history of the locality. Open 2pm to 6pm on Tuesdays to Thursdays and Saturdays; 11am to 6pm on Sundays and Bank Holidays between Easter and end-September; admission charge payable.

From Henfield, we headed north along the A281 Horsham road for two miles before turning west onto the B2116 and then northwest onto the B2135. Our next destination was **West Grinstead**, a scattered community with a fine country house and two interesting churches: designed in the early 1800s by the famous Regency architect John Nash, **West Grinstead Park** is now an established racehorse breeding centre which is part of the National Stud. The parish church of St George dates from early-Norman times and has an unusual 15th-century timbered porch; the stability of early-19th-century life in this part of rural Sussex is reflected in the names of the local farms which can still be seen painted on the backs of the church pews. A long-established centre of Catholicism, West Grinstead also possesses a Catholic church which was regularly visited by the writer Hilaire Belloc when he was resident at nearby Shipley.

One mile to the west of West Grinstead, the busy **A24** runs alongside the stark ruin of **Knepp Castle**, the fortification built by William de Braose of Bramber to defend the upper reaches of the River Adur. All that remains of this once-impressive Norman keep is a solitary wall standing on top of a low earthwork mound, or *motte*, which in turn is surrounded by a dry moat. The rest of the castle was demolished in 1726 and the rubble used to form the base for a new road between Horsham and Steyning above which motorists still travel today.

Three miles to the northeast of West Grinstead, the attractive village of **Cowfold** stands at the busy junction of the **A272** and **A281**. The parish church of St Peter is surrounded by some charming

73

domestic buildings and contains an exceptional 15th-century monumental brass of the prior of St Pancras Priory in Lewes; this renowned monastic house belonged to the rare Cluniac order and was home to the talented team of artists who, a couple of centuries earlier, were responsible for painting some of the most exceptional ecclesiastical murals in Sussex.

It is hard to believe today that Cowfold was once an important centre of the iron industry. The abundance of timber for fuel and reliable streams to drive the bellows and heavy hammers made this an active iron-smelting area from mediaeval times to the end of the 18th-century. In order to secure a steady supply of water to these early foundries, small rivers were dammed to form triangular mill- or hammer ponds, and a number of disused examples can still be seen in the surrounding woodlands, especially around **Crabtree**, a couple of miles to the north.

The beautiful **Leonardslee Gardens** lie in a natural valley on the eastern side of the A281, half-a-mile north of Crabtree. Laid out in the early 19th-century, this spectacular spring-flowering garden has been extensively planted with rhododendrons, azaleas, magnolias and other specimen shrubs. The valley also contains a series of small lakes, possibly disused hammer ponds, around which deer and wallabies live in semi-wild conditions. Open daily in spring, and at weekends in summer and autumn; admission charge payable.

South Lodge Hotel, Lower Beeding, Near Horsham, West Sussex
RH13 6PS 0403 891711 Map Ref : 3D

Situated in the heart of West Sussex countryside on the **A281** at Lower Beeding, **South Lodge Hotel** is a magnificent Victorian house standing in 90 acres of beautifully parkland and gardens. Originally built by Frederick Ducane Godman, a noted explorer and botanist, it is him we can thank for the variety of rare shrubs and plants that fill the hotel grounds. Here you will find luxurious

74

elegance in every room. The spacious dining room boasts lovely views of the rolling Sussex countryside, the source of much of the fine fresh produce served, whilst the 39 individually designed bedrooms provide an atmosphere of luxurious comfort ensuring total relaxation. An area steeped in history, Sussex is full of wonderful places to visit and you would be hard put to find a finer touring base than South Lodge Hotel.

Another distinctive hammer pond can be found just to the north of Lower Beeding on the southern fringe of **St Leonard's Forest**. This 10,000-acre wooded heath is one of the few treed areas to survive the long-term ravages of the timber-fuelled iron industry. Rising in places to around 500ft, the forest lies on the undulating sandstone ridge bounded by Horsham, Crawley and Handcross. According to local folklore, St Leonard's Forest is the home of a legendary 9ft dragon which roamed the heath and terrorised the surrounding villagers. Coincidentally, the bones of a prehistoric iguanodon have since been discovered in the Forest by the Sussex-based geologist, Dr Gideon Mantell.

The Old Posthouse can be found on the **A279** between Handcross and Lower Beeding, just 13 miles from Gatwick Airport and 4 miles from Horsham. As the local General Store and Post Office, this charming 19th century house was the centre of the community until 1987 when it was converted into the spacious guest house it is today. The accommodation comprises one triple, three en-suite double/twin and two single rooms, all attractively furnished and well-equipped. Your friendly hostess Molly Murby, a keen member of the W.I., runs a welcoming house based on traditional values. She is an avid cactus collector and keeps over 1500 in a greenhouse at the back, whilst the garden provides homegrown vegetables to accompany the evening meal.

The Old Posthouse, Handcross Road, Plummers Plain, Lower Beeding, Near Horsham, Surrey   RH13 6NU 0403 891776 Map Ref:3D

From Lower Beeding, we drove northeast along the A279 to **Handcross**, home of the celebrated National Trust-owned **Nymans Garden**. Set around the ruins of a country mansion, this splendid thirty-acre landscaped area incorporates a walled garden, sunken garden, old rose garden, topiary garden, laurel walk and pinetum. Together, these contain a wonderful collection of specimen trees, shrubs and flowering plants, many of which are native to other continents. Open daily (except Fridays and non-Bank Holiday

Mondays), 11am to 7pm between April 1st and end-October; admission charge payable (free to National Trust members).

On leaving Nymans, we joined the **B2114** and drove southeast for four miles to reach **Cuckfield**, a sizable village with an exceptional Elizabethan and Georgian centre. The Norman lords of Lewes who once used to hunt deer and wild boar in the forest around Cuckfield also founded a church on high ground; this was rebuilt in the 13th-century with a shingled broach spire and Horsham 'slate' roof and became Cuckfield's parish church. It was again altered in Victorian times and today, contains some fine carved monuments and stained-glass windows.

Before a new turnpike road was built in 1807, Cuckfield stood on the main London to south coast coaching route and a number of fine buildings remain from this era of genteel prosperity, including the King's Head coaching inn in the High Street, the **Talbot** former law courts and civic centre, and **Ockenden Manor**, now a hotel. Cuckfield's gradual development has given rise to an unusually wide assortment of building styles and materials, including brick, local sandstone, weatherboarding and tile-hanging. Those interested in discovering more about the history of this fine old settlement should make a point of visiting **Cuckfield Museum** in Queen's Hall in the High Street. Open Tuesdays, Wednesdays and Saturdays, 10am to 12.30pm; admission free. Situated near Ansty, two miles to the southwest of Cuckfield, the impressive Sussex Archeological Society-affiliated **Legh Manor** is open to visitors from 2.30pm to 5.30pm on the second and third Wednesday and second Saturday of the month between May and September.

During the Elizabethan era, the leading Cuckfield iron-master, Henry Bowyer, built **Cuckfield Park**. This substantial country house and estate was subsequently acquired by the Sergison family who, during the 1840s, refused permission for the new South Coast Railway to cross their land. As a result, the railway was forced to the east and a station built at **Haywards Heath**, a then-remote settlement on exposed heathland which within a few years had grown sufficiently to depose Cuckfield as the area's main market town.

On entering Haywards Heath from the west along the A272, we passed through the conservation area around **Muster Green**, a pleasant open space surrounded by trees which is believed to take its name from the obligatory annual 17th-century custom of 'mustering the militia'. Close by, we came across the 16th-century Sergison Arms, perhaps the oldest building in the town, which takes its name from the landed family who once owned Cuckfield Park.

Just a little way to the east from Hayward's Heath is Freshfield

Lock where you will find **The Sloop Inn.** Freshfield Lock could hardly be called a 'hidden place' to anyone who lives in this part of England, but for those of you visiting Sussex it is a place you just might miss, which would be sad. It would be even sadder if you did not call in at the Sloop Inn, which was originally for bargees, and has been constantly used as a good traditional pub in the two hundred years of its life span. You can imagine what it must have been like back in those days as you sit in the comfortable, friendly bar enjoying a drink. It has a slight Victorian air about it, but is far lighter than one would expect from a building of this age. There are three separate beer gardens, and whichever one you choose to sit in on a sunny day will reward you with a variety of trees and colourful plants to look at. The gardens are very sheltered, and are complete sun traps. We watched children playing safely and happily on the climbing frames whilst their parents refreshed themselves from the exertions of a holiday with a well-earned drink! The pub is surrounded by farmland, and there are many kinds of farm animals as well as loads of wildlife. You can eat extremely well at The Sloop, either at lunch or dinner. The blackboard menu has no less than 40 different dishes available; anything from quiches to steaks, or seafood. People living in the area use the pub regularly for meals, and many are greeted by name; but have no fear, you will have just as friendly a welcome. The pub would rightly be described as picturesque, and sitting alongside the canal it is real postcard material. It is very pleasant to take a walk around here, either along the canal bank or lightly further afield. To get there just go off the A272 from Scaynes Hill and just one and a half miles on you will find Freshfield Lock. Go along Church Road and just follow the signs.

The Sloop Inn, Freshfield Lock, Hayward's Heath, Sussex
RH17 7NP 0444 831219 Map Ref : 3G

It's well worth making the short diversion to visit **Borde Hill**

Garden, an award-winning landscaped estate which can be found on the Balcombe road, one-and-a-half miles north of Haywards Heath. As well as a superb collection of late-spring flowering shrubs, the garden offers some delightful woodland walks, a lake with an adjoining picnic area, a children's adventure playground, an attractive plant sales area, and some spectacular views over the surrounding Sussex Weald. Open daily, 10am to 6pm between late-March to late-October; admission charge payable.

Despite lying only a mile or so to the northeast of central Haywards Heath, the ancient village of **Lindfield** could not be more dissimilar in character. Like Cuckfield three miles to the west, Lindfield resisted the onslaught of the railway, instead preferring to retain its rural gentility. Today, the village rises from a well-manicured common, complete with village pond and cricket pitch, along a High Street, complete with listed Georgian redbrick and older timber-framed buildings, to an impressive 14th-century parish church, complete with shingled broach spire. Indeed, there are a great many noteworthy buildings in Lindfield, particularly around the church and along the High Street, although ironically we somehow found the atmosphere here to be a little *over*-perfect.

The church house adjacent to the parish church is a former inn which still retains its original name, the Tiger, and further down Lindfield High Street, the Old Brewery now houses a private museum dedicated to the valve-operated radio, the **Wireless Museum**; this contains a large collection of receivers made prior to the introduction of the transistor in the early 1960s, as well as crystal sets, wind-up gramophones and wireless accessories. Open Tuesdays, Thursdays and Fridays, 10am to 5pm, all year round; small admission charge payable.

Continuing northwards along the **B2028**, after a mile or so we passed the imposing redbrick edifice of **Ardingly** (pronounced Arding-*lye*) **College**, the famous public school which, like Lancing College, was founded by the pioneering churchman Nathaniel Woodard. A mile-and-a-half further north, the parish church in Ardingly village contains some fine monumental brasses of the Wakehurst and Culpeper families, the former owners of nearby Wakehurst Place. To the west of the village, a tributary of the River Ouse has been dammed to form **Ardingly Reservoir**, a 200-acre lake which offers some good fishing, and on a permanent site to the northwest, the three-day **South of England Show** takes place each year in early June. As well as being the venue for the region's premier agricultural event, the showground hosts a range of other attractions, including showjumping competitions and antiques' fairs.

Situated beside the B2028 a mile-and-a-half north of Ardingly, the National Trust-owned **Wakehurst Place** is sometimes referred to as 'Kew in the Country'. This beautiful Elizabethan country mansion and estate was originally built for Sir Edward Culpeper in 1590 and is now managed by the Royal Botanic Gardens, Kew. The grounds contain an unrivalled collection of rare trees, flowering shrubs and plants which are laid out in a variety of imaginative settings; there is a Winter Garden, a nature reserve, a Rock Walk and a famous water garden consisting of a series of lakes, ponds and streams linked by a nature trail. Open daily, 10am to 7pm (or dusk if earlier), all year round; admission charge payable (free to National Trust members).

On leaving Wakehurst Place, we retraced our steps southwards for a short distance before turning northeast onto the narrow country road leading to **West Hoathly** (sometimes pronounced Hoath-*lye*, sometimes Hoath-*lee*). Standing at an ancient road junction almost 600ft up on a ridge of the High Weald, this historic settlement has some panoramic views of the South Downs. It also contains some outstanding old buildings: the Norman church was founded around 1090 and rebuilt in the 13th-century, the Cat Inn was the haunt of smugglers in the 18th-century, and the stone-built Gravetye Manor was constructed around 1627 for a local iron-master and is now a first-class country house hotel.

Perhaps most exceptional, however, is the **Priest House**, a delightful early-15th-century timber-framed residence with a hefty Horsham 'slate' roof. The house was originally built with a large open hall, but was altered to its present layout in Elizabethan times; inside, there is a fine collection of 18th- and 19th-century furniture and a charming museum of village life. The building is surrounded by a traditional English country garden and is now owned by the Sussex Archeological Society; it is open to the public daily (except Tuesdays), 11am (2pm Sundays) to 5.30pm, between late-March and end-October; admission charge payable.

The pleasant village of **Turner's Hill** stands at the junction of the **B2028** and **B2110**, two miles to the northwest of West Hoathly. This is where we discovered the impressive **Tulley's Farm Shop**. With 125 acres of carefully cultivated 'pick your own' produce, Tulleys Farm leaves you spoilt for choice. This superb farm can be found by taking the B2110 from Turners Hill and following the right hand fork signposted Crawley for about 1 mile. In addition to acres of produce, there are 14 acres of parking space, conveniently placed around the site for maximum convenience. The emphasis here is on quality and attention to detail and the staff are most friendly and helpful. As well as 'pick your own', the attractive farm shop which is open all year, is a fascinating place housed within a refurbished milking parlour which offers a wide selection of fruit, vegetables, cakes and confectionery. With picnic places, children's play areas and toilet facilities dotted around the site, a visit here soon becomes a fun day out for the whole family.

Tulleys Farmshop and Pick Your Own, Tulleys Farm, Turners Hill, West Sussex RH10 4PE
Farm shop: 0342 718472 Pick Your Own: 0342 715365 Map Ref: 2G

For those with a particular interest in historic churches, it's well worth venturing westwards to the eastern fringe of Crawley to visit **Worth**. This ancient settlement contains one of the most complete Saxon churches in the country which, despite having been 'restored' and having had a reproduction spire added during Victorian times, retains its original Saxon walls, windows and arches, the largest of which is 22ft high. St Nicholas' Church was built between 950 and 1050, but for some reason isn't mentioned in the Domesday Book. It's still in use today and is open daily during daylight hours. Worth, a Saxon term meaning 'enclosure in the forest', was once an important centre of the iron-smelting industry, and **Rowfant House** on the eastern edge of the village was built for a successful local iron-master during the late-Elizabethan era.

Three miles east of Turner's Hill, we turned south off the **B2110** to reach the exceptional National Trust-owned house and garden, **Standen**. This remarkable late-Victorian country mansion was built by architect, Philip Webb, using a variety of traditional local building materials, including brick, stone, weatherboarding and facing tiles. It was completed in 1894 for a prosperous London solicitor who used it as a family retreat before retiring here some years later. Webb was a colleague of William Morris, the famous founder of the English Arts and Crafts Movement, and the house was fitted with carpets, wallpaper and textiles designed by him. The interior has now been completely restored and, as well as the Morris furnishings, visitors can see the original electric fittings, billiard room and conservatory, all designed in the same lively style which was to become fashionable during the 1920s. The house is set within a beautiful hillside garden and enjoys spectacular views over Ashdown Forest and the valley of the upper Medway river. Open Wednesdays to Sundays (and Bank Holiday Mondays), 1.30pm to 5.30pm between 1st April and end-October; admission charge payable (free to National Trust members).

One-and-a-half miles north of Standen lies the old Sussex market town of **East Grinstead**. Despite its suburban-sounding name, East Grinstead has a surprisingly long and rich history; the town was granted its market charter in 1221 and throughout the late Middle Ages it was one of the most important mercantile and iron-founding centres in the High Weald. The surrounding forest and sandstone ridge provided some excellent building materials and a surprising number of sizable domestic structures from this period survive to this day. Some of the finest can be seen in a group on the southern side of the High Street; these timber-framed buildings are characteristic of the Sussex 'hall' houses which were popular in the 15th- and 16th-centuries and include Amherst House, Sackville House and the imposing **Cromwell House** which was built in 1599 with distinctive oriel windows, brick chimneys and overhanging timbering.

Opposite stands **Sackville College**, a development of Jacobean almshouses built around a courtyard in 1609; this attractive quadrangle, with its sandstone walls, Horsham 'slate' roofs and redbrick chimneys, was constructed for retired workers from the Sackville estates at Buckhurst and Knole. The college was renovated in the 19th-century and continues to house a number of local elderly people; visitors are however permitted to view the public rooms, including the old banqueting hall with its magnificent hammerbeam roof.

The Georgian parish church of **St Swithin** was constructed by James Wyatt in 1789 after the tower of its predecessor had twice collapsed, on the second occasion taking with it the majority of the building. The replacement structure is a striking example of early Gothic revival; it has a spacious interior and a unusually tall tower which is believed to have been built at the request (and expense) of Charles Abbot, the then Speaker of the House of Commons, so that it could be seen from his nearby country estate.

Before the 1832 Reform Act, only the occupants of East Grinstead's 48 original *burgage* plots (long narrow housing allotments) were eligible to vote, making this a notorious rotten borough. As was common practice elsewhere where voting rights were dependent on the ownership of small plots of land, the local landed family, in this case the Sackvilles, would ensure they acquired enough of them to guarantee a comfortable majority. Following a century or so of gradual decline, the coming of the railway in 1855 led to a revival and today, East Grinstead is a flourishing country town with good shopping facilities and some excellent amenities for sports and recreation. There is also an interesting museum of local history in East Court, College Lane which is open on Wednesdays and Saturdays, 2pm to 4pm, all year round; admission free.

CHAPTER THREE

East Sussex.

From Ashdown Forest to the Seven Sisters.

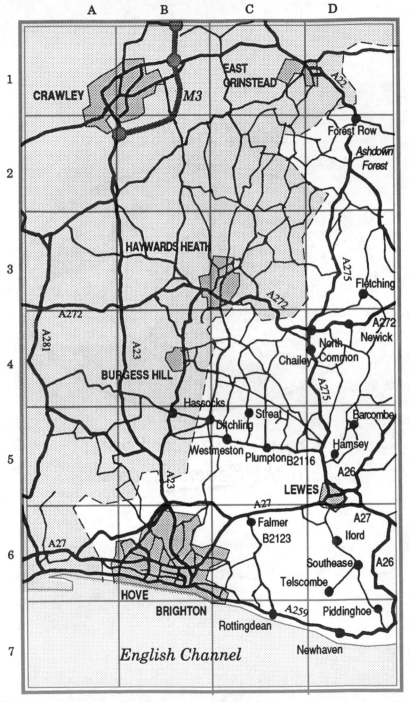

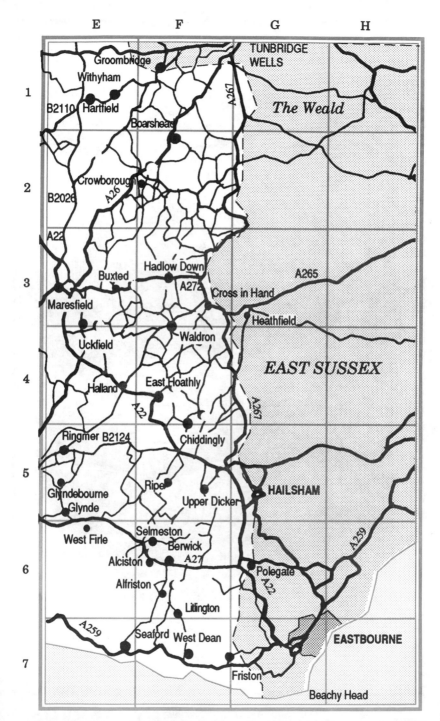

85

Ashdown Forest.

CHAPTER THREE

East Sussex.
From Ashdown Forest to the Seven Sisters.

We crossed into the county of East Sussex near **Forest Row**, a scattered community standing at the junction of the **B2110** and the **A22** London to Eastbourne road. This pioneering 'waste-edge' settlement was founded in the late Middle Ages as a single row of cottages on the fringe of **Ashdown Forest**. At that time the forest was part of the dense and, in places, impenetrable swathe of vegetation which covered the Weald and effectively separated the Thames Valley from the south coast. The Romans knew the forest as *Silva Anderida* and were the first to cut a way through to connect the city of Londinium with their fortified settlement on the south coast at Pevensey. Following the Norman invasion, Ashdown Forest became a royal hunting ground, and the vantage point known as **King's Standing** is believed to have been used by both Edward II and Edward III for observing the chase. In 1372, the whole area was fenced off and given by Edward III to his son, the Duke of Lancaster; modern place names such as Chelwood Gate and Friar's Gate mark the sites of former entrance points.

In common with other parts of the Weald, the plentiful supply of water power and timber for fuel made the fringes of Ashdown Forest into an important centre of the iron industry. The high-temperature smelting process developed in Tudor times required huge quantities of charcoal, making it more economical to bring the iron ore to the fuel source rather than vice-versa. Demand from the iron industry, and to a lesser extent from the shipbuilding and glass-making industries, devastated the forests of the Weald during the centuries leading up to the Industrial Revolution. Ashdown Forest was, however, one of the last areas to be seriously affected and indeed, it survived largely intact until the arrival of new coal-fired technology during the 18th-century finally halted the encroachment of the charcoal burner's axe. Today, Ashdown Forest's 14,000 acres of wildlife-filled woodland and heath are crisscrossed by a network of footpaths which offer some wonderful woodland walking. Further information on what to do and see in the forest can be found at the **Ashdown Forest Centre**, one mile east of Wych Cross on the Coleman's Hatch road.

Forest Row provides an excellent base for exploring the area; it is also surrounded by a number of interesting country houses, including **Kidbrooke Park**, three-quarters-of-a-mile to the southwest, which dates from the early 18th-century and has a garden designed by Repton, **Ashdown House**, one mile to the northeast, which was designed in the 1790s by the architect responsible for several fine buildings in Baltimore and Philadelphia, and **Brambletye House**, half-a-mile to the northwest, which was built in Jacobean style in 1631 and fell into disrepair after its former owner, Sir James Richards, was forced to flee the country in 1683 under suspicion of treason; several impressive towers and wall sections remain.

From Forest Row, we drove eastwards along the B2110 to **Hartfield**, on old hunting settlement which takes its name from the adult male red deer, or hart. The 13th-century village church has a tower with a shingled broach spire and an unusual roofed churchyard gate, and close by stands an early 16th-century timber-framed cottage with an overhanging upper storey which appropriately is known as the Lychgate. Two lovely old pubs can be found towards the centre of the village, the Hay Wagon and the Anchor Inn; the latter dates from the 16th-century and was originally built as a 'house of correction for wayward women'.

Bolebroke Mill, Edenbridge Road, Hartfield, East Sussex TN7 4JP
0892 770425 Map Ref : 1E

For a holiday base with character which offers tranquil surroundings and superb facilities, **Bolebroke Mill** in Hartfield has to be seen to be believed. Heading south along the B2026 towards Hartfield, turn left immediately past Perryhill Nursery down an unmade road and bear right after about 50 yards. Here you will discover the Mill, Miller's Barn and Mill House, the unusual home of Christine and David Cooper. The four beautiful en-suite guest rooms are all unique. For example, guests in the Watermill have a lounge built around old mill machinery and the guest dining room is accessed through a trapdoor which passes the water wheel! The four-course breakfast won the Best Breakfast in Britain award in the BTA's "In Britain" magazine and when you treat yourself to a break here, you will soon understand why.

A A Milne, the author of the much-loved *Winnie The Pooh* stories, lived at Cotchford Farm, half-a-mile south of Hartfield. Along with the artist E H Shepard, he made the landscape of Ashdown Forest come alive to millions of young readers throughout the world. The timber bridge spanning the small tributary of the Medway where Milne's son, Christopher Robin, would meet with his fictitious friends to play *Pooh Sticks* has recently been restored by Milne's publishers and East Sussex County Council.

If like us, you are a fan of Winnie-the-Pooh, then you will want to come to Hartfield and visit **"Pooh Corner"**. You will certainly find your tastes catered for as the shop is full of "Pooh-phanalia". The building was built at around 1690 and has low ceilings. If you are tall, beware of banging your head as you cross the threshold. It is situated in the village where, over sixty years ago, A.A. Milne wrote the famous Pooh stories - on the edge of Ashdown Forest where the stories were set.

Pooh Corner, High Street, Hartfield, East Sussex TN7 4AE
0892 770453 Map Ref : 1E

Inside Pooh Corner is "Piglet's Parlour" Tea Room where you can take a seat at a table with a pink and white table cloth. Apart from delicious Cream Teas you can enjoy locally made Dairy Ice Creams in a dozen different flavours. One of the popular features is, of course, the sweets. When Christopher Robin Milne visited the shop with his

Nanny, 'Alice', on their weekly trips to the village it was bulls-eyes that were their favourites. You can still buy bulls-eyes and nowadays children can choose sweets from glass jars within easy reach. Then there is "Poohsticks Bridge" and the "Enchanted Places" in and around Ashdown Forest. If you prepare yourselves with Wellington boots and an armful of Poohsticks, and promise to be well behaved, a good way to start your "Expotition" is to read the map in the shop window. Opening times: Monday to Saturday 9.00-5.00, Sunday and Bank Holidays 1.30-5.00. Pooh Corner has a Mail Order service. Full colour catalogue £1.00. Proprietor: Mike Ridley.

You will find there are three very good reasons for visiting **Stairs Farm** in Hartfield, since it houses three businesses under one roof. Set back from the village High Street in an elevated position, parts of this delightful building date from the 17th century and the Sackville Crest can be seen on the 1835 frontage. Charming hostess Geraldine Pring enjoys welcoming guests into her lovely home and provides non-smoking accommodation in three very comfortable guest rooms, each offering lovely views. The patio outside forms part of her country style tearoom and here you can savour mouthwatering homemade scones, cakes and traditional hot and cold meals. The third part of her business, the farmshop, provides the organically grown fruit, vegetables and home produced meat etc.

Stairs Farm, High Street, Hartfield, East Sussex TN7 4AB
0892 770793 Map Ref : 1E

One mile east of Hartfield on the B2110, we came to **Withyham**, another pleasant community which is loosely arranged around an attractive green. The village church was built in the mid-17th-century to replace an earlier structure which burnt down after having been struck by lightning. Inside, there is an impressive mural of the *Last Judgment* painted by the Earl de la Warr, the rector here in the mid 19th-century. The surrounding area, and indeed much of Ashdown
90

Forest, was once owned by the Earls' family, the Sackvilles, several of whom are buried in the Sackville Chapel. This section of the church contains an exceptional group of carved stone monuments, including an inscribed slate memorial to Vita Sackville-West, the writer and co-owner of Sissinghurst Garden in Kent who died in 1962, as well as an unusual collection of 18th-century flags belonging to the Dukes of Dorset.

Situated on the B2110 at Withyham you will find a delightful country pub and restaurant called **The Dorset Arms**. Originally an Elizabethan farmhouse, it became an inn during the 18th century then called The Ale House. The cosy bar features open fires and beamed ceilings, providing a lovely setting for a quiet drink and tasty bar snack. The adjoining restaurant is a picture, with lovely pictures and plates on the walls and freshly picked flowers on the tables. The menu is excellent, combining traditional English fare with more unusual dishes, all freshly prepared using the finest local produce. Bar food is available at all times, but the restaurant is closed on Sunday evenings and all day Monday.

The Dorset Arms, Withyham, Near Hartfield, East Sussex TN7 4BD
0892 770278 Map Ref : Map Ref : 1E

A couple of miles further east, the well-groomed village of **Groombridge** stands on the Sussex-Kent border (in fact, the older, more interesting part of the village lies across the river in Kent.) At the centre of the village there is a triangular green which is surrounded by a group of attractive 18th-century cottages, a handsome 17th-century Dower House and a church which began life as the chapel of nearby Groombridge Place. This impressive moated redbrick country mansion lies a short distance away across open parkland and was built to a characteristic 'H' design in the mid 17th-century on the site of an earlier structure. It is set within beautiful terraced gardens (open certain days) which are believed to have been planned by John Evelyn, the 17th-century English diarist.

From Groombridge, we followed the country lanes southeastwards to the **A26** Tunbridge Wells to Crowborough road. Turning southwest, we passed close by the site of the Bowles Outdoor Centre, a residential centre which runs courses for young people and adults in rock climbing, skiing and canoeing. A little further on at **Boarshead**, we took the opportunity of calling in at the charming village pub and eating place, the **Boar's Head Inn**, a traditional English pub dating back to 1636. Here an atmosphere of olde worlde charm is enhanced by exposed oak beams and a lovely inglenook fireplace, whilst outside in the summer you can relax with a drink on the patio beer garden. This is a place where fine ale goes hand in hand with first class homecooked fare, freshly prepared using local produce wherever possible. The pub is thought to have smuggling links and judging by its age and character, you can't help but feel that "there must be a ghost somewhere!"

The Boar's Head Inn, Boarshead, Near Crowborough, East Sussex
TN6 3HD 0892 652412 Map Ref : 2F

The scattered community of **Crowborough** lies on the A26, a couple of miles to the southwest of Boarshead. Its position at over 750ft above sea level makes it is one of the highest towns in Sussex and some splendid views over the High Weald can be enjoyed from the summit of **Crowborough Beacon** near the centre of town. Before the arrival of the railway in the 1860s, all that existed here was a lonely settlement populated by iron-smelters and brigands. However, the new rail link soon attracted commuters keen to escape the grime of Victorian London and gradually transformed Crowborough into a flourishing residential town. Its convenient location also attracted a number of well-known writers around this time, in particular Arthur Conan Doyle, the author of the Sherlock Holmes stories.

Recent residential and retail developments have made Crowborough into a prosperous modern town with good shopping and recreational facilities. An establishment which drew our particular attention was **Chillies Granary**, the delightful and somewhat unusual home of June and Alan Peck. Standing on a hill overlooking open countryside, it can be found off the A26 on Chillies Lane 2 miles from High Hurstwood. An 18th century granary over a carthouse, Chillies Granary has been sympathetically converted and refurbished by the owners and now offers very comfortable accommodation in several guest rooms situated around a minstrel's gallery, some rooms still featuring old "dragon ties and braces" in the corner.. The entrance to the spacious hall faces the stairs which lead to the lovely beamed gallery. Breakfast is served in the hall with its splendid inglenook fireplace and where the original granary wheel is still evident.

Chillies Granary, Chillies Lane, Crowborough, East Sussex
TN6 3TB 0892 655560 Map Ref : 2F

The undulating lanes to the southeast of Crowborough took us through some of loveliest countryside in the Weald and eventually led us onto the **A272** near **Hadlow Down**, just outside Hadlow Down, we discovered **Wilderness Wood**, sixty acres of working woodland which are run as a living museum of woodland management.

Enjoying a peaceful location on the south side of the A272 to the east of Hadlow Down, Wilderness Wood is a rare find indeed. Run by Christopher Yarrow, this wonderful working wood is a 'tree farm' where wood has been grown for almost 1000 years. The barn, built using genuine medieval techniques of wattle and daub, houses a detailed display about the growth and use of wood, as well as refreshments and souvenirs. The woodland trail changes seasonally and here you can test your knowledge of nature by completing the quiz sheets, whilst the play area provides adventure and excitement for the children. There are picnic tables and barbecue stands available and these, the barn, WC and yard area are all accessible to the disabled.

Wilderness Wood, Hadlow Down, Near Uckfield, East Sussex TN22 4HJ 0825 830509 Map Ref : 3F

Situated on the outskirts of the village of Hadlow Down, **Smallberry Hill**, a former Tudor Ironmaster's house dates back to 1542. This charming house is owned by John and Fiona Bickerton who enjoy welcoming guests into their home. The house is beautifully decorated, with lovely antique furniture and paintings adding to the elegance of the splendid drawing room and beamed dining room. From the rear terrace you can enjoy magnificent views across the valley towards Ashdown Forest, an area of Outstanding Natural Beauty. Smallberry Hill is ideally located for those attending Glyndebourne Opera and, a member herself, Fiona is highly praised for the tasty and imaginative dinners and hampers she prepares for her guests.

Smallberry Hill, Five Chimneys Lane, Hadlow Down, Uckfield, East Sussex TN22 4DX 0825 830302 Map Ref : 3F

94

From Hadlow Down, we drove west along the A272 to **Buxted**, a village which was rebuilt in its present position in the early 19th-century when Lord Liverpool, the owner of nearby Buxted Park, wanted to clear his estate of unsightly domestic dwellings. The much-restored 13th-century church of St Margaret remained within the grounds; it features an 18th-century shingled broach spire and a Jacobean pulpit which was used by William Wordsworth's brother when he was vicar here. Lord Liverpool's Georgian country mansion, Buxted House, was almost destroyed by fire in 1940.

A couple of miles further west, **Maresfield** is a sizable village which, thankfully, is now bypassed by the main A22 London to Eastbourne road. This was a remote spot before the road builders finally managed to conquer the dense forest of the Weald in the 18th-century. With the coming of the new roads, however, Maresfield's position at the junction of two through routes helped it grow into an important staging point, and the Georgian Chequers Inn, perhaps the oldest building in Maresfield, is a fine example of a former coaching inn which survives from this period.

In the centre of Maresfield, entering Maresfield Park through the Lodge Arch opposite the church, you will find a delightful place to stay at **South Paddock**, situated 200 yards on the left. This is the elegant home of Major and Mrs. Allt who offer traditional hospitality to guests from all over the world. Set in three and a half acres of beautiful landscaped gardens, there are "staddle stones" outside the front gates and within the house, welcoming log fires for those chillier days. There are two spacious and well-equipped south facing guest rooms, large enough to accommodate a family. A feature at the breakfast table is Mrs. Allt's homemade preserves of which a sample can be bought as a souvenir of your visit here.

South Paddock, Maresfield Park, Maresfield, East Sussex
TN22 2HA 0825 762335 Map Ref : 3E

Two miles south of Maresfield, the scattered community of **Uckfield** also now benefits from being bypassed by the A22. Like Crowborough, Uckfield is a thriving residential town which underwent a rapid development after it was joined to the rail network in the mid-19th-century (although the line now terminates here, until the 1960s it continued on to Lewes). Thanks in part to the efforts of the Uckfield Preservation Society, a small number of buildings survive from the pre-railway period; these include the Georgian Maiden's Head Hotel, and Hook Hall, with its unusual chequered façade. During the 1980s, the Society was also responsible for restoring nearby Nutley post windmill to working order.

Sliders Farm, Furners Green, Uckfield, East Sussex TN22 3RT
0825 790258 Map Ref : 3E

Surrounded by its own fields and woodland, **Sliders Farm** in Furners Green is a real gem where you are assured of a friendly welcome from hosts Jean and David Salmon. Situated 400 yards down Sliders Lane which lies off the A275 East Grinstead to Lewes road, this 16th century listed farmhouse provides beautifully furnished accommodation in well-equipped en-suite guest rooms, which like the rest of the house, are full of character and charm. Within the farmhouse grounds there is also a first class self-catering cottage which was converted from a part 16th century barn and sleeps six. Additional attractions include a tennis court, heated outdoor swimming pool, private trout lake and free range ducks, geese and hens, providers of the eggs for breakfast!

At **Buckham Hill**, one-and-a-half miles to the west of Uckfield, **Beeches Farm** is a charming 16th-century farmhouse set within beautiful lawned grounds which contain a sunken garden, an impressive collection of yew trees and a delightful rose garden. Open daily, 10am to 5pm, all year round; admission charge payable.

The narrow lanes to the northwest of Beeches Farm led us to the village of **Piltdown**, a place notorious in academic circles for being the site of one the greatest archeological hoaxes of all time. In 1912, an ancient skull was discovered by the amateur archeologist, Charles Dawson, which was believed to form the missing link between man and the apes. The Piltdown Skull was believed to be about 150,000 years old; however, the improved methods of dating which came in during the 1950s revealed that the jaw bone in fact belonged to a modern ape, whilst the rest was a human skull dating from around 50,000 BC. The perpetrator of the hoax was never discovered; however, various theories point the finger at Sir Arthur Conan Doyle, at an evangelical Christian fundamentalist, or perhaps most likely, at Charles Dawson himself.

Just off the A272 midway between Haywards Heath and Uckfield, you will find **Barkham Manor Vineyard**, well signposted. The site was mentioned in the Domesday Book and has quite a history. Visitors can see where in 1911, the first fossilised remains of Piltdown Man were discovered here. Today, Barkham has one of the most modern wineries in England. Run by Mark de Gruchy Lambert, there are guided tours, tutored wine-tastings, and a vineyard trail for you to enjoy at your leisure and beautiful grounds for a picnic. The tastefully restored 18th century Great Barn, with its oak timbers and minstrel's gallery is now used for wedding receptions, wine tastings and banquets. The adjoining shop has souvenirs and international award-winning wines for you to try.

Barkham Manor Vineyard, Piltdown, Uckfield, East Sussex
TN22 3XE 0825 722103 Map Ref : 3E

From Piltdown, we crossed the A272 Maresfield to Haywards Heath road and followed the narrow country lanes northwestwards to the historic village of **Fletching**. During mediaeval times, this was an important arrow-making, or *fletching*, centre and indeed, the settlement probably takes its name from this ancient craft. This convenient supply of ammunition may have contributed to Simon de Montfort's decision to billet his troops here the night before the Battle of Lewes in 1264. (De Montfort went on to defeat Henry III and take his son, the future Edward I, hostage, a result which helped establish England's first representative parliament.)

The earth below the nave of the 13th-century village church is believed to contain the remains of several knights who were killed in battle and then buried here in full armour. The church also contains a number of unusual monuments, including one to a local glove-maker, Peter Denot, who took part in Jack Cade's ill-fated rebellion against Henry IV in the 15th-century; he is remembered in a small memorial brass engraved with two gloves. The Earl of Sheffield, whose family owned nearby Sheffield Park, added a mausoleum during the 18th-century which contains a number of family tombs and the grave of friend-of-the-family Edward Gibbon, the author of *The Decline And Fall Of The Roman Empire*.

Fletching's pleasant main street contains a number of other noteworthy buildings, including Fletching Lodge, Corner Cottage and St Andrews House. The last-named has a timbered upper floor which was added in the 19th-century to match its older next-door neighbour and was once the family home of the Maryon-Wilson family, rival landowners to the Sheffields. On November 5th each year, people come from a wide area to join in the village Bonfire Night celebrations, a tradition which once had more sinister religious overtones. At the bottom of Fletching's main street, there is an imposing, though closed, stone gateway to **Sheffield Park Gardens**.

The public entrance to this 100-acre National Trust-owned property is instead located a couple of miles away on the western side of the estate. During the late 18th-century, the grounds of Sheffield Park were laid out in a grand style, at first by Capability Brown and then by Humphry Repton, on the instructions of John Baker Holroyd MP, the first Earl of Sheffield. At around the same time, he also commissioned James Wyatt to build Sheffield Park House, an impressive mansion which can be seen from a distance but is not open to the public. The third Earl of Sheffield was an enthusiastic cricketer who organised the first test tours of England by the Australians. He also established a tradition (which lasted only twenty years or so) where the Australian team would play the first match of their tour at Sheffield Park against an Earl of Sheffield's XI. The former cricket field, now studded with specimen trees and shrubs, can still be made out on a rise above the main lake.

The gardens lie within a steep-sided valley and contain a series of five lakes with connecting cascades which were constructed over a period of 100 years. In spring, the ground is covered with bluebells and daffodils, in early summer there is a wonderful show of azaleas and rhododendrons, and later in the year, the autumn foliage creates a spectacular blaze of colour. Sheffield Park Gardens are undeniably impressive; however, there is something about the fairy-tale nature of some of the features and the presence of palms and other exotic trees which seems to create a slightly artificial atmosphere. Open Tuesdays to Saturdays, 11am to 6pm, and Sundays and Bank Holiday Mondays 2pm to 6pm, between April and early-November; admission charge payable (free to National Trust members).

The way to Heaven.....isn't it a super name? Actually it is **Heaven Farm**, and you will find it on the A275 from Wych Cross going towards Sheffield Park. The history of this unique farm is well documented back to the year 1387. The present farm buildings originate from just over 150 years ago, when a wealthy landowner created his home farm. The many buildings and their original contents are now, through a series of the most unusual coincidences, preserved as a museum portraying farming life as it was before the existence of mains water, gas, electricity or telephone, and when the only means of transport was by way of the horse. Within these buildings and others, Heaven Farm still has a variety of animals and free range chickens on the farm. We spent a very happy day there. The Farm Trail is delightful from the entrance with its rhododendrons and laurels, which were probably planted for pheasant cover, then along beside the woodland stream, with its high banks, crossing over the Greenwich meridian line nought degrees from east to western hemisphere, to find deep in these beautiful woods, Knee Holly, sometimes called the Butchers Broom, because it was used to clean butcher's chopping blocks. It is now very rare, so it was particularly pleasing to find it at Heaven Farm. Towards the end of the trail, you will come to an artificial pond, which is home to a wide variety of pond life, especially dragonflies. We were told that a carp, which is the enormous weight of 2.25 kilograms, sometimes puts in an appearance. A cross country runner could get around the trail in eight minutes, but he would have missed all the delights and interesting things that we saw. You need to take time to stand and quietly observe all that is there anyway, especially the lovely old country mansion, which stands as a superb backcloth to the ancient parkland. This all forms part of an absolutely delightful countryside experience. John Butler, who owns Heaven Farm, will tell you that you are welcome to spend all day wandering around, providing that you observe the country code. It is an excellent place for groups to visit, as well as individuals. There are conducted tours if they are required, but you do need to book those in advance. The telephone number is 0825 790226. The restaurant serves very good ploughmans' lunches, and wickedly fattening cream teas. There is a seating capacity for 60 people. Do take note that it is ideal for the disabled, with easily accessible facilities. In addition to just paying a visit, you can take caravans and tents there on a secluded site. You are so near many attractions, like the Bluebell Railway and Sheffield Park Gardens, that it makes sense to use Heaven Farm as a base.

Did You Know...

There is a full
Town and Village Index
at the back of the book?

Heaven Farm, Furners Green, Uckfield, Sussex TN22 3RG
0825 790226 Map Ref : 3E

On leaving Heaven Farm, we retraced our steps southwards along the **A275** to **Sheffield Park Station**, the southern terminus of the famous **Bluebell Railway** (the entrance is almost opposite Sheffield Park Gardens). This privately-owned stretch of the former East Grinstead to Lewes line runs for five miles through a delightful wooded valley which, as the name suggests, is carpeted with bluebells in springtime. One of the first of the new generation of private steam railways, the line was acquired by the Bluebell Railway Preservation Company in 1961 and is largely staffed by a team of dedicated volunteers.

Sheffield Park Station dates from around 1882 and is undergoing an ongoing programme of restoration. The engine sheds house a unique collection of around thirty vintage locomotives, some of which are over 100 years old, and there is also a fascinating museum of railway memorabilia, a signal box, shops and a café. Steam trains run daily between June and September, as well as during Easter week; weekends and Wednesdays in May; weekends only in March, April and November; Sundays only in January and February. Those travelling to the northern terminus at Horsted Keynes will find an interesting collection of railway carriages and an attractive picnic area.

From Sheffield Park Station, we continued our journey southwards and after a couple of miles came to **North Common**, a pleasant settlement which stands at the busy junction of the A275 and A272. The common, a designated nature reserve, features a well-preserved smock windmill; it is also the location of the famous **Chailey Heritage Crafts School**, a learning centre which was established in 1903 to instruct seven physically disabled children from the East End of London. It now has a roll of over 200 students and a worldwide reputation. It also has a highly individual Edwardian chapel which was designed by Sir Ninian Comper shortly before the First World War. **Chailey** village, a little further to the south, has some impressive old buildings, including a 13th-century parish church, a moated rectory, a late-17th-century residence, the Hooke, and a Georgian country house, Ades.

In the centre of North Common, we turned east onto the A272 to reach **Newick**, a large and sprawling village which is centred around a broad triangular green. On the green, there is an unusual village pump which was erected to mark Queen Victoria's diamond jubilee in 1897 and a pub, the Bull Inn, which claims to be haunted by the spirit of a dead skittles player whose heavy ball can sometimes be heard rolling across the floor of the bar. Newick's other noteworthy features include a Norman church with a Perpendicular sandstone tower, an Old Rectory with distinctive wrought-iron railings, Founthill House, and the former Lady Vernon's School (now School Cottage) which was founded in 1771 as a school for 'poor girls'. The actor Dirk Bogarde was brought up in the area and was given his first big part in an amateur production at Newick in the 1930s.

The delightful village of Newick was once the stopping-off point for pilgrims travelling between Winchester and Canterbury cathedrals, and it is here that you will find an ideal stopping-off point in your own journey, when you call in at **The Royal Oak**. This charming 17th century half-timbered Grade 2 listed building overlooks the village green and is a popular watering-hole with locals and tourists alike. Festooned with hanging baskets and covered in climbing roses, the exterior is a riot of colour in the summer months and provides a lovely setting for visitors to enjoy a drink and watch village life go by, whilst inside, exposed beams and an inglenook fireplace help to create a cosy, welcoming atmosphere in which to savour fine ale and wholesome pub fare.

The Royal Oak, 1 Church Road, Newick, Near Lewes, East Sussex BN8 4JU 0825 722506 Map Ref : 4D

On leaving the Royal Oak, we turned south into the network of country lanes which connect the many small farming settlements of the fertile Ouse Valley. After passing through Barcombe Cross, we found ourselves in **Barcombe**, a peaceful community which is locally-renowned for its excellent freshwater fishing. Like many of its contemporaries in Sussex, the village church dates from the 13th-century, is dedicated to St Mary, has a shingled broach spire, and was heavily restored by the Victorians. More unusual is **Shelley's Folly**, a striking private residence dating from around 1700 which, sadly, is not open to visitors.

The Anchor Inn at Barcombe is renowned as "the smallest pub in Sussex". This delightful hostelry enjoys an idyllic location on the west bank of the River Ouse and has exclusive boating rights over a three mile stretch of the river. Visitors can hire a boat by the hour or the day to paddle the round trip to the fish ladder "Falls" and back, which takes about two hours. Inside the Inn, pictures of aeroplanes and classic cars adorn the walls, including a painting of the original proprietor, Wing Commander Bovet-White, returning from France in his Mosquito on only one engine. The Anchor is popular with traditional jazz enthusiasts and car lovers - the Vintage Sports Car Club and the Jaguar Drivers Club both hold their monthly meetings here. The parents of the present proprietor have been here since 1963 and have created a haven of peace where you can enjoy a quiet drink and restaurant or bar lunch, leaving the stresses and strains of everyday life far behind you. You can book an intimate dinner in the Pagoda Room, where the emphasis is on excellent homecooked fare, then afterwards retire to one of the four attractive guest rooms, which include a honeymoon suite complete with patio balcony. The family aims to provide a relaxing country retreat with a homely atmosphere and friendly welcome.

The Anchor Inn, Barcombe, Nr. Lewes, East Sussex BN8 5BS
Barcombe 400414 Map Ref : 5D

Nearby **Barcombe Mills** has been a popular picnicking place since the Edwardian era. At that time, artists would come from miles around to paint the dilapidated mill buildings in this splendid Ouse Valley setting. Although the old mills have now been removed, there are still some wonderful views over the surrounding landscape towards Mount Caburn, the chalky outcrop which can be seen rising sharply from the valley floor to the southeast. The charming hamlet of **Hamsey** is situated another mile to the southwest; here, the old church stands in a wonderful position overlooking the Ouse and is approached through the neighbouring farmyard.

From Hamsey, we continued southwest onto the **A275** near Offham, where instead of turning south to Lewes, we turned north and soon after, west onto the **B2166**, to allow us to have a look at the settlements lying along the foot of this section of the South Downs escarpment. **Plumpton** has an elegant 16th-century moated manor house, Plumpton Place, which was substantially remodelled in the 1920s by Sir Edwin Lutyens. The then owner, Edward Hudson, was a wealthy magazine proprietor who had previously commissioned Lutyens to renovate his other country property, Lindisfarne Castle, off the Northumberland coast. Plumpton's famous National Hunt Racecourse is situated a mile-and-a-half to the north; spectators arriving by train should look out for the Victorian signal box which has recently been designated a listed building following the persistent efforts of local railway enthusiasts. The regular customers at

Plumpton's Half Moon pub feature in an unusual mural painted in 1977.

From Plumpton, we continued west along the B2166 for a mile before turning north to reach the peaceful hamlet of **Streat**. This tiny hamlet is mentioned in the Domesday Book and here you will find **North Acres**, a rambling Victorian country house owned by John and Valerie Eastwood. John is a recently retired lecturer in Animal Physiology at a nearby college and he and Valerie keep Vietnamese pot-bellied pigs as pets, which apparently get on very well with their cat! The Eastwoods live in part of the house, but there is a large lounge/conference room, dining room and small lounge for guest's use, in addition to the six comfortable guest bedrooms. The peaceful location of North Acres which lies about a mile and a half north of the South Downs, makes it an ideal base for country lovers and walkers.

North Acres, Streat, Sussex BN6 8RX 0273 890278 Map Ref: 5C

After returning to the main road, we turned west along the B2166 and soon arrived in the village of **Westmeston**. The village church has an unusual shingled bell turret and a series of early murals which have been attributed to the celebrated team of artists from St Pancras Priory in Lewes. The village also boasts two fine country houses: the part-15th-century Westmeston Place and the early-19th-century Middleton Manor, now an arts and crafts training centre for young people with learning difficulties.

On the western edge of Westmeston, the **B2116** turns sharply to the north and after another mile or so, arrives in the historic village of **Ditchling**. The lands around Ditchling were once part of a royal estate belonging to King Alfred who is also believed to have owned a small palace here. The parish church of St Margaret of Antioch has a shingled Sussex Cap spire and was rebuilt in Caen stone, flint and chalk in the 13th-century (it was again much altered during the 1860s). Opposite the church gate stands **Wings Place**, an unusual

104

Tudor house built of flint, timbering and brickwork which is also referred to as Anne of Cleves House. This is because it is thought to have formed part of Henry VIII's divorce settlement with his fourth wife, although there is no evidence of her ever having stayed here.

Country lovers will enjoy a day out at **Stoneywish Country Park** which can be found by taking the B2116 Lewes road out of Ditchling, turning left after about half a mile into Spatham Lane and Stoneywish car park lies a short distance up on the left. Comprising 52 acres of farmland, Stoneywish is an open plan country park where visitors of all ages can enjoy watching a variety of bird and animal life, ranging from Whooper Swans, and ducks to donkeys, Vietnamese pot-bellied pigs and Mr. T, one of the biggest shire horses in Sussex. Children can play with the rabbits and guinea pigs and there are various displays of old farming tools. With a tea room to relax in and children's play areas to keep younger family members entertained, your visit to Stoneywish is complete.

Stoneywish Country Park, Spatham Lane, Ditchling, East Sussex
0273 843498 Map Ref : 5B

Old Ditchling is arranged around an ancient road junction and the area to the west of this contains some exceptional early buildings. **Cotterlings** dates from the Regency period and has a striking façade of redbrick window surrounds interspersed with black glazed tiles, **Pardons** has an unusual gazebo in the grounds, and **Court Farm** incorporates a village green and the foundations of an old tithe barn. The Five Mile Act of 1665 which banned Nonconformist worship within five miles of a town made Ditchling into something of a religious centre; the **Old Meeting House** in the Twitten is a handsome survivor from this period.

During the 1920s, Ditchling became home to a lively group of artists, printers and Bohemians whose number included the sculptor, designer and typographer Eric Gill, the painter Frank Brangwyn, and

105

the calligrapher Edward Johnston. The village is still inhabited by a thriving population of artists and craftspeople whose work can be seen in Ditchling's many studios, galleries and antique shops. Visitors wanting to discover more about the locality's long and interesting history should make a point of calling in at the museum in the old village school; opening times displayed on site.

Garden Pride Garden Centre, Common Lane, Ditchling, East Sussex BN6 8TN 0273 846844 Map Ref : 5B

Just outside the village of Ditchling, **Garden Pride Garden Centre** is a former wholesale nursery transformed by its owners into a garden centre of excellence. An attractive display of outdoor plants greets your arrival, whilst inside the large retail area you will find an extensive range of house plants, mainly from Garden Pride's own nurseries. You can relax with light refreshments in the comfortable coffee shop, then browse round the extensive gift area which has something for everyone, ranging from own label rum butter and shortbread, to glassware and toiletries. Beautiful cedar wood sheds and conservatories, barbecue equipment and garden furniture are just some of the other items available and easy access for the disabled means everyone can enjoy a trip to Garden Pride Garden Centre.

To the south of Ditchling, the land rises sharply onto the 813ft summit of **Ditchling Beacon**, the third highest point in the South Downs. Once the site of Neolithic hill fort and later, an Admiralty fire beacon, on a clear day this long-established vantage point offers a thirty-mile view northwards across the Weald to the North Downs. Following World War II, the site was donated to the National Trust in memory of a young flyer who had been killed in action. A steep twisting lane extends from Ditchling's South Street to a car park on the crest of the ridge. This road then continues southwards down the shallow dip slope of the Downs all the way to **Brighton**.

Before Dr Richard Russell of Lewes published his famous

dissertation on *The Use Of Sea Water In Diseases Of The Glands* in 1753, Brighton was a small and unassuming fishing village which went under the name of Brighthelmstone. At that time, the sea front was constantly under threat from the encroachment of the sea and those not directly involved in fishing, settled on higher ground in the area of densely-packed streets and alleyways now known as **The Lanes**. Although most of the buildings here were renewed in the early 19th-century, this highly picturesque quarter between West, North and East Streets retains its maze-like mediaeval street plan. The present-day Lanes are inhabited by an interesting assortment of antique shops, street cafés and specialist retailers which together form a fascinating attraction.

During the 1750s, Dr Russell moved to Brighton and began to extol the virtues of both bathing in and drinking sea water (the original chalybeate spring where he treated his patients can still be seen in St Anne's Well Gardens in Hove). His ideas gradually gained favour amongst the rich and influential until in 1783, the fashionable status of the town was affirmed when the Prince of Wales chose to sample the beneficial effects of the new resort for himself. The young prince, who was later to become the Prince Regent and then George IV, was so taken with the place that he decided to build a permanent **Royal Pavilion** in the resort. In 1787, architect Henry Holland designed a classical-style building with a dome and rotunda; however in 1815, John Nash, the architect responsible for London's Regent's Park and the Mall, was asked to remodel the building.

Nash came up with a radical and exotic scheme based on an Indian maharajah's palace complete with minarets, onion-shaped domes and pinnacles (not to everyone's liking, the upper part of the new building was once unkindly described as 'a large Norfolk turnip with four onions'). Inside, the flavour of the building moves from the Indian subcontinent to the Far East in what must be one of the finest examples of Regency chinoiserie in the world. This highly-individual style reaches its zenith in the banqueting hall whose towering domed ceiling contains an elaborate chandelier from which a silver dragon can be seen hanging by its claws. The Great Kitchen with its huge array of special cooking utensils is another part of this extraordinary building which should not be missed. Open daily, 10am to 6pm (5pm in winter), all year round; admission charge payable.

The nearby **Dome** was once an arena for exercising the royal horses and is now a major concert venue; likewise, the old stables in Church Street have been converted into Brighton's acclaimed **Museum and Art Gallery**. The town contains a number of other splendid Regency developments, most of which are dotted along the sea front

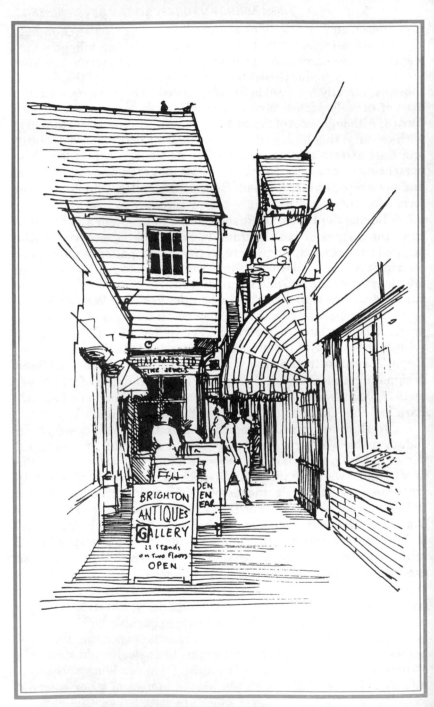

The Lanes, Brighton.

on either side of the old mediaeval centre. Among the better known are Bedford Square, Regency Square, Russell Square, Kemp Town and, perhaps most famous of all, Royal Crescent; this elegant row of terraced houses is faced with dark 'mathematical' tiles, a characteristic feature of this part of East Sussex.

Brighton also has a couple of noteworthy churches: St Nicholas' in Dyke Road is a rare survivor from the 14th-century which has some interesting monuments and a superb carved Norman font, and St Peter's, a short distance to the north of the Royal Pavilion, was designed in lavish neo-Gothic style in the 1820s by Charles Barry, the future architect of the Houses of Parliament. At 135ft, the walls of St Bartholomew's Church near the railway station are the tallest of any parish church in England; the building is visible from the London train and is rumoured to have been designed in this manner to remind potentially wayward trippers of the omnipresence of the Lord.

A hidden place which may be of interest to those keen on antique toys and model railways is situated in the arches underneath Brighton station. The **Sussex Toy and Model Museum** is open daily, 10am to 5pm (closed 1pm to 2pm), all year round; admission charge payable. Alternatively, an interesting exhibition of steam engines, some of which can be seen in operation, can be found at the **British Engineerium** in Hove.

Modern Brighton is a vibrant seaside town which offers visitors an enormous range of recreational activities. Apart from its long shingle beach, there are two splendid Victorian piers (one of which is no longer open to the public), a combined aquarium and dolphinarium which was founded in 1872, a popular race course, an electric railway which was the first of its kind in the country, and an impressive marina which at 126 acres, is the largest such development in Europe. Further information on these well-established attractions is widely available in other publications.

One of Brighton's lesser-known attractions is **Preston Manor**, a 13th-century manor house which is set within beautiful landscaped grounds on the northern approaches to the town. The house was rebuilt in the 1730s and was left to the people of Brighton in 1932 on condition that it would remain an 'English country home'. The interior contains a permanent display of 18th-century furnishings, silverware and porcelain, and the grounds have been preserved in period style and contain some fine water-lily ponds and a famous scented rose garden.

Visitors entering the town along the nearby London Road pass a sandstone pillar with the charming inscription:-

Hail guest, we know not what thou art,
If friend, we greet you hand and heart,
If stranger such no longer be,
If foe... our love shall conquer thee.

Further to the west, a unique view of the Downs can be seen through a recently-installed *camera obscura* at the **Foredown Tower Countryside Centre** on the outskirts of Hove.

We finally left Brighton along the Lewes road and after about three miles, paused in Falmer to take a quick look at **Sussex University**. This impressive collection of concrete and redbrick buildings occupies part of **Stanmer Park**, a sizable country estate which is now owned by Brighton Borough Council. This, the first of the new generation of universities to be founded during the 1960s and 70s, was designed by Sir Basil Spence, the architect of Coventry Cathedral. The site incorporates an excellent theatre, the **Gardner Centre**, which offers the public a wide range of top class drama, dance and musical productions throughout the year.

To the east of Falmer, the **A27** drops down to **Lewes**, the county town of East Sussex. This historic settlement stands at the strategically important point where the River Ouse is crossed by an ancient east-west land route. Because of the area's close proximity to Normandy, William the Conqueror divided his newly acquired Sussex estates amongst some of his most trusted lieutenants. The lands around Lewes were granted to William de Warenne and his wife, Gundrada, who not only constructed a substantial double motte and bailey castle on a hillside above the river, but also founded St Pancras Priory on the southern edge of the town. This once-magnificent monastic house belonged to the abbey of Cluny in Burgundy and had a great church as large as Chichester Cathedral. The priory was the home of the renowned team of artists who painted the famous ecclesiastical murals at Hardham and Clayton during the 12th-century. Following Henry VIII's Dissolution of the Monasteries in 1537, the building was forcibly demolished and its stone used for constructing residential dwellings in the town.

One building thought to have benefited in this way is **Southover Grange**, in Southover Road, a substantial gabled residence which was built in 1572 and was the childhood home of the famous 17th-century diarist, John Evelyn. Today, the house is perhaps best known for its wonderful walled garden whose beautiful lawns, trees and

Southover Grange Gardens.

flowering plants provide a secluded haven in the heart of the town. Garden open daily, 7am till dusk, all year round; admission free.

Although very little of the priory has survived, a substantial part of **Lewes Castle** still remains, including a section of the keep with two flanking towers dating from the 13th-century and a fortified gateway, or Barbican, dating from the 14th-century. Visitors climbing onto the battlements are rewarded with magnificent views over the surrounding town and countryside; the castle gardens also offer an attractive area for relaxing or picnicking. Open daily, 10am (11am Sundays) to 5.30pm, all year round (closed Sundays in winter). Nearby Barbican House contains both the **Museum of Sussex Archeology** and Lewes' **Living History Model**. The former charts human development from early hunting cultures, through the Roman, Saxon and Norman incursions, to the end of the mediaeval era; the latter is an audio-visual presentation which tells the story of Lewes since 1066 using a remarkable scale model of the town. Open daily, 11am to 5.30pm between Easter and mid-September (museum also open weekdays in winter).

In 1264, Lewes was the site of a particularly bloody confrontation between the armies of Henry III and Simon de Montfort. The **Battle of Lewes** took place on Mount Harry, an exposed hillside on the western side of the town, and resulted in the deaths of as many as 5000 troops (years later, the skeletons of an estimated 1500 men were unearthed near Lewes gaol, and hundreds more were discovered by railway engineers in a field near Plumpton). Henry's defeat led to his enforced signing of the *Mise of Lewes*, a document which strengthened the importance of the barons and laid the foundations of modern parliamentary democracy.

Like Ditchling, Lewes has an **Anne of Cleves House,** an early 16th-century Wealden 'hall' house which formed part of Henry VIII's divorce settlement with his fourth wife (also like Ditchling, the property was never lived in by the estranged queen). The structure has been much altered over the centuries and has evolved into an attractive concoction of buildings set around a reconstructed Tudor garden. Now a museum run by the Sussex Archeological Society, its rooms and galleries have been arranged to create an impression of domestic and working life in Lewes in the 17th- and 18th-centuries. Open daily, 10am (2pm Sundays) to 5.30pm between Easter and October; admission charge payable.

Lewes developed strong Protestant roots following the Reformation and the burning of over a dozen Protestant martyrs in the town during the reign of Mary I established an anti-Catholic fanaticism which can still be detected in the town's modern bonfire night festivities. In what must be the most extravagant 5th November celebrations in the country, rival bonfire societies march through the streets carrying flaming torches and specially-made 'guys', often thinly-disguised effigies of the Pope. These are then carried to the edge of town and thrown onto huge bonfires - a spectacular, if somewhat sinister, annual custom.

In the 18th-century, Lewes became something of a centre for radical political thought. During this period, a local excise officer, Tom Paine, became renowned as a human rights campaigner and leading supporter of the American and French Revolutions. Paine lived at Bull House in the High Street, now a restaurant, and married the daughter of his landlord before settling in America. On his return, he wrote the revolutionary work in support of the French Revolution, *The Rights of Man* in 1792 and was forced to flee across the Channel.

At around this time, Lewes was establishing itself as a prosperous county town and a number of its finest residential buildings, including Lewes House and School Hill House, were constructed by wealthy professional people who lived and worked in the town. Many older timber-framed buildings were refaced with characteristic 'mathematical' tiles, small hanging tiles which were designed to resemble fine brickwork. The streets of old Lewes are connected by a number of narrow pedestrian alleys, or *twittens*, which provide a fascinating walking tour of the town (a guide published by Lewes Town Council is available at the Tourist Information Centre). Lewes also possesses a renowned independent brewery, **Harvey's Bridge Wharf Brewery**, which was founded on the banks of the Ouse in Georgian times and was rebuilt in Victorian Gothic style during the 1880s.

Tucked in a fold of the Sussex Downs just off the A27 near the historic County Town of Lewes, you will find a very special 'hidden place' indeed. **Southerham Old Barns** is the deceptive name given to four superbly equipped houses which provide luxury self catering accommodation which has been justifiably awarded the ETB five key Highly Commended rating. Originally created from a range of old agricultural buildings, these impressive holiday homes are every housewife's dream, tastefully incorporating original features of the buildings, whilst providing every modern household convenience. Each house has a fully fitted kitchen, whilst the furnishings throughout are beautifully coordinated and of the highest quality. On your arrival the house is immaculate, with a bowl of fresh fruit and a bottle of quality English wine to welcome you. The many additional facilities available include a maid service and babysitting arrangements, whilst for the health-conscious guest, Southerham Old Barns has its

Anne of Cleves House, Ditchling.

own complete fitness complex. During your stay here you have exclusive use of a 30-acre bluebell wood for private walks and picnics, whilst a pleasant ten minute walk along the banks of the River Ouse will lead you to Lewes where Anne of Cleves house is always a popular attraction. Further afield a trip to the delightful country village of Alfriston is a must, home to The National Trust's first property The Clergy House. Whatever your interests, one taste of the idyllic country setting and luxurious accommodation of Southerham Old Barns will have you eager to return, and many guests do.

Southerham Old Barns, Southerham, Lewes, East Sussex
0444 440774 Map Ref : 5H

On leaving Lewes, we were careful to join the minor road which runs southwards through Kingston-near-Lewes along the western side of the River Ouse. This road connects a number of exceptional villages and hamlets, the first of which is **Iford**, a charming settlement with a flint-built Norman church and a 16th-century manor house which is the official residence of the Vice-Chancellor of Sussex University.

The influential Bloomsbury group figures Virginia and Leonard Woolf once owned a country retreat at **Rodmell**, a little further to the south. The Woolfs acquired the **Monk's House** in 1919 and gradually converted it from a primitive cottage without running water or sanitation into pleasant, if modest, village house. Throughout the following twenty years, Virginia Woolf, the author of such works as *To The Lighthouse* and *Orlando*, suffered from increasingly serious bouts of depression and mental illness, until in 1941 she tragically committed suicide by drowning herself in the River Ouse. The Monk's House is now administered by tenants on behalf of the National Trust. Open Wednesdays and Saturdays, 2pm to 5.30pm between April and end-October; admission charge payable (free to National Trust members).

The church at **Southease** is one of only three in Sussex with a round tower (the others are located within a few miles of here at Lewes and Piddinghoe). Although the building was originally thought to be pre-Norman, it is likely that it was rebuilt in the late 11th-century on the site of a Saxon predecessor. Inside, there are some fine mediaeval wall paintings and in the tower, a peal of bells dating from the 13th-century.

A two-mile long cul-de-sac leads southwestwards from Southease to the remarkably well-preserved village of **Telscombe**. This ancient downland settlement owes its unspoilt nature to Ambrose Gorham, a local landowner who, in 1933, left most of the village to Brighton Borough Council in his will. The locality was formerly an important sheep rearing and horse-training centre; the last man in England to be hanged for sheep stealing in 1819 is believed to have come from the village, and nearby Telscombe Tye was a popular exercising ground for locally-trained racehorses.

After returning to the main road, we continued southwards to **Piddinghoe**, a village containing the third of the three round-towered churches in Sussex. The tower is topped by a weather vane in the shape of a golden fish (despite having been referred to by Kipling as a 'dolphin', it is widely understood to be a sea trout). The narrow main street winds past an assortment of buildings, both ancient and modern, including a malthouse and an old forge; a recently-restored brick kiln can also be seen near the church. Now the domain of pleasure craft, the old village quay was once a bustling port which was popular both with legitimate and non-legitimate traders. Indeed, such was the incidence of smuggling that a unique series of folk stories and sayings grew up here in the 17th- and 18th-centuries; for example, the local expression for 'going to see a man about a dog' is 'going down to Piddinghoe to shoe magpies'.

The busy port and fishing town of **Newhaven** lies at the mouth of the River Ouse, another mile to the southeast. Prior to the 16th-century, the river flowed into the sea at Seaford, two-and-a-half miles away; however, the combined efforts of a great sea storm and a team of Elizabethan civil engineers succeeded in rerouting the river. A 'new haven' was then created at a place formerly occupied by the small village of Meeching. Despite its recent origins, a number of Bronze Age tools and Roman artefacts have since been discovered in and around Newhaven, indicating that the site has in fact been in occupation for many thousands of years.

During the 18th- and 19th-centuries, Newhaven underwent a period of rapid development as its importance as a cross-Channel port grew. Louis Philippe, King of the French, landed here after being forced to flee the forces of republicanism in 1848. The 'Citizen King' stayed overnight at the Bridge Hotel, the renowned 16th-century hostelry which still stands beside the harbour bridge. After further alterations to the port were completed at the turn of the century, Newhaven established a regular cross-Channel passenger and cargo service with the Normandy port of Dieppe, four hours away to the south.

Fort Newhaven was built around 1860 as part of Palmerston's little-used coastal defence system. Originally designed to defend the port against attack from the sea, the vast ten-acre structure was built with a network of underground passages, a parade ground and a series of massive gun installations. Now restored, the fortress incorporates a pub, picnic area and children's assault course, along with an interesting museum of military history; this contains a large collection of historic armaments and a special room devoted to the Allied raid on Dieppe in 1942. Open Wednesdays to Sundays, 10.30am to 6pm between mid-April and early-October.

Garden Paradise and Planet Earth in Avis Road, Newhaven are twin all-weather attractions which provide a fascinating insight into the natural history of the world. Visitors can see displays of replica dinosaurs, exotic plants, flowering cacti, and a 144 million year-old fossil tree which weighs over two tons. Open daily, 10am to 6pm (4.30pm in winter), all year round. Just off the A26 one mile north of the town centre, we discovered Chris Lewis' pottery at **South Heighton**. Here, he produces a wide range of handmade stoneware which is fired in a special wood-fired kiln. Showroom open Mondays to Fridays, 10am to 5pm, all year round, plus most weekends in summer.

The **A259** to the east of Newhaven led us to **Seaford**, a once-thriving coastal port which went into decline after the River Ouse diverted to its present course in the 16th-century. The town underwent a gradual revival following the arrival of the railway in the mid-19th-century and today, it is a comfortable seaside resort of Victorian and between-the-wars buildings which is popular with older holidaymakers.

The Old Plough in Seaford is, as its name suggests, an old traditional country pub. The foundations apparently date back to the 13th century, but the main building is 17th century and was possibly once a Manse or coaching inn. Friendly host John Boots is a third generation publican and has been in the trade since 1953. His experience shows, with good quality ale and first class pub fare provided in a warm, relaxed atmosphere. The menu includes fresh local fish from Newhaven when available and has something to tempt every palate at very reasonable prices and in the 'Elbow Room' you can reserve a table for a traditional roast dinner.

The Old Plough, 20 Church Street, Seaford, East Sussex
BN25 1HG 0323 892379 Map Ref : 7E

To the southeast of Seaford, the cliffs rise dramatically to around 300ft at **Seaford Head**, the promontory which lies at the western end of one of the most spectacular stretches of coastline in the British Isles. Evidence of a prehistoric hilltop encampment and a Roman burial ground have been discovered on the site which now forms part of the **Seaford Head Nature Reserve**; this 300-acre statutory reserve extends to the River Cuckmere and offers some of the most scenic cliff-top walking in Sussex.

The small settlement of **Exceat** stands on the River Cuckmere at the northeastern corner of the reserve. Here, we discovered **The Living World**, a unique natural history centre which contains a fascinating collection of live butterflies, spiders, reptiles, stick insects and marine creatures, all of which can be viewed at close quarters and sometimes even handled. The centre is located in a group of converted farm buildings and is open daily, 10am to 5pm between mid-March and 1st November (also weekends and school holidays in winter); admission charge payable (free to under fives).

Exceat has had an unusually turbulent history; during the 14th-century, it was almost wiped out by the Black Death, then 120 years later, a violent cross-Channel raid almost achieved the same result. Between the hamlet and the sea, the River Cuckmere makes a spectacular serpentine meander through the area known as **Cuckmere Haven**. This striking flood plain forms the western boundary of the **Seven Sisters Country Park**, a broad tract of County Council and National Trust-owned Heritage Coastline which incorporates the famous **Seven Sisters** chain of white chalk cliffs. The cliffs, which are now receding at around three feet per year, can

118

also be accessed from the top of the Downs at **Crowlink** and from the east at the popular picnicking spot of **Birling Gap**. The downland above the Seven Sisters is strewn with evidence of early settlement, including a number of Neolithic bowl and round barrows.

A mile or so inland, the village of **Friston** has a part-Norman church with a low capped tower. The churchyard contains the grave of the composer, Frank Bridge, and is entered through a rare tapsel gate, a gate which pivots around a central upright. The nearby pond was the first in England to be designated an ancient monument. The village also contains an impressive manor house, Friston Place, which was built in the mid 17th-century around an existing timber-framed structure.

The 1600-acre **Friston Forest** lies to the west of the village between Friston and Exceat. When this ancient beechwood forest was acquired by the Forestry Commission in the 1920s, they planted a number of quick-growing conifers to protect the young broadleaved trees from the fierce coastal winds. Over the years, the conifers have gradually been removed to reveal a magnificent mature beech forest which now incorporates some delightful waymarked walks and picnic areas.

After returning to the **A259**, we retraced our steps to the foot of the hill near Exceat before turning north along the Cuckmere Valley. The nearby village of **Westdean** lies at the end of a narrow cul-de-sac and is believed to have once contained a palace belonging to Alfred the Great. The village church is part-Norman and has a broad, rectangular tower with an unusual 'half-hipped' spire. Inside, there is a bronze head which was sculpted by Jacob Epstein in memory of Sir John Anderson, later Lord Waverley, after whom the Anderson air-raid shelter was named. Other noteworthy buildings in the vicinity include the flint-built church rectory which dates from the 13th-century, and **Charleston Manor** which features a combination of Norman, Tudor and Georgian building styles and lies half-a-mile to the north.

A mile or so further on, the small village of **Litlington** is perhaps best known for its Victorian tea gardens. This elegant outdoor café was founded over 150 years ago making it the oldest such establishment in Sussex. Here, customers are offered the finest English cream teas and homemade refreshments in a relaxed old-fashioned atmosphere. Open daily, 11am to 5.30pm between Good Friday and end-October. Litlington's 13th-century village church contains a font made from 'Sussex marble', the distinctive limestone which is found around Petworth. An outline of a white horse, the only example of its kind in the county, is carved into the chalk hillside on the western bank of the Cuckmere opposite Litlington; during the Second World War, this was covered up to prevent it being used as a navigational aid by enemy bomber pilots.

Continuing north, we soon passed through **Lullington**, a hamlet which is renowned for having one of the smallest churches in Britain. The 16ft-square structure is in fact the chancel of a much larger mediaeval church which fell into disrepair following the Black Death. The Victorians rescued what remained of the building and converted it into its present form. The chalky heathland above Lullington is a National Nature Reserve which is noted for its distinctive downland flora and fauna.

Half-a-mile after forking west at Lullington, we turned west across the Cuckmere and followed the signs to **Alfriston**, one of the oldest and best-preserved (and consequently, most popular) villages in Sussex. The settlement was founded in Saxon times and grew to become an important river port and market town. The old market cross, or at least the substantial part of it which remains, stands beside a tall chestnut tree in the middle of Waterloo Square; it is one of only two such structures to survive in Sussex (the other, somewhat grander example is at Chichester). This delightful market square, along with the old High Street leading off to the south, is lined with ancient inns, shops and residential buildings which were constructed in an assortment of materials and styles over the centuries. Perhaps the most striking is the 15th-century **Star Inn**, a former hostel for mendicant friars, whose ceiling timbers are decorated with wonderful carved animals. Others include the 15th-century George, the timber-framed Ship, and the Market Cross, a popular smugglers' haunt which has no fewer than six staircases and a room with five separate means of escape (indeed, it is also known as Ye Olde Smugglers). In the early 19th-century, this was the base of a notorious gang led by Stanton Collins, a ruthless local villain who is said to have lured an excise officer to his death on the cliffs above Seaford and was eventually transported to Australia for stealing sheep.

At one time, large quantities of contraband were brought upriver to Alfriston in the dead of night and unloaded onto waiting packhorses. Such atmospheric scenes inspired Rudyard Kipling, a one-time resident of Rottingdean near Brighton, to pen his evocative poem, *A Smuggler's Song*:

> If you wake at midnight, and hear a horse's feet,
> Don't go drawing back the blind, or looking in the street.
> Them that asks no questions, isn't told a lie,
> Watch the wall my darling, while the gentlemen go by!

> Five and twenty ponies, trotting though the dark,
> Brandy for the parson, baccy for the clerk,
> Laces for the lady, letters for a spy,
> Watch the wall my darling, while the gentlemen go by!

Alfriston's former status as a market town is reflected in the scale of its 14th-century parish church, an unusually spacious structure which is often referred to as 'the cathedral of the Downs'. **St Andrew's Church** stands in a prominent position beside the Cuckmere at the centre of a raised green known as the Tye. As recently as the 1930s, local shepherds would be buried here with a scrap of raw wool in their hand, a custom which served to inform the keeper of the gates of heaven that the deceased's poor church attendance was due to the obligations of his occupation.

The old **Clergy House** stands within an attractive herbaceous cottage garden on the southern edge of the Tye. This charming thatched and timber-framed building was constructed as a mediaeval 'hall' house in the 14th-century and was the first property to be acquired by the National Trust in 1896, reputedly for a price of only £10. Thanks to Alfred Powell's skilful renovation, its crown post roof and original timbers have been saved. Today, the building houses an interesting exhibition on mediaeval construction techniques. Open daily, 11am to 6pm between April and end-October; admission charge payable (free to National Trust members).

Other noteworthy buildings in Alfriston are its early-19th-century **Congregational Church** and the **Heritage Centre and Blacksmiths' Museum**; this interesting museum on the social history of the locality is housed in a restored 15th-century blacksmith's forge and can be found next to the Dene car park, a little to the north of Waterloo Square. Open daily, 11am to 5pm between Easter and end-October.

On leaving Alfriston, we retraced our steps back onto the eastern side of the Cuckmere and returned to the fork near Lullington before turning northeast to reach our next destination, the historic remains of **Wilmington Priory**. This once-imposing Benedictine priory was built between the 12th- and 14th-centuries and is rumoured to be inhabited by a number of legendary ghosts. Parts of the building, including the hall, gatehouse and courtyard, have now been restored by the Sussex Archeological Society and the site includes an interesting museum of agricultural history.

The mysterious figure of the **Long Man of Wilmington** can be seen from the priory grounds. This remarkable 226ft-high outline of a man carrying a staff in each hand was carved into the chalky hillside of Windover Hill sometime between pre-Roman times and 1779, the year it was first documented. Perhaps most astonishing is the fact that the design takes account of the slope of the hill, and so accurately maintains the proportions of a man even when viewed from below. To date, no one knows who was responsible for the carving or why it was done; various theories suggest that it is a figure of a pilgrim, a Saxon chieftain and even the 'Midsummer Man' of pagan folklore. In 1969, the carving was strengthened with over 700 concrete blocks.

From Wilmington, we continued north to the **A27** and then turned west towards Lewes. After about a mile we came to **Drusillas Park**, a charming small zoo which is renowned for its collections of exotic birds and smaller mammals. There is also a children's adventure play area, a miniature railway and an award-winning family restaurant. Open daily, 10am to 5pm, all year round; admission charge payable. The zoo is located within a few yards of the **English Wine Centre**, a working vineyard which hosts an annual English Wine Festival in early September. Tours of the vineyard, cellars and an interesting museum of wine making can be arranged throughout the year, and a wide range of (mostly English) wines can be purchased.

Just south of the A27 half-a-mile to the west, we made a short detour to visit **Berwick** (pronounced *Bur-wick*), a village whose Norman church contains a famous series of contemporary wall paintings. Despite the church having been built in the 12th-century and restored in the 1850s, the murals are firmly rooted in the 20th-century. They were commissioned, somewhat controversially, by the Bishop of Chichester shortly after he came to office in 1929. The Bishop made the brave decision to engage the Bloomsbury Group painters Duncan Grant and Vanessa Bell who, with the help of Bell's children, Quentin and Angelica, finally completed their task in 1943. In keeping with a long tradition, the artists placed a number of clearly identifiable local people and places within a set of familiar biblical settings.

The 'forgotten village' of **Alciston** lies in a similar position off the A27, another mile to the west. The original settlement was abandoned following the Black Death and a new one built some years later on the opposite side of the 13th-century church. To avoid the likelihood of flooding, this was built on the foundations of an earlier Saxon structure which stood at the top of a small hill. The remains of a substantial mediaeval dovecote can be seen nearby; during the late Middle Ages, large numbers of pigeons were kept here to provide a much-prized supplement to the dreary winter diet.

The fertile agricultural land around Alciston once belonged to the estates of Battle Abbey. At that time, the tenant farmers paid 'rent' to the abbot in the form of one tenth of their annual farm output, and at harvest time each year, this was brought to Alciston and deposited in the abbey's huge mediaeval **tithe barn**. This magnificent structure is over 170ft long and is one of the largest of its type in Sussex; it can be seen in a delightful farmyard setting on the southern side of the village, close to the point where the road into the hamlet narrows to a rough track. As well as being the focus of the estate, the adjacent farmhouse once served as a retirement home for the monks.

In more recent times, the inhabitants of Alciston have established the custom of village skipping on Good Friday, a tradition which involves people of all ages skipping over a long rope in front of the local inn.

Rose Cottage, Alciston, Near Polegate, East Sussex BN26 6UW
0323 870377 Map Ref : 6F

Enjoying a tranquil location on the outskirts of the pretty village of Alciston, **Rose Cottage** is the unlikely name given to a superb country pub and restaurant. This delightful establishment was originally a cottage built some 300 years ago and was formerly the thatched village shop. Today however, it provides a peaceful interlude in your journey where you can enjoy a refreshing drink and delicious food in picturesque surroundings. The covered outdoor seating area overlooks the paddock and duck pond, where you will see chickens scratching about. Inside the decor is true country pub style, with church pews to sit on and thatchers blades as ornaments. The restaurant is only open in the evenings but offers an unusual and regularly changing menu, including fresh fish from Newhaven whenever possible.

On the other side of the A27 to the north of Alciston, we came to the ancient hamlet of **Selmeston**. During the 1930s, archeologists discovered tools, weapons and pottery fragments in the local churchyard

123

which are thought to date from the New Stone Age. Despite having been heavily 'restored' by the Victorians, the church still retains its original octagonal carved-oak roof supports.

An unexpected treat at Selmeston, pronounced 'Simson', was **Silletts Cottage**, a grade II listed Sussex farmhouse, with part of the building dating back to 1602 when it was first built and actually named 'Church Farm' because its land was adjacent to the church. The date of the building is known, as it has been found carved on an exposed beam in the loft. The original building consisted simply of two downstairs front rooms, which are now a marvellous restaurant offering all the ingredients for a perfect meal in this lovely country setting. It is open for lunch and dinner seven days a week. We had a wonderful home-cooked meal with a fine bottle of wine in a quiet, charming, relaxed atmosphere, which would be as pleasurable in summer as winter. In the summer you can feast your eyes on the panoramic views of the Downs, and in the winter we could just imagine relaxing in front of the crackling log fire in the cocktail lounge. Ron Sillett prepares all the dishes offered with the assistance of the chef Neil Wakefield. Ron told us that they are always looking for new recipes, so if you have any tucked away in a kitchen drawer do take it with you and show him. Silletts Cottage is quite small, and only accommodates a maximum of forty customers. Lunch is from a snack to a full a la carte with no minimum charge. Dinner is a fixed price with no hidden extra costs. If you wish to indulge yourself then you can accept the offer of overnight accommodation in a comfortable en-suite bedroom with colour TV at very reasonable prices. You can imagine how charming a room in a house this old would be, with its beams and nice farmhouse atmosphere. Personal service is terribly important to Ron and his staff. They looked after us superbly and genuinely wanted to know if there was anything they could do to please us further. It would be hard to do so. We loved every minute of our visit there. Silletts Carriages is another part of the business run by Ron's father, Frank Sillett, who has spent his entire life with horses and who literally talks, sleeps, dreams and lives for horses. He has marvellous tales to tell, and will keep you entertained and interested all the time. Ask him about the various services he offers. For a wedding day or any other important occasion with the help of his black Welsh cob and 1910 phaeton carriage, you can hire him, or indeed if you just want a quiet afternoon drive or a picnic in the Sussex countryside, then he will take you. We wished we had known about him before we went to Glyndebourne, because he would have taken us and Ron Sillett would have provided a super picnic hamper for the interval. Then there is Fred, a miniature Shetland pony, who is as much of a character as his master. He is used a lot for promotional and advertising work. We had a great day at Silletts Cottage and hope to return for dinner and a night's stay in the near future.

Silletts Cottage Restaurant, Church Farm, Selmeston, Nr. Polegate, East Sussex BN26 6TZ 0323 811343 Map Ref : 6F

From Selmeston, we made a two-mile detour northwards through the country lanes to visit the attractive community of **Ripe**. The Perpendicular village church contains several references to the local landed family, the Pelhams, and there is also an exceptional building known as the Old Cottage which is faced with a remarkable set of wooden carvings

Lulham Cottage, Ripe, Near Lewes, East Sussex 0323 811438 Map Ref: 5F

Walkers and country lovers looking for a quiet and peaceful spot will discover the ideal place to stay at **Lulham Cottage** in the picturesque village of Ripe, near Lewes. As you enter Ripe from the south, you will come to a crossroads and if you take the road signposted 'Narrow Road', you will soon come to this welcoming haven. Friendly hosts Gavin and Susan Wood offer their guests lovely home from home accommodation in two attractively furnished letting rooms, from which lovely views are enjoyed over the surrounding countryside to the Downs. The Wood's warmth and hospitality will have you relaxing immediately and after savouring Susan's excellent breakfast in the morning, you will find yourself feeling refreshed and ready for a day's exploring.

From Ripe, we retraced our steps back to Selmeston and then onto the A27. Continuing westwards, we soon passed the English Farm Cider Centre, a retail farm shop specialising in real farm cider from all over southern England. Our next major destination was the extraordinary country home of the Bloomsbury Group members Clive Bell, Vanessa Bell and Duncan Grant, two of whom were responsible for the murals at Berwick. **Charleston Farmhouse** (which shouldn't be confused with Charleston Manor near Westdean) is located at the end of a long driveway, the entrance to which is on the southern side of the A27 approximately one mile west of Selmeston. During the 1930s, the occupants transformed the interior of this unexceptional building into a work of art by utilising their skills as painters and designers. They covered almost every wall, floor and ceiling with their own murals, fabrics, carpets and wallpapers, and then completed the job with some fine original framed paintings, including a self-portrait by Vanessa Bell and one of Grace Higgens, their valued housekeeper.

They also created a delightful flint-walled cottage garden around the farmhouse which they carefully laid out with mosaic pathways, tiled pools, sculptures and a scented rose garden. During the 1930s, this unique country retreat welcomed some of the most eminent artists and thinkers of the day, including the economist John Maynard Keynes and the young composer Benjamin Britten. In more recent times, Charleston has been restored by a wealthy American patron and is now open to the public from 2pm to 6pm on Wednesdays, Thursdays, Saturdays, Sundays and Bank Holiday Mondays between April and October; admission charge payable.

Charleston Farmhouse lies at the base of **Firle Beacon** which at 712ft, is one of the highest points in the eastern South Downs. One of the Admiralty fire beacons which warned of the approaching Spanish Armada was sited on this exposed hilltop in the 16th-century, and several ancient remains have also been discovered here, including a 100ft Stone Age long barrow, a group of Bronze Age round barrows (known locally as the *Lord's Burghs*), and a Roman observation post. A number of Iron Age field terraces, or *lynchets*, can also be be made out, although modern farming methods are now placing these under threat. The summit can be reached by making a short detour from the

South Downs Way or by climbing one of the steep paths from Alciston or West Firle; those making it to the top are rewarded with breathtaking views over the Downs to the English Channel.

A mile or so to the west, the hamlet of **West Firle** has a good pub and a noteworthy part-Norman church which contains several impressive monuments to the Gage family, the owners of nearby **Firle Place**. This elegant country mansion was built in the 16th-century by Sir John Gage who, somewhat surprisingly for a Roman Catholic, was Henry VIII's Vice-Chamberlain. Two striking alabaster effigies of Sir John and Lady Philippa are among the finest features in the church. Another notable member of the family is General Sir Thomas Gage, the commander-in-chief of the British forces at the outset of the American War of Independence in the 1770s. Firle Place was significantly remodelled around this time and when Sir Thomas returned to this country, he brought with him a collection of early American artefacts which were used to furnish the house. Open 2pm to 5pm on Sundays, Wednesdays, Thursdays and Bank Holiday Sundays and Mondays between May and end-September; admission charge payable.

You approach Firle Place by way of a long drive, which is very beautiful, in spite of its once fine elms having suffered as have so many others. The core of the house is a Tudor manor house and must have been built by Sir John Gage (1479-1556). The drawing for Sir John's tomb, by Gerard Johnson, in the church can be viewed hanging in the house. The exterior of the house is certainly part of Sir John's house and still has the original hammerbeam roof above the 18th century plaster ceilings. There is one remaining Tudor gable on the south aspect. The Georgian remodelling occurred in two phases between 1713 and 1744 under Sir William Gage, and completed in 1744 to 1754 by the first Viscount, Thomas Gage, who added the Long Gallery for his collection of pictures. Firle is very much a family house, and because of that its warmth provides a wonderful setting for the collection of paintings by Europeans and British Old Masters. It is an important collection, considered to be one of the finest in south east England. There are rare and notable examples of French and English furniture and Sèvres porcelain. The magnificence of some of the paintings by Van Dyck, Gainsborough, Fra Bartolommeo, Corregio, De Koninck, Reynolds, Reubens, Puligo, Zoffany and a host of other wonderful painters left us breathless. We can well understand why Firle Place has been used for programmes on antiques, and why it also provided the setting for the film of Rebecca West's novel, 'The Return of the Soldier'. There is a special Connoisseurs Day on the first Wednesday of the month, which gives a longer unguided tour.

*Firle Place, Firle, Near Lewes, East Sussex BN8 6LP House 0273
858335 Restaurant 0273 858307 Map Ref : 6E*

Normally visitors are admitted to the house in groups for approximately fifty minutes guided tour, which is not nearly long enough to take it all in. The licensed restaurant will provide you with a very good cold buffet luncheon from 12.30 to 2.00pm, or a Sussex cream tea from 3.00pm. The House is open from May to the end of September, Sundays, Wednesdays and Thursdays. Also, Easter, May, Spring and August Bank Holiday Sundays and Mondays, from 2.00pm to the last tickets sold at 5.00pm. The Gage family are interesting. Sir John rose to distinction in the reign of Henry VIII when he held high military posts in wars against the French and Scots. He became Constable of the Tower of London, where he had charge of Lady Jane Grey before her execution, and was one of the Council of Regency during the minority of Edward VI. He was again Constable under Queen Mary when Princess Elizabeth was kept under his surveillance in the Tower for two months. It was his standing at court that enabled Sir John to enlarge Firle Place. The family were staunch Catholics until the eighteenth century, when they conformed to the Church of England and once more took part in public life. The first Viscount had two sons, one of whom succeeded him. The other, Thomas, became Commander-in -Chief of the British Forces in America. He was in command at the outbreak of the War of Independence, including the battle of Bunker Hill. His eldest son Henry succeeded as third Viscount, and it is from him that the present family are descended. The Gages held another property; Hengrave Hall in Suffolk. It was from this branch of Gages that Sir Thomas Gage, a well known botanist, ordered various plums to be sent from France, in the nineteenth century. These were planted at Hengrave but due to a label being mislaid from off a green plum, the gardeners then renamed it "Greengage". There is still a shoot from the original 'plum' to be seen at Hengrave Hall.

On leaving Firle Place, we returned once again to the A27, and after turning west and very soon after north, we arrived in the internationally-renowned village of **Glynde**. Although the settlement is filled with well-preserved traditional Sussex cottages, the 18th-century village church is very untypical of the area in that it is built in Palladian style. The churchyard contains the grave of one of Glynde's most noted sons, John Ellman, who was a pioneer of selective breeding and was responsible for producing the black-faced Southdown sheep, the breed on which most of the flocks in New Zealand and Australia are based.

Glynde Place, the imposing brick and flint mansion near the church, was built in the mid-16th-century for William Morley. Two centuries later, it was acquired by Richard Trevor, the Bishop of Durham, who added the stable block, remodelled the house and built the neoclassical parish church. (The village pub, the Trevor Arms, is named after the Bishop's family.) The house has an elegant wood-panelled long gallery and contains some exceptional works of art, and the grounds are beautifully laid out and incorporate an aviary and a pottery. Glynde Place is now owned by Lord Hampden and is open to the public on a limited number of days each year (opening times displayed on site).

The distinctive local landmark known as **Mount Caburn** lies to the west of Glynde and can be reached along a footpath from the village. Many thousands of years ago, this steep-sided chalk outcrop was separated from the rest of the Downs by the action of the River Glynde. This process created an artificial-looking mound almost 500ft in height whose natural defensive properties have long been exploited by man. The earthwork defences of an Iron Age hill-fort can still be made out near the summit, and evidence of an earlier Stone Age settlement has also been detected.

The part-Tudor, part-Victorian country house lying one mile to the north of Glynde village is the home of the world-famous **Glyndebourne Opera House**. This unique institution was founded by John and Audrey Christie in 1934, and since then it has built up an international reputation for presenting the finest opera in the most idyllic of English surroundings. Each summer season, audiences wearing evening dress arrive by train from London and leave their champagne to cool in the lake while they listen to the first half of the evening's performance; they then picnic in the grounds during the long interval before returning to the auditorium to enjoy the second

Glynde Place.

half. Fans preferring their opera in a less precious atmosphere often choose to attend the autumn performances by Glyndebourne's Touring Company. The beautiful grounds of Glyndebourne are regularly open to visitors throughout the year.

A couple of miles further north, **Ringmer** is a sizable village centred around a pleasant green which still retains a genteel charm despite having undergone considerable development in recent years. The parish church of St Mary contains a poignant memorial to the acclaimed village cricket team who joined up en masse to fight in World War I; of the 34 club members who went to war, only 6 were to return alive.

During the 17th-century, Ringmer played an important, if roundabout, part in early American history. Two young women brought up here married men who went on to become influential figures in the development of the United States: Ann Sadler married John Harvard, the founder of Harvard University, and Guglielma Springett married William Penn, the founder of Philadelphia. However, Ringmer's most famous inhabitant appears to have been Timothy, a tortoise belonging to the aunt of the 18th-century naturalist, Gilbert White, which was the subject of a long and engaging study; Timothy's shell is now part of the natural history collection at the British Museum.

From Ringmer, we continued northeast along the B2192 and after three miles, came to the renowned **Bentley Wildfowl and Motor Museum** near **Halland**. The estate covers some 100 acres in the heart of beautiful Sussex countryside and has something to spark everyone's interest.

Bentley House is a magnificent Palladian-style mansion surrounded by lush green fields and woodland. An architectural masterpiece, this beautiful building started life as a Tudor farmhouse and has since been extended and sympathetically altered to create the splendid building you see today. Exquisitely furnished throughout, the house is particularly renowned for its Chinese room and the Philip Rickman gallery which houses a collection of over 150 of the Sussex artist's watercolours of wildfowl.

Outside, the formal gardens are similarly laid out to Bentley House, as a series of rooms, separated by hedges of yew and often themed by colour, for example, the blue garden. Exploring the grounds still further will lead you to Glyndebourne Wood, a cool tranquil place with conifers and various broad leaved trees providing shade between the sunny glades.

Children will find the small animal section on the estate particularly appealing, with many young farm animals to touch and observe. Afterwards, the adventure playground gives parents the chance to relax while their offspring burn off some excess energy and the miniature steam railway which runs from April to September proves popular with the whole family.

Bentley is also renowned for its outstanding wildfowl reserve, which boasts more than 150 different species, eleven of which are listed as endangered.

Motoring enthusiasts will love Bentley Motor Museum which houses a magnificent collection of 50 cars and 25 motor bikes, ranging from veteran, Edwardian and vintage to modern day Lamborghini. Many of the vintage models are regular participants in the London to Brighton run and some are very rare models indeed.

Bentley Wildfowl and Motor Museum, Halland, Near Lewes, East Sussex BN8 5AF 0825 84057 Map Ref : 4E

After continuing into the centre of Halland, we turned southeast onto the A22 Eastbourne road and after a couple of miles, came to the pleasant village of **East Hoathly**. Situated on the High Street **Clara's Tearooms** is a delightful establishment run by a cheerful lady, Jane Seabrook. The building dates back to the mid-18th century and was built at a time when East Hoathly was one of the country's major smocking areas. Today it is more than just a tearoom and after savouring a freshly baked cake and cup of tea in attractive, country-style surroundings, you will find time disappearing as you browse around Jane's wide selection of local crafts, antiques and gifts. There is also a lovely beamed gallery upstairs which stocks a wide range of the up-market Rowan knitting yarn along with a few select items of designer knitwear.

Clara's Tearooms, 9 High Street, East Hoathly, near Lewes
BN8 6DR 0825 840339 Map Ref : 4E

Michelham Priory.

The church at **Chiddingly**, two miles to the east, has a towering 128ft stone spire which can be seen for miles around. From the churchyard, there are wonderful views in all directions and inside, there is a monument to the Sir John Jefferay, Queen Elizabeth I's

Chancellor of the Exchequer. The Jefferay family used to reside at nearby **Chiddingly Place**, a once-splendid Tudor mansion which, sadly, is now in ruins; a large timber-framed barn from the same era has, however, been saved from dilapidation. Another Tudor residence which has managed to survive the ravages of time is **Stonehill House**, a mile-and-a-half to the northeast.

From Chiddingly, we made our way southeastwards through the narrow country lanes and after crossing the A22, continued on to the village of **Upper Dicker**, the site of one of the loveliest old monastic houses in Sussex, **Michelham Priory**. This surprisingly well-preserved Augustinian priory was founded in 1229 by Gilbert de Aquila, the Norman lord of Pevensey, and continued to flourish until Henry VIII's Dissolution of the Monasteries in 1537. It then became the focal point of a large agricultural estate which for nearly three centuries belonged to the Sackville family.

The six-acre priory site is situated on a small peninsula which is surrounded on three sides by the River Cuckmere. The remaining side is separated from the mainland by a slow-flowing moat whose water is still used to power an old mill where traditionally-ground flour is produced in small batches to this day. Those entering the priory make their way across an old stone bridge and through a magnificent 14th-century gatehouse. A number of other structures have been incorporated into the original monastic buildings over the centuries, including a large Elizabethan barn, a blacksmith's workshop, a wheelwright's shop, a rope museum and a Tudor wing which has been converted into an interesting exhibition area.

The priory grounds are beautifully laid out and include separate herbaceous, rose and evergreen borders; there is also an unusual physic garden which is planted with a variety of early medicinal herbs. The river and moat attract many different species of wildfowl and other water-loving birds throughout the year. Michelham Priory is now under the ownership of the Sussex Archeological Society and is open daily, 11am to 5.30pm between 25th March and end-October (also Sundays, 11am to 4pm in February, March and November); admission charge payable.

On leaving Michelham Priory, we made our way back onto the A22 near Hailsham and continued southwards into the area covered in our next chapter.

CHAPTER FOUR

East Sussex.

From Eastbourne to Rye and the Kent Border.

135

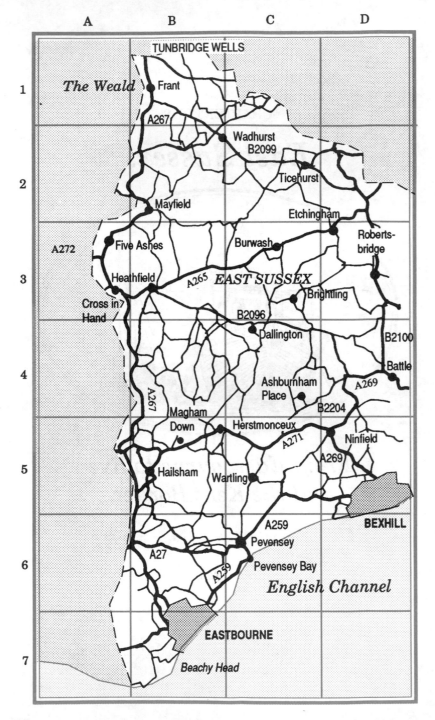

A B C D

TUNBRIDGE WELLS

The Weald   Frant

1

A267

Wadhurst
B2099

2

Ticehurst

Mayfield

Etchingham

A272   Five Ashes

Burwash

Roberts-
bridge

Heathfield   *EAST SUSSEX*

A265

3

Cross in?
Hand

Brightling

B2096

Dallington

B2100

Battle

4

A267

Ashburnham
Place

A269

Magham
Down

B2204

Herstmonceux

Ninfield

A271

A269

5

Hailsham   Wartling

BEXHILL

A259

6

A27   Pevensey

A259   Pevensey Bay

English Channel

7

EASTBOURNE

Beachy Head

136

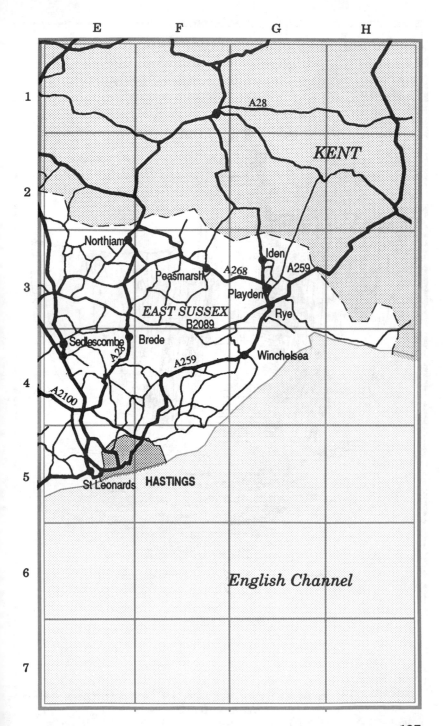

Beachy Head.

CHAPTER FOUR

East Sussex.
From Eastbourne to Rye
and the Kent Border.

After joining the **A22** near Hailsham, we continued southwards until we reached the coast at **Eastbourne**. This stylish and genteel seaside resort takes its name from the stream, or *bourne*, which has its source in the old reservoir in the area of open land now known as Motcombe Gardens. The town developed relatively recently as a seaside resort. Prior to 1780 when the children of George III spent the summer here, Eastbourne consisted of two separate villages, the larger of which lay over a mile inland. A period of gradual development then followed which gained momentum after the town was connected to the railway network in 1849.

The development of Eastbourne's sea front was relatively controlled, largely because most of the land belonged to only two individuals, the 7th Duke of Devonshire, and to a lesser extent, Carew Davis Gilbert. Between them, they were able to plan the wide thoroughfares, graceful stuccoed buildings and spacious gardens which characterise the town's three-mile-long esplanade. Among the noteworthy buildings constructed around this time are the handsome Regency-style Burlington Hotel, St Saviour's Church, the town hall, and the unusually elegant railway station. Eastbourne's classic seaside pier was built in 1880s and is one of the finest examples of its type in the country.

Despite its distinctive Victorian flavour, a settlement has existed on the site for many centuries. The remains of a Roman ship were discovered here in the 1960s, and the parish church of St Mary dates from around 1200. Other pre-Regency buildings include the flint- and cobble-built Old Rectory and the 13th-century Lambe Inn in the High Street. A total of fourteen Martello towers were built along the sea front in the early 19th-century when a Napoleonic invasion seemed likely. One of these, the **Wish Tower**, has been restored and now houses the **Coastal Defence Museum**, an interesting museum which chronicles Britain's attempts over the centuries to resist invasion from the sea. It can be found just to the west of the pier, approximately half way along the esplanade; open daily, Easter to October.

The circular **Redoubt Tower** in Royal Parade is another, even larger, Martello tower which has been converted for modern use. As well as containing an aquarium and the popular Treasure Island children's play centre, it is also the home of the **Sussex Combined Services Museum**, an informative museum on the history of Sussex-based military units. Open daily, Easter to end-October. The **Royal National Lifeboat Museum** lies on the sea front within a few yards of the Wish Tower; when it first opened in 1937, it was the first of its kind in the country. Open daily, April to December; weekends only, January to March.

Eastbourne has a proud reputation for its floral gardens and indeed, it would be hard to find a more typically-British display of spring bulbs and summer bedding plants than here. The **Carpet Gardens** beside the pier have an international reputation and are one of the finest remaining examples of the art of carpet gardening, a style which first became popular in the 18th-century. Both **Helen Gardens**, with their fine views along the cliffs to Beachy Head, and the **Italian Gardens**, a place much-visited by George V and Queen Mary during their stay in 1935, can be found at Holywell, at the western end of the esplanade; **Princes Park**, at the opposite end, has a popular boating lake with rowing boats for hire; **Hampden Park** further inland incorporates a lake and bird sanctuary.

The acclaimed **Towner Art Gallery** and local history museum is housed in an 18th-century manor house which also enjoys an attractive landscaped setting. It contains an impressive collection of work by 19th- and 20th-century British sculptors and painters, including Henry Moore, Elizabeth Frink and John Piper. Open daily, all year round (closed Mondays in winter). An international women's tennis tournament takes place prior to Wimbledon each year on the celebrated grass courts of **Devonshire Park**, and the famous **Grand Parade Bandstand** on the front holds traditional brass and military band concerts throughout the year. Eastbourne's all-weather attractions include the Butterfly Centre on the promenade, the Sovereign pool and leisure complex, and the 'How We Lived Then' museum of shops in Cornfield Terrace. Further information on these and the town's many other holiday attractions can be obtained at the Tourist Information Centre.

A wonderful excursion from Eastbourne is to the summit of **Beachy Head**, three miles to the west of the town centre. This magnificent white chalk cliff marks the eastern end of the South Downs and from the pleasant grassy picnicking area at the top, there's an almost sheer drop of well over 500ft to the waves below. The views from here are superb: to the east it is possible to see as far as Dungeness, to the west as far as Selsey Bill and the Isle of Wight, and to the south as far as the distant cargo ships which ply the busy shipping lanes of the English Channel.

The colossal mass of Beachy Head dwarfs the red and white banded lighthouse which stands on the wave-cut platform at its base. Notwithstanding, this distinctive granite-built structure throws out a beam of light which can be seen over fifteen miles out to sea. This stretch of coastline was once known as the 'Devil's Cape' because of its danger to shipping, and to this day the lighthouse has to continue its vital task of deterring ships from straying too close to the cliffs.

From the top of Beachy Head, we retraced our steps down the winding **B2103** towards the centre of Eastbourne, before joining the **A259** Pevensey road and continuing eastwards along the coast. After a couple of miles we turned northwest onto the **B2104** to reach the charming former iron-founding settlement of **Friday Street**. The hamlet's industrial past has left a surprisingly picturesque legacy in the form of a large hammer pond, an artificial lake which was formed by damming the Tilling Bourne stream. Around 300 years ago, water from the pond would have provided the power to drive the bellows and mechanical hammers in a nearby iron foundry. Today, however, the area around the tranquil tree-lined lake offers some excellent woodland walks through mature evergreen and broadleaved trees, some of which were planted by the 17th-century diarist and arboriculturist, John Evelyn. A good place to end a walk is the Stephen Langton Inn, a pleasant timber-framed building which is named after the Archbishop of Canterbury who was born here in 1150.

From Friday Street, we retraced our steps southwards for half-a-mile before turning northeast onto the **B2191** near the village of Langney. Our next stop was one of the gems of East Sussex, the old Roman garrison town of **Pevensey**. The low-lying land around Pevensey proved a good landing place for the invading Roman legions, and in order to protect their strategic anchorage, the Romans erected a massive fortification (they went on to build ten such strongholds along the southern shores of Britain). Although **Pevensey Castle** now lies almost two miles inland, it once stood on the shoreline within a few yards of the Roman landing stages. However, the steady eastward drift of the shingle beach gradually isolated Pevensey from the English Channel, a process which was inadvertently accelerated by the draining of the Pevensey Levels during Tudor times.

In 1066, the invading forces of William the Conqueror also landed in Pevensey Bay and used the castle to billet his troops prior to the Battle of Hastings. Then after the Norman Conquest, the surrounding lands were granted to the Count of Mortain who constructed a smaller fortification within the original Roman ramparts using stone from the earlier structure. Two centuries later, this castle successfully resisted a siege by Simon de Montfort's forces who were attempting to oust the supporters of Henry III following the Battle of Lewes in 1264. The structure then gradually fell into disrepair as it became increasingly isolated from the sea, although it was briefly reoccupied at around the time of the Spanish Armada, and again during the Second World War. The ruins of Pevensey Castle are now under the ownership of English Heritage and are open daily, 9.30am (2pm on Sundays) to 6.30pm (4pm in winter), all year round.

The village of Pevensey contains an unusual number of fine mediaeval buildings, including the **Mint House** which was built in the 1340s on the site of a Norman mint, and the **Court House** which served the borough as a combined courtroom and gaol; both buildings now house interesting museums of local history. There are also a number of excellent old inns in the village, and **Glyndley Manor** on the edge of Pevensey is renowned for its mysterious atmosphere and celebrated colony of herons. In the days prior to the founding of the Royal Navy, Pevensey served as one of the nation's *Cinque Ports*, that is to say it was granted certain privileges by the Crown in return for providing ships and men in defence of the Channel coast. Several centuries later, a series of Martello towers was built along the coast to the east of Pevensey to defend the shore against a possible attack from the forces of Napoleon.

On leaving Pevensey, we drove inland across the area of drained marshland known as the **Pevensey Levels**. At one time, this was an area of tidal mud flats which were covered in shallow salt pans; since then, however, it has been reclaimed for agricultural use and is now covered in fertile arable fields. Our journey northwards took us through the village of **Wartling** you will discover a welcome stopping-off point in your journey when you call in at the **Lamb Inn**. Standing beside the village church, not far from the castle, this is a delightful 17th century inn which also boasts a fine restaurant. Here, in a warm friendly atmosphere with the delicious aroma of freshly cooked food mingling with the smell of the log fire, you can soak up the olde worlde ambience whilst sampling a wide range of beers and lagers. The à la carte menu is both extensive and varied, including an excellent selection of fish dishes and has something to suit every palate at a very reasonable price. Whether you want a refreshing drink or a tasty meal out, at the Lamb Inn, a warm welcome and first class hospitality are assured.

Lamb Inn, Wartling, East Sussex 0323 832116 Map Ref : 5C

From Wartling, we continued northwards for a couple of miles and turned west onto the **A271** Hailsham road. After passing though the village of **Windmill Hill**, and shortly before reaching Herstmonceux (pronounced *Herst-mon-soo*) village, we turned south into a narrow country lane to reach the famous **Herstmonceux Castle** and **Observatory**. The castle was built on the site of an earlier Norman manor house in 1440 and was one of the first large-scale buildings in Britain to be constructed from redbrick; it was also one of the first fortifications to take into account both the defensive needs and the comfort of its residents.

Later, the castle passed into the hands of the Hare family who presided over a long period of decline which culminated in its virtual dismantling in 1777. The structure then remained in a state of dilapidation for some 150 years until a major programme of restoration began in the 1930s under the supervision of the Lewes architect, W H Godfrey. His careful and inspired work helped to restore the turrets and battlements to their former glory and today, the fully-refurbished castle stands in pristine condition at the centre of its highly-photogenic moat.

Herstmonceux Castle is said to be haunted by a 9ft phantom drummer who can occasionally be seen marching slowly across the battlements on misty winter's nights. According to different versions of the story, he is either the ghost of a former owner who beat the drum to warn off his young wife's admirers, or the invention of an 18th-century member of the Hare family who is alleged to have been involved in shady smuggling activities and who is said to have contrived the legend of the 'Herstmonceux Drummer' to discourage unwanted visitors.

Herstmonceux Castle.

In 1948, the Royal Greenwich Observatory moved here from its original home in Greenwich Park, London to get away from the residual glare of the city. Over the following twenty years, the mighty Isaac Newton telescope was planned and built in the grounds which, when it was officially opened in 1967, was one of the five largest telescopes in the world. Recent advances in the field of astronomy necessitated a further move, and the Royal Greenwich Observatory is now located in Cambridge. The observatory and grounds are open daily, Easter to end-September; the castle is open on a limited number of days each year (opening times displayed on site).

Opposite the entrance to Herstmonceux Castle stands the parish church of All Saints, a handsome building dating from 1180 which was built on the site of an earlier Saxon structure. Inside, there is an unusual rectangular font which was carved from Wealden sandstone around 1380 and a number of exceptional memorials, including a monumental brass of Sir William Fiennes dated 1402 and an elaborate carved Gothic tomb which contains the reclining figures of Thomas, 8th Lord Dacre and his son, Sir Thomas Fiennes who predeceased his father in 1528.

Waldernheath Country Restaurant, Amberstone Corner, Magham Down, Hailsham, Sussex 0323 840143 Map Ref : 5B

Instead of returning to the **A271** at Herstmonceux village, we turned west through the lanes to reach **Magham Down**, home of the renowned **Waldernheath Country Restaurant**, two miles outside Hailsham. This charming 15th century house boasts views over the rolling Sussex Downs and provides a relaxed and informal setting for that 'special' meal out. Run by Paul Hill and his family, Waldernheath offers the finest English and French cuisine, beautifully presented in a cosy, candlelit atmosphere. Paul holds the prestigious Hotel and Catering Management Diploma, received after training in Lausanne, Switzerland - an indication of the quality guests can expect. There is ample parking space and an extensive garden, the source of much of the restaurant's produce, but there is also a patio and garden area for guests to enjoy their meal 'al fresco', weather permitting, with Patio Platters proving to be Summer favourites.

Herstmonceux is renowned for its traditional woodworking and in particular, for the making of 'trugs', handmade wooden gardeners' baskets which are made from broad bands of willow on an ash or chestnut frame. Though appearing ancient in origin, these in fact only date from the Great Exhibition of 1851.

A delightful place to stay can be found just south of the village on the road to the castle and church. **Cleaver's Lyng** is a lovely old stone cottage which was built in 1580. You will discover a real haven of peace and tranquility when you stay at Cleavers Lyng, a delightful 16th century country hotel enjoying a secluded countryside location two miles outside Herstmonceux. Following the A271 east towards Herstmonceux, take the turning signposted for the church and after about a mile and a half, you will find Cleavers Lyng on the right. The name Cleavers Lyng means 'woodcutter's house on the hill overlooking the marsh' and today some of the eight attractively furnished guest rooms have a private balcony overlooking the South Downs. The restaurant with its beamed ceiling and inglenook fireplace provides the perfect setting for the excellent menu, all freshly prepared using local produce, including Carr Taylor Sussex wines.

Cleavers Lyng, Church Road, Herstmonceux, East Sussex
BN27 1QJ 0323 833131 Fax: 0323 833617 Map Ref : 5B

From Herstmonceux, we drove eastwards along the A271 and retraced our steps through Windmill Hill. Those interested in rural history should make a detour here to visit the **Sussex Farm Heritage Centre** which can be found three-quarters-of-a-mile to the north of the main road. A mile or so further east, we passed through the village of Boreham Street and soon after, turned northeast onto the Battle road. Our next destination was the hamlet of **Ashburnham**, a truly hidden place which lies in the country lanes between the **B2204** and the hamlet of Ponts Green. One of the last surviving centres of the Sussex iron industry, a sizable foundry operated here for around three centuries until the beginning of the 19th-century. The old foundry buildings are still in existence, along with the remains of the great hammer ponds which once channelled water to the mechanical hammers and bellows.

Ashburnham Forge stands on the northern edge of the privately-owned **Ashburnham Park**, a 1000-acre country estate which was landscaped by Capability Brown in the 18th-century. One of his finest creations is the series of artificial lakes which he constructed in the shallow valley in front of **Ashburnham Place**. The church within the grounds contains a number of fine monuments to the Ashburnham family. House and estate not open to the public.

Kitchenham Farm, Ashburnham, Battle, Sussex TN33 9NP
0424 892221 Map Ref : 4C

Travelling on the **A271**, just past Ashburnham Place as you come south of Battle, you will find **Kitchenham Farm**, the charming home of Amanda Worssam who offers a warm welcome to her many guests. The beautiful Georgian farmhouse built in 1770 is surrounded by an Oast House and traditional buildings which offer a lovely backdrop to the spectacular views. The farm is a 700 acre working farm, mainly arable, sheep and cattle and is part of the Ashburnham Estate. Guests are welcome to stroll down to the river through the meadows or in the woods where blue bells and primroses abound in the Spring. The house provides very comfortable accommodation in three spacious, traditionally furnished guest rooms and a drawing room and dining room with open log fires for those cool evenings.

After returning to the **B2204**, we made our way southwards through the country lanes to Ninfield where we joined the **A269** and

147

continued southeastwards for four miles to **Bexhill**. In common with most other seaside resorts on the Channel coast, Bexhill was not much more than a fishing and smuggling community before the arrival of the railway in the 19th-century. A good number of pre-Victorian features have managed to survive, including the old weather-boarded cottages and commercial buildings in Church Street, the 14th-century Manor House, and the part-Norman parish church of St Peter which stands on the site of an ancient Neolithic earthwork.

Modern Bexhill owes its character to the local landed family, the Earls De la Warr, who developed the town in the 1880s. (Many years before, a branch of the family had an influence in the naming the American state of Delaware.) Most of the features characteristic of an English seaside resort date from this late-Victorian period, including the promenade and the floral gardens in Egerton Park. Perhaps the most striking feature of the town, however, wasn't built until the 1930s, the **De la Warr Pavilion**. This was designed by the acclaimed German architects Mendelsohn and Chermayeff in a style reminiscent of an ocean-going liner, and contains a theatre, concert hall, ballroom and elegant terrace bar. Now Grade I listed, it still attracts an international lineup of performing artists throughout the year.

Bexhill was the first resort to allow mixed bathing on its beaches in 1900 and was regarded as very progressive in its day; today however, it is more the domain of the traditional and unadventurous. Nevertheless, the gently sloping shingle beaches offer clean and safe bathing, and there are also good facilities for windsurfing and other watersports. **Bexhill Museum** on the edge of Egerton Park houses an interesting collection of artefacts pertaining to the natural history, geology and archeology of the area. Open Tuesdays to Sundays (and Bank Holiday Mondays), 10am (2pm weekends) to 5pm, all year round (closed January); small admission charge payable. The Manor Gardens in the old town contain an aviary, open-air theatre, walled garden and the renowned **Bexhill Museum of Costume and Social History**. This unique collection of historic costumes is arranged in a series of imaginative settings covering the period from 1740s to the 1940s. Open daily, 10.30am (2pm weekends) to 5pm between Easter and end-October; admission charge payable.

Our journey eastwards from Bexhill took us through **St Leonards**, a western suburb of Hastings which was founded in the 1820s as a fashionable seaside resort. It was created by James Burton, the celebrated London architect who was responsible for designing much of Bloomsbury. With the assistance of his son, Decimus, a talented architect in his own right who went on to design the Wellington arch at Hyde Park Corner in London, he created a model seaside town which was designed to attract the wealthy and aristocratic.

The focus of regency St Leonards is the **Royal Victoria Hotel** on the seafront, a handsome stuccoed brick building which was designed in classical style with a broad pedimented façade. At one time, the hotel looked out onto the Royal Baths where guests would go to take the chilly waters of the English Channel in relative privacy. The low colonnade on either side of the hotel creates a striking formal promenade, the unity of which has been spoiled to some degree by the close proximity of oversized 20th-century apartment blocks. Unfortunately, one of these stands beside Crown House, Burton's original seaside residence which he gave up to Princess (later Queen) Victoria when she visited St Leonards in 1834.

In its heyday, the resort's formal social activities took place in the **Assembly Rooms** (now the Masonic Hall), a building which was connected by tunnel to the hotel kitchens so that provisions could be brought in for social functions. The delightfully informal **St Leonards Gardens** stand a little inland from here. Originally private gardens maintained by the subscriptions of local residents, they were acquired by the local authority in 1880 and now provide a delightfully tranquil area with lakes, mature trees and gently sloping lawns. The gardens also contain a number of fine Regency buildings, including the **Clock House**, which appears to be three storeys high from the park but only one from the road behind, **Allegria Court**, Burton's subsequent private home, and **Gloucester Lodge**, the former residence of Princess Sophia of Gloucester.

North Lodge, a castellated gatehouse to the north of the park, was built to guard the northern entrance to the town. It was also once the home of Sir Henry Rider Haggard, the author of *King Solomon's Mines* and other classic adventure stories. Victorian St Leonards even had its own service areas: **Mercatoria**, the tradesmen's quarter, and **Lavatoria**, the laundry-women's quarter. **Burton's Tomb**, the curious pyramid-shaped vault where James Burton and several member of his family were buried, can be found In the grounds of the old parish church in West Hill. Guided walking tours of this fascinating resort depart from the Royal Victoria Hotel at 2.15pm on summer Thursdays; a detailed written guide is also available from bookshops and the tourist information centre.

A mile or so further east, the ancient town of **Hastings** is quite different in character. Long before William the Conqueror made his well-publicised landing on the beaches of nearby Pevensey Bay, Hastings was the principal town of a small semi-independent Saxon province which straddled the Kent-Sussex border. By the mid 10th-

Fishing Boats at Hastings.

century, it was an important port and it even had its own mint. Following the Battle of Hastings, which in fact took place six miles inland at the place now called Battle, the Normans chose a promontory to the west of the old town to build their first stone castle in England. Sections of the north and east walls, a gatehouse, tower and dungeons still remain, and the stiff walk up to the castle site is rewarded with some magnificent views of the town and surrounding coastline. Open daily, April to end-September.

Over the centuries, Hastings has been subjected to periodic attack from the sea, both from cross-Channel raids, which on at least one occasion left the town a smouldering ruin, and from the waves themselves, which would regularly flood the streets during stormy conditions. The town's busy fishing harbour started to silt up during the Elizabethan era and now lies buried beneath a 20th-century shopping development. Nevertheless, the industry managed to survive and today, fishing vessels continue to be hoisted onto the shingle beach by motor winch. One of Hastings' most characteristic features are the tall, narrow wooded huts which are used for for dying nets and storing fishing tackle; these date from the 17th-century and are known as *net shops* or *deezes*. The old fishermen's church of St Nicholas now houses the **Fishermen's Museum**, an interesting exhibition which includes the full-sized sailing lugger, *Enterprise*. This was the last vessel to be built in Hastings before the shipyard closed in 1909 and was actively involved in the Dunkirk evacuation of 1940. Open daily (except Fridays), May to end-September.

The old part of Hastings consists of a network of narrow streets and alleyways, or *twittens*, which lie between Castle Hill and East Hill. The best way discover the many interesting old residential buildings, inns and churches is to take a walking tour along the High Street and All Saints Street. (Those especially interested in churches should follow the 'Hastings Church Trail', a pleasant walk which takes in seven churches, most of them mediaeval.) St Clement's Church in the High Street has two cannonballs embedded in its tower, one of which was fired from a French warship, and the Stag Inn in All Saints Street has a concealed entrance to a smugglers' secret passage and a pair of macabre 400 year-old mummified cats.

There are two cliff railways in Hastings, one on each side of the old town. The West Hill railway runs underground and carries passengers up to the castle, the lighthouse and the famous **St Clement's Caves**, a three-acre network of sandstone caves which was opened up in the 1820s and now contains an ingenious multi-media museum known as the Smugglers' Adventure. Open daily, 10am to 5.30pm, all year round.

Hastings also contains a variety of attractions for the traditional seaside holidaymaker. The 600ft long **Pier** was completed in 1872 and had to be repaired after the Second World War when it was deliberately holed in two places to prevent it being used as a landing stage by Hitler's forces. According to local legend, the **Conqueror's Stone** at the head of the pier was used by William the Conqueror as a dining table for this for his first meal on English soil in 1066. 81 events spanning 900 years of the town's history are remembered in the impressive **Hastings Embroidery** in the town hall. Inspired by the Bayeux Tapestry, this remarkable 240ft long embroidery was made by the Royal School of Needlework in 1966 to commemorate the ninth centenary of the Norman Invasion. Among the characters to be depicted is John Logie Baird, the pioneer of television who carried out his early experiments here in the 1920s.

Parkside House, 59 Lower Park Road, Hastings, East Sussex TN34 2LD 0424 433096 Map Ref : 5E

For visitors to the historic town of Hastings, **Parkside House** on Lower Park Road provides absolutely first class accommodation and is one of only seven houses in the South of England to carry the coveted 'deluxe' award from the English Tourist Board. Run by friendly hosts Janet and Brian Kent this charming Victorian house is a non-smoking establishment offering lovely views across Alexandra Park and easy access to the centre and seafront of this busy coastal town. The house is beautifully furnished throughout with lovely antique furniture and the decor of the guest rooms is colour-themed, giving each one its name. All are en-suite and one even boasts a french bed, but they all offer extra facilities such as bathrobes, hairdryer and video. The comfortable guest lounge is the perfect place to relax, whilst the option of an excellent homecooked dinner with wine, means you really have everything you could possibly need under one roof.

The 600-acre **Hastings Country Park** to the east of the town offers some spectacular clifftop walking along two-and-a-half miles of unspoilt coastline. Guided walks through this attractive area of woodland and heath are provided by the local ranger service throughout the summer.

Seven miles along the **A259** to the northeast of Hastings, we came to the ancient Cinque Port of **Winchelsea**, the smallest town in England and one of the earliest to be subjected to the machinations of the town planner. Until the 13th-century, Winchelsea lay several miles to the south on a site which was eventually engulfed by the sea following a series of violent storms. In its place, a new town was laid out its present position on Iham Hill which was designed to a rigid grid plan drawn up in part by Edward I. Built along Roman lines, the ambitious rectangular pattern of 39 squares covered a total area of 89 acres and for two centuries, became home to some 6000 inhabitants, around ten times the present number.

For a short period in the early 14th-century, Winchelsea was perhaps the most important of the Channel ports, carrying on a thriving wine trade and supplying thirteen of the fifty ships which made up the total Cinque Port fleet. However, the unpredictable forces of nature caused the sea to retreat once again, an occurrence which stranded Winchelsea without a port and a means of sustaining its economy. Neither the town walls nor the sizable parish church of St Thomas were ever completed, and the town gradually shrank into an area of a dozen or so blocks in the northeastern quarter of the Edward's original layout. Of the town's three surviving gateways, Strand Gate, Pipewell Gate and New Gate, the last-named now stands some distance south of the nearest buildings. The town's decline wasn't helped by a series of devastating cross-Channel raids which reduced the town to smouldering ruins on more than one occasion.

Assisted by a gradual recovery which began in the mid 19th-century, present-day Winchelsea is a place with great historic beauty. The town has its own special atmosphere which has long attracted artists and writers, including Turner, Millais, Thackeray and Conrad. Of the town's many historic buildings, **Court Hall** is among the oldest in the county and now contains a small, yet informative, local history museum. The ruins of a 14th-century Franciscan Friary, the **Grey Friars**, can also be seen within the grounds of a home for the elderly in Friars Road. Further details can be obtained by studying the information board on the green, or by following the instructive walking guide published by the local council.

Since the time of the Romans, the ancient Cinque Port town of Winchelsea has been vulnerable to marauding invaders, but today the

Strand Gate at Winchelsea.

only invasion is by visitors keen to absorb its fascinating history. Enjoying a central location here, **The New Inn** is a charming 18th century family pub whose character is enhanced by exposed beams and an open log fire. A popular haunt, this welcoming establishment serves a fine selection of well-kept ale and is renowned for its excellent lunchtime and evening menu, specialities being the homemade pies and fresh local fish. Children are well-catered for with their own menu, dining area and even a play area in the large beer garden. With accommodation available in several comfortably furnished guest rooms, The New Inn really has everything you could need.

The New Inn, German Street, Winchelsea, East Sussex TN36 4EN
0797 276252 Map Ref : 4G

In 1975, the National Trust acquired **Wickham Manor Farm**, a broad ring of farmland which surrounds Winchelsea on all sides except the north. This acquisition will hopefully conserve the unique setting of this truly exceptional hilltop settlement for all time.

The Country House at Winchelsea is a very special place, perfect for that quiet break away from it all. Set back from the A259, this delightful 17th century listed building exudes a friendly warmth and offers lovely home-style accommodation. The beautifully furnished guest rooms are all en-suite with every modern facility to ensure complete comfort, whilst the cosy sitting room with its log fire provides a relaxing setting for a pre-dinner drink. An excellent homecooked dinner is available by prior arrangement and can be enjoyed in the elegant candlelit dining room. With two acres of beautiful walled gardens providing a haven for a variety of birds and butterflies, The Country House at Winchelsea seems an idyllic hideaway for all its guests.

The Country House at Winchelsea, Hastings Road, Winchelsea, East Sussex TN36 4AD 0797 226669 Map Ref : 4G

Our journey northeastwards from Winchelsea to Rye took us past the ruins of **Camber Castle**, a fortification built in 1539 by Henry VIII as part of the Tudor coastal defences. Although originally constructed near the shoreline, the shifting sands have marooned the structure over a mile inland.

In many respects, the history of the delightful town of **Rye** mirrors that of Winchelsea. Along with its once-eminent neighbour to the southwest, Rye was added to the five existing Cinque Ports of Hastings, Romney, Hythe, Dover and Sandwich in the 12th-century. The town was also subjected to ferocious cross-Channel raids and indeed, almost every non-stone-built structure in the town was burnt to the ground in the notorious French raid of 1377. Later, the harbour suffered from the problems of a receding coastline, a dilemma which eventually required the building of a new port, Rye Harbour, closer to the repositioned mouth of the River Rother.

Rye's prominent hilltop site is partially ringed by the rivers Rother, Brede and Tillingham, a factor which has made it an easily defendable hill fort since early times. A substantial perimeter wall was built to defend the open northern approaches, and one of its four great gateways, the **Land Gate**, still survives in the northeastern corner of the old town. This imposing 14th-century structure once had oak gates, a drawbridge and a portcullis, the movement of which carved deep grooves in its stone walls. The clock was added in 1863 in memory of Prince Albert, and after a long period of neglect, it was restored at the time of the Royal Wedding in 1981.

Visitors to the historic town of Rye will discover a first class restaurant when they call at the **Landgate Bistro**. Housed in a grade

156

II listed building and run by Nick Parkin and Toni Ferguson-Lees, the Bistro specialises in fresh locally caught fish, seasonal game and Romney Marsh Lamb. Popular dishes include Local Squid cooked with white wine, tomatoes and garlic, Very Fishy Stew and Wild Rabbit with Rosemary. Toni Ferguson-Lees is superb chef and has been included in the book 'Woman Chefs of Britain'. There is a well chosen and fairly priced wine list. A local architectural feature of the restaurant is the late Georgian "mathematical" tiling on the exterior of the building.

The Landgate Bistro, 5 / 6 Landgate, Rye, East Sussex TN31 7LH
0797 222829 Map Ref : 3G

Rye grew prosperous in the late mediaeval period due to the activities of its fishing and merchant fleets who brought in fish and cloth and sent out wool and processed iron to continental Europe. However, the silting up of the harbour gradually denied the town a means of earning a living and heralded a lengthy period of decline. This economic downturn halted the process of organic change in Rye and many of the buildings which would have been updated in more prosperous circumstances remained unchanged.

As a result, present-day Rye has inherited a superb legacy of late-mediaeval buildings, most of which have been restored in the years since the town was 'rediscovered' in the 19th-century. The local council now publishes an informative walking guide of the old town which is available from the public library or the bookshop in the High Street. Alternatively, the **Heritage Centre** on Strand Quay offers a unique sound and light show which tells the story of Rye using a remarkable scale model of the town. Open daily April to October, weekends only November to March; admission charge payable

The ancient seafaring town of Rye is full of cobbled streets and antique shops and here on Watchbell Street, you will find a lovely place to stay at **The Hope Anchor Hotel**. This 17th century Grade

Rye.

II listed building is run by Lena and Derrick Baldock and stands at the top of the hill which dominates Rye. There are 15 well-equipped, attractively furnished guest rooms with lovely views, nine of which have en-suite facilities and two with four-poster beds. Lena does all the cooking and offers tasty bar meals as well as a full table d'hote and a la carte menu which can be enjoyed in the comfortable restaurant. Open to non-residents, the restaurant is very popular locally, so booking is advisable, particularly for Sunday lunch.

The Hope Anchor Hotel, Watchbell Street, Rye, East Sussex
TN31 7HA   0797 222216 Map Ref : 3G

The Hope Anchor Hotel is located just a few yards from the foot of **Mermaid Street**, one of the finest examples of an unspoilt mediaeval thoroughfare in Rye. This delightful cobbled lane is lined with early timbered buildings including the famous **Mermaid Inn**, a wonderful old hostelry which was rebuilt in 1420 following the devastating French raid of forty years before. In the 18th-century, the inn became the headquarters of the Hawkhurst Gang, one of the most infamous and powerful bands of smugglers on the south coast. Local legend has it that they always sat with their pistols at the ready in case of a sudden excisemen's raid. A series of events recording the inn's past are displayed on boards at the front of the building.

On turning right at the top of Mermaid Street, we came to the National Trust-owned **Lamb House**, a handsome redbrick Georgian residence which was built by a local wine merchant, James Lamb, in 1723. The new building incorporated a number of earlier structures, including a 'deese' for drying herrings and a brewery which occupied the site of what is now the walled garden. In 1726, George I paid an impromptu visit to Lamb House after his ship was driven onto nearby Camber Sands during a storm. He ended up being snowed in for four nights during which time Lamb's wife, Martha, gave birth to a son; the king agreed to be child's godfather and two days later he was baptised

159

'George'. An inscribed silver bowl given by the king as a christening present was later revealed to be silver plate.

In 1742, an attempt was made on James Lamb's life by a local butcher, John Breads. As mayor, Lamb had fined Breads for selling short measures and in revenge, Breads attacked a man wearing the red mayoral cloak as he was walking through the churchyard late one night. The man turned out to be Lamb's brother-in-law, Allen Grebell, who had agreed to represent him at a dinner on board a visiting ship. Grebell later died from his injuries and Breads was tried and hanged. His body was then chained to a public gibbet as a deterrent to others. Later, the murderer's bones were taken down and boiled into an infusion which was thought to cure rheumatism, and the remainder of the his skull, still in its gibbet cage, was put on display in Rye's 18th-century town hall where it can still be seen to this day. The ghost of Allen Grebell has been known to appear both in Lamb House and in Rye Churchyard.

Lamb House became the home of the American writer Henry James from 1898 until his death in 1916, and indeed many of his finest later novels were dictated to his secretary either in the Green Room, or during warmer weather, in the Garden Room. James laid out the delightful walled garden and invited many of his literary friends to the house, including H G Wells, Rudyard Kipling, G K Chesterton and Joseph Conrad. During the 1920s, Lamb House was leased to another writer, E F Benson, the author of the *Mapp and Lucia* books, who thinly disguised the house as 'Mallards' and the town as 'Tilling'. Today, Lamb House contains a number of Henry James' personal effects and is open to the public on Wednesdays and Saturdays, 2pm to 6pm between April and end-October; admission charge payable (free to National Trust members).

From Lamb House, it is only a very short walk to **Church Square**, Rye's wonderful centrepiece which contains some of the town's finest late-mediaeval buildings. The parish church of St Mary the Virgin was severely damaged during the French raid of 1377, although not before its church bells were taken down and carried off to Normandy. However, a retaliatory raid the following year not only inflicted a similar fate on two French towns, but succeeded in recapturing the bells of St Mary. The church was sympathetically restored during the Victorian era and contains some fine features, including a 16th-century turret clock with a spectacular 18ft pendulum, some interesting 20th-century stained-glass windows, and the original 'quarter boys', 18th-century cherubs which once stood above the clock face, but which have now been replaced by fibreglass replicas; these golden reproductions still come out to strike on the quarter hour (but *not* on the hour).

A highly unusual oval structure can be found close to the town hall at the eastern end of the churchyard. Built of red brick in 1735, the Town Cistern, or **Water House**, stands on top of an underground tank which once held the town's water supply. The tank was filled by raising water through wooden pipes from the bottom of Conduit Hill using horse drawn machinery. A little to the southwest of here, we came to the **Ypres Tower and Museum**; one of the oldest surviving buildings in Rye, it was constructed around 1250 as a defensive fort. Two centuries later, it was acquired by John de Ypres as a private residence, then subsequently it became the town's courthouse, gaol and mortuary. Today, it houses the award-winning **Rye Museum** and offers some magnificent views over the surrounding coastal plain. Open 10.30am to 5.30pm between April and end-October.

We returned to the Water House and walked down into Rye's shopping district via the **Flushing Inn** and the old **Apothecary's Shop** in East Street. Having crossed the High Street, we decided to have a look at the old Augustinian friary in Conduit Hill. The remains of this 14th-century monastery are now occupied by a fascinating establishment, the **Cinque Ports Pottery**.

Cinque Ports Pottery, The Monastery, Conduit Hill, Rye, East Sussex TN317LE 0797 222033 Map Ref : 3G

Cinque Ports Pottery is one place where you will definitely find yourself enticed in. Originally built as a friary in 1377 by Augustinian Monks, today it is a superb pottery with a public gallery where you can watch the complete process of pottery making. Each item is individually handcrafted and in the showroom you will find many ideas for gifts and mementos. In a building of this age, it comes as no surprise to learn that there is a resident ghost. Apparently he was a choir singer who ran off with a local maiden and was caught and bricked up alive by the monks! The showroom is open daily and viewing times are from 10.00am-12.00pm and 1.30pm-4.30pm, weekdays only.

The nearby Dormy House Club stands on the site of the old Tower House, the former home of a beautiful young woman who is said to have fallen in love with a friar with a particularly fine singing voice. The pair ran away together, but were caught, brought back and punished by being buried alive. Years later, the skeletons of the lovers, still wrapped in each other's arms, were discovered during excavations for the railway. Their ghosts, who regularly haunted nearby Turkey Cock Lane, have not been seen since their remains were given a formal re-burial.

It would be hard to find a more charming place to stay in Rye, than **Jeake's House** in Mermaid Street, a beautiful listed building set in one of Britain's most picturesque medieval cobbled streets. The oldest part of this delightful house dates back to 1689 with original wood panelling and exposed beams enhancing its character and charm. The twelve guest rooms are individually furnished to a very high standard, in keeping with the age of Jeake's House and provide en-suite bath/shower facilities. The galleried breakfast room, formerly an 18th century chapel and Quaker meeting house, provides a lovely airy setting in which to enjoy breakfast, its white walls, high windows and beautifully laid tables, with a backdrop of soothing classical music ensuring a perfect start to the day.

Jeake's House, Mermaid Street, Rye, East Sussex TN31 ET
0797 222828 Map Ref : 3G

For bed and breakfast accommodation with a difference, **Furnace Lane Oast** is somewhere rather special. Situated off the **A28** north of the village of Broadoak, this was originally a working oast house until 15 years ago and is now a family-run business owned by Robert Sevastopulo. This magnificent house offers first class accommodation in beautifully secluded rural surroundings. Guests

162

here can also enjoy croquet on the lawn followed by tea on the terrace if they wish. If it sounds rather wonderful, it is. An ideal base for walking in the area with the lovely town of Rye and all its facilities close at hand.

Furnace Lane Oast, Broadoak, Brede, Rye, East Sussex TN31 6ET
0424 882407 Map Ref : 3G

The hamlet of **Playden**, one mile to the north of Rye, has a 13th-century church with a shingled broach spire. Inside, there is an unusual memorial to a 16th-century Flemish brewer which is engraved with a pair of beer barrels; these would originally have been inlaid with brass. The settlement also contains a couple of elegant country residences: **Leasam House**, which was constructed of red brick in the 1800s, and **The Cherries**, which contains an interesting private museum of rural history.

Playden Cottage Guest House, Military Road, Rye, East Sussex
TN31 7NY 0797 222234 Map Ref : 3G

For first class accommodation in picturesque surroundings, **Playden Cottage Guest House** seems to have it all. Enjoying a hillside setting overlooking the River Rother, there was once a Roman settlement in the field behind where a bronze griffin's head was recently found. This charming cottage has three beautifully furnished en-suite guest rooms, but what makes this house so special are extra features such as the peaceful guest's writing room and the Long Sitting Room, both with their own patio. You can choose to hire a barbecue and prepare your own supper, or take advantage of the simple but tasty meals that hostess Sheelagh Fox prepares. Sheelagh is a mine of information and is happy to help you plan your stay in this lovely ancient town.

Visitors to the historic town of Rye, famous as a port during the 14th century, will discover a real gem at the **Playden Oasts Hotel** which lies just outside the town. A delightful establishment with rounded oast towers, it makes a charming alternative to the usual town hotels. Here you will find the facilities normally associated with a top class hotel chain, but all provided in an atmosphere of friendly hospitality. The eight attractively furnished bedrooms are all en-suite and well-equipped, with two of them featuring King-Size round beds! The hotel restaurant, renowned for its excellent cuisine, is open to non-residents and provides an extensive and imaginative menu, with local fish dishes a speciality and delicious homemade desserts making a refreshing change from the usual mass-produced frozen selection.

The Playden Oasts Hotel, Playden, Rye, East Sussex TN31 7UL
0797 223502 Map Ref : 3G

The country lanes to the northeast of Playden led us to the start of the **Royal Military Canal**, an unusual inland waterway which was built in 1804 as part of the nation's defences against Napoleon. The twenty-mile towpath between Rye and Hythe offers some easy and attractive walking along the northern fringe of the now-drained Walland and Romney Marshes. There are some pleasant picnic spots along the length of the canal, a section of which is now owned by the National Trust.

For the best in farmhouse accommodation you need look no further than Barons Grange in **Iden**, a somewhat 'hidden place' that can be found by taking the B2082 into Iden village, then turning left after the village store into Church Lane. After about 1/2 a mile you turn down Readers Lane on the right, passing between apple orchards this wonderful listed Georgian farmhouse stands 400 yards on your left. With charming hosts and a relaxed informal atmosphere, you immediately feel you are with friends here. The guest wing provides two first class en-suite rooms, where you are requested not to smoke, whilst additional facilities include a sun loggia overlooking attractive gardens with swimming pool and hard tennis court which you are welcome to use. All these factors ensure you leave Barons Grange completely relaxed and refreshed.

Barons Grange, Readers Lane, Iden, Near Rye, East Sussex
TN31 7UU 0797 280478 Map Ref : 3G

The narrow road to the west of Iden led us back onto the A268, and after driving west for another mile, we found ourselves in the village of **Peasmarsh**. Here, we called in at **New House Farm**, a charming establishment which offers top quality farmhouse accommodation. This traditional weather-boarded farmhouse is the charming home of Diana Ashby and was built circa 1663 around an enormous central chimney which boasts large inglenook fireplaces within the farmhouse. The age and character of this lovely house is evident in the low, beamed ceilings and original oak floorboards which slope steeply in the two comfortably furnished guest bedrooms. A working sheep and arable farm, New House provides a tranquil touring base and guests are welcome to stroll down to the river Rother which borders the farmland or take a look around the 17th century oast which stands alongside the farmhouse.

New House Farm, Wittersham Lane, Peasmarsh, Rye, East Sussex TN31 6TD 0797 230201 Map Ref : 3F

From Peasmarsh, we continued northwest along the **A268** for three miles, then just before reaching the junction of the **A28**, we turned west into a minor road to reach **Northiam**, a large and picturesque village which is known for its characteristic white weatherboarded buildings. At the heart of the community is a sizable village green which is surrounded by a number of fine 17th- and 18th-century buildings. Perhaps the most impressive of these is a substantial three-storey white-boarded house which stands on the edge of the green behind an unusual carved stone monument. Elizabeth I is reputed to have rested under the branches of Northiam's great oak whilst journeying to Rye in August 1573 (the tree is now believed to be over 1000 years old). Her green high-heeled shoes must have been particularly uncomfortable for she left them behind, magnanimously donating to the villagers who saved them as a memento of her brief royal visit.

Northiam contains a surprising number of well-preserved late-mediaeval buildings, including Strawberry Hole Farmhouse, Silverden Manor, Wellhouse and the Hayes Arms Hotel. The nave and chancel of St Mary's parish church were built of ironstone in the 14th-century, and the tower has an unusual turreted staircase and a stone-built spire, a feature rarely found in Sussex. Inside, there is an impressive mid-19th-century mausoleum dedicated to the Frewen family, the local rectors and lords-of-the-manor who lived at nearby **Brickwall House**. This imposing 17th-century residence is noted for its fine plasterwork ceilings and stands within beautiful grounds which contain a chess garden, a rare early-18th-century bowling alley, a sunken topiary garden and a charming formal garden with an unusually grand entrance.   Open Saturdays and Bank Holiday Mondays, 2pm to 5pm between April and end-September; admission charge payable. One 17th-century member of the Frewen family was a strict Puritan who named his two sons 'Accepted' and 'Thankful'. Accepted went on to become president of Magdalen College, Oxford and then the Archbishop of York, and Thankful is remembered for having donated the communion rails to the church in 1683.

The southern terminus of the **Kent and East Sussex Railway** can be found on the A28, a mile to the north of the village. Reopened in 1974, steam trains run from here to Tenterden in Kent throughout the summer. At one time, the nearby River Rother was navigable to this point and barges were brought upstream to be unloaded at the busy quay. This practice must has gone for centuries for in 1822, the remains of a 60ft Viking long ship were discovered in the mud beside the river where it had lain since the 9th-century.

Great Dixter, one of the finest examples of a late-mediaeval 'hall' house, can be found three-quarters-of-a-mile to the northwest of Northiam. This superb building dates from around 1450 and was bought in 1911 by the architectural historian, Nathaniel Lloyd, after it had been on the market for ten years. Lloyd commissioned his friend, Edwin Lutyens, to remodel the house and he immediately set to work restoring the great hall and solar. Lutyens' stroke of genius was to incorporate a 16th-century timbered house which he and Lloyd discovered eight miles away in Benenden, in Kent. The building, which had previously been covered in corrugated iron and used as a barn, was carefully re-erected alongside the original manor house and combined with it to form a single residence of delightful proportions. Part oak-timbered and part tile-hung, Great Dixter is now furnished with a carefully chosen collection of antique furniture, tapestries and oriental carpets.

When Lutyens was also asked to lay out the gardens at Great Dixter he came up with a truly imaginative design which retained several existing outbuildings and introduced a number of exciting new features, including a sunken garden, topiary lawn, orchards, horse pond and meadow garden. The estate is still in the hands of the Lloyd family, the gardens being the responsibility of Christopher Lloyd, the celebrated gardening writer and historian. Many rare and unusual plants are on sale to the public at Great Dixter's own nursery. Open Tuesdays to Sundays (and Bank Holiday Mondays), 2pm to 5pm between 1st April and end-October; admission charge payable.

After returning to Northiam, we made our way westwards through the country lanes to our next destination, the impressive National Trust-owned **Bodiam Castle**. With its imposing stone walls, castellated turrets and lily-filled moat, this must be the epitome of a classic romantic castle. Bodiam was one of the last great mediaeval fortifications to be built in Britain; it was constructed in 1385 by Sir Edward Dalyngrigge to defend the upper Rother valley against possible attack from the French following the infamous cross-Channel raid on Rye eight years before. The castle was very well-appointed for its day, but never saw hostile fire until nearly three centuries later when the Parliamentarian forces of General Waller reduced it to a shell to avoid it becoming a Royalist stronghold during the English Civil War.

A long period of decay then followed until in 1829, plans to completely dismantle the castle were thwarted by 'Mad' Jack Fuller of Brightling. A programme of external restoration was begun by George Cubitt towards the end of the 19th-century and completed by Lord Curzon, a former Viceroy of India, between 1917 and 1919. On his death in 1926, Curzon bequeathed Bodiam to the National Trust who have carried on the process of restoration and conservation. Several floors in the towers have now been replaced enabling visitors to climb to the top of the battlements. An audio-visual display about life in a mediaeval castle has also been installed, along with two 'education rooms' for school students; there is also a small museum near the ticket office. Open daily (closed Sundays in winter), 10am to 6pm (or dusk if earlier), all year round; admission charge payable (free to National Trust members).

On the southern side of the River Rother three-quarters-of-a-mile south of Bodiam, we discovered **Quarry Farm**, a 200-acre open farm which offers an entertaining day out for those with an interest in rural life. As well as a wide assortment of farm animals, there is an exhibition on the farmer's year, a collection of steam traction engines and a children's adventure play area. Open Wednesdays to Sundays (and Bank Holiday Mondays), 11am to 5pm between Easter and end-September; admission charge payable.

Continuing southwards from Bodiam, we followed the country roads through Staple Cross and Cripp's Corner to our next stopping place, the delightful village of **Sedlescombe**. This former iron-founding settlement is stretched out along a long, gently-sloping green with a part-14th-century church at the top and a pillared pump house built in 1900 near the bottom. The brick and tile-hung houses lining the green are mostly 16th- and 17th-century, and there are also couple of good hostelries, the Brickwall Hotel and the Queen's Head Inn.

The internationally-renowned **Pestalozzi Children's Village** is situated on a country estate to the southeast of Sedlescombe. It was founded in 1959 to carry on the work of the 19th-century Swiss educational reformer, Johann Heinrich Pestalozzi, on the premise that young people of all nationalities should learn together. The village now specialises in educating children from the Third World in the belief that their newly learnt skills will help them contribute to the development of their home countries.

Enjoying a peaceful location, **Sedlescombe Vineyard** is the only wholly organic vineyard in the East Sussex area and producer of excellent English wines. This is a fascinating place to visit, or even to stay since hosts Irma and Roy provide bed and breakfast accommodation in a simply furnished cabin-style house which overlooks the vineyards. Whilst here, you can follow the vineyard trails, sample some of the products at the winetasting, or follow the beautiful nature trail within the vineyard grounds, before calling in at the shop to purchase a bottle or two as a memento. Sedlescombe was chosen by Egon Ronay in 1987 to launch his 'Guide to Healthy Eating Out', which is a sure sign of the quality you can expect.

Sedlescombe Vineyard, Sedlescombe, Robertsbridge, East Sussex
TN32 5SA 0580 830715 Map Ref : 4E

The village of **Brede**, two-and-a-half miles to the east of Sedlescombe, has a history shrouded in myth and tales of the supernatural. The legend of the Brede Giant is based around the 16th-century figure of Sir Goddard Oxenbridge, by all accounts a normal, God-fearing member of society except for his unusual height - over seven feet. Some time after his death, the story spread that he had been a terrible child-devouring monster who was eventually done away with by a band of vengeful children who fed him strong ale and then cut him in half using a two-handled wooden saw. Oxenbridge's remains lie in a tomb in the parish church, but his ghost still haunts his late-mediaeval family home, Brede Place.

The historic settlement of **Battle** lies a similar distance from Sedlescombe, but to the southwest. The town is renowned as the location of the momentous battle on 14th October 1066 between the forces of Harold, the Saxon King of England and William, Duke of Normandy. The Battle of Hastings actually took place on a hill which the Normans named Senlac, meaning *lake of blood*, and even today, some believe in the myth that blood seeps from the battlefield after heavy rain (any discolouring of the water is, in fact, due to iron oxide in the subsoil).

A visit to Battle has to start with **The Almonry** on the High Street. Here you can follow a tour of Battle through the town model,

Monks Common Room, Battle Abbey.

where the viewer's eye is synchronised with a pre-recorded commentary and a guiding spotlight. The Almonry is a 14th century, 5-bay medieval hall house and is one of only four oak-framed buildings remaining in East Sussex with an internal courtyard and a 70ft well still containing water. The 17th century panelled staircase features a 300 year old Guy Fawkes and beneath the house, a secret passage links the building directly with the Abbey. With a wealth of gifts and souvenirs to choose from, you are sure to find a fitting memento of your visit to this fascinating place.

The Almonry, High Street, Battle, East Sussex TN33 0EA
0424 772727 Map Ref : 4D

Prior to 1066, the site of Battle was virtually uninhabited; however, one of William the Conqueror's first tasks on becoming king of England was to found a substantial Benedictine abbey on this exposed hillside in order to make amends for the loss of life in battle and so secure his future salvation. St Martin's Abbey was finally consecrated in 1094, the high alter in the great church being placed on the very spot where Harold was struck in the eye by an arrow from a Norman bow. Throughout the late Middle Ages, the abbey grew wealthy and powerful as it extended its influence over a wide area of East Sussex. This period of prosperity came to an abrupt end, however, following Henry VIII's Dissolution of the Monasteries in 1537.

The abbey site is now under the ownership of English Heritage and several of the old monastic buildings are open to visitors, including the towering 13th-century dormitory and the monks' common room with its magnificent vaulted ceiling. The imposing 14th-century gatehouse contains a recently-opened exhibition which brings the history of the abbey to life, and the mile-long 'Battlefield Walk' guides visitors around the edge of Senlac Hill and describes the course of the battle with the help of models and information boards. Open daily,

171

10am to 6pm (4pm in winter), all year round; admission charge payable (free to members of English Heritage). The restored abbot's house and cloister have been part of a girls' private school since 1922 and are not open to the public.

In the ancient and picturesque town of Battle, next door to the Abbey, you will find **The Pilgrims Rest**, an outstanding tearoom and restaurant which is steeped in history. This black and white timbered, 14th century medieval hallhouse features the original Kingpost, and wattle and daub is still exposed above head height. Built as part of the Abbey by the monks, this Grade II listed building was known as the "monks hospital" because of the hospitality the monks showed to pilgrims and travellers who couldn't afford to stay at the local inns. Today it is a delightful restaurant full of character, where you can savour excellent homecooked English fare, which in the Summer can be enjoyed in the lovely, flower-filled garden.

The Pilgrims Rest, 1A High Street, Battle East Sussex TN33 0AE
0424 772314 Map Ref : 4D

Battle offers a number of other noteworthy attractions. The parish church of **St Mary the Virgin** was built early in the 12th-century and, like many of its contemporaries, was restored by the Victorians. Inside, there is an unusual covered Norman font, some fine stained-glass windows and a series of wall paintings dating back to the 13th-century. The **Battle Museum of Local History** in Langton House contains a half-size reproduction of the Bayeux Tapestry, a facsimile of the Sussex volume of the Domesday Book, and an interesting collection of old maps, coins, toys and games. Open daily between Easter and end-September. **Buckley's Yesterday's World** in Battle High Street has a display of around 100,000 historic artefacts and items of memorabilia dating from between 1850 and 1950. Open daily, 10am to 5.30pm, all year round. A number of good small shops and inns can be found in the High Street and the old market place, and in May there is a mediaeval fair and a ten-day arts festival.

Enjoying a central location on the High Street in Battle, you will find **Inglenooks**, a delightful hotel and restaurant. This attractive stone-clad building was taken over last year by an enthusiastic young couple, Rob and Sue Eustace who are friendly, cheerful hosts full of ideas for developing their new business. Inglenooks has a warm, welcoming atmosphere and the attractively decorated restaurant makes the ideal venue whether you want a mid-morning coffee, lunch with a friend, or an intimate dinner for two. In the small bar to the rear with its splendid inglenook fireplace, you can relax with a drink after dinner before retiring to one of the five spacious and tastefully furnished guest rooms for a comfortable night's rest.

Inglenooks, 27, High Street, Battle, East Sussex TN33 0EA
0424 775171 Map Ref : 4D

From Battle, we made our way northwestwards through the country lanes for approximately five miles to our next port of call, the extraordinary village of **Brightling**. The village is perhaps best known for one of its former residents, the Georgian eccentric, 'Mad' Jack Fuller, who was not only a local iron-master and squire, but was also a generous philanthropist and the long-serving MP for East Sussex. He was also one of the first people to recognise the talent of the artist J M W Turner, and was responsible for saving Bodiam Castle from complete destruction. (He also weighed some 22 stone and was affectionately referred to as the 'Hippopotamus'.)

Perhaps Fuller's most visible legacy is the series of imaginative follies which he commissioned to provide employment for his workers during the decline of the local iron industry. Among these is the Brightling Observatory, now a private house, the Rotunda Temple in Brightling Park, and the Brightling Needle, a 65ft stone obelisk which was erected on a rise to the north of the village which at 646ft above sea level is the second highest point in Sussex. Another of Fuller's follies was built as a result of a wager. After having laid a bet on the number of church spires which were visible from Brightling Park, he returned home to discover that one he had taken into account, Dallington, could not in fact be seen. He solved the problem by getting a party of workmen to hastily erect a 35ft mock spire in a meadow near Woods Corner which is now referred to as the Sugar Loaf.

The parish church of St Thomas Becket contains an impressive Gothic-style barrel organ which Fuller presented to the parish in 1820. Ten years earlier, and 24 years before his death, Fuller erected a personal mausoleum in the churchyard in the shape of a 25ft pyramid. When he finally passed away in 1834 at the age of 77, local legend has it that he left instructions that he should be placed inside sitting upright, wearing a top hat and clutching a bottle of claret in one hand and a glass in the other. When the tomb was opened in 1938, sadly there was no evidence of Fuller or his carefully-specified props.

Dallington's genuine church spire can be found just off the **B2096** Battle to Heathfield road two miles to the southwest of Brightling. St Giles church possesses one of only a handful of stone-built spires in Sussex and is adjoined by an attractive timber-framed house.

Turners Farm, just outside Dallington on the B2096, is the delightful part 16th century farmhouse home of Helena and Henry Grissell, where you will find very comfortable, traditional farmhouse accommodation in two pretty guest rooms. The house is set in 500 acres, part of Brightling Park which was originally owned and built by "Mad Jack" Fuller and is ideal for walkers and nature lovers. The interior has a lovely old-fashioned feel, with low beamed ceilings throughout and an inglenook fireplace in the lounge. You have the luxury of tea and coffee brought to your room each morning and the farm chickens provide freshly laid eggs for breakfast which is served in the large, flagstoned kitchen, complete with AGA.

Turners Farm, Dallington, Heathfield, East Sussex TN21 9LF
0424 82207 Map Ref : 4C

From Dallington, we continued westwards along the B2096 for four miles to **Heathfield**, a sprawling settlement which grew to become an important market town on the former Tunbridge Wells to Eastbourne railway. The parish church in old Heathfield has a 13th-century tower with a shingled spire, and the nearby Heathfield Park estate was once owned by General (later Lord) Eliot, the commander of the British garrison during the Siege of Gibraltar in 1779-83. Gibraltar Tower in the grounds was erected in his honour. The main house was remodelled in the 19th-century and incorporates parts of earlier 17th- and 18th-century structures. A good day to visit the town is April 14th, Heathfield, or *Hefful*, Fair Day.

Runt in Tun, Hailsham Road, Maynards Green, Heathfield, East Sussex TN21 0DT 0435 864284 Map Ref : 3B

Runt in Tun is the unusual name given to a pleasant country pub on the B2203 just outside Heathfield village. An ideal stopping-off point for a refreshing drink or tasty pub lunch, this is a traditional establishment run by welcoming hosts Bill and Pauline Gibbon and their friendly staff. The pub's name appears to be a pun on the original name of the village - Runtington, and the sign shows a 'runt' pig inside a barrel or 'tun'. Outside the paved beer has a children's play area and behind the pub, the "Cuckoo Walk" follows the route of the now disused Cuckoo Railway and, after enjoying a drink and some lunch, provides you with a beautiful walk, close to the South Downs Way.

The intriguingly-named community of **Cross in Hand** lies just off the A267, two miles to the west of Heathfield. Here, we discovered a windmill, which at one time stood five miles to the west at Uckfield, and a first-class pub and eating place, the **Cross in Hand Inn**. Parts of this charming establishment date back some 500 years and careful renovation by the present owners Maurice and Jackie Chatfield has exposed original oak beams and wood panelling. Here, whether you call in for a quick drink or park up for an overnight stay, a large breakfast is available to all-comers! The two guest rooms are clean and cosy, with beams and sloping floors confirming the age of the building, whilst downstairs in the bars, crackling log fires are a welcome sight on colder days, tempting you to linger despite the reputed presence of the Cross in Hand ghost!

The Cross in Hand Inn, Cross in Hand, Heathfield, East Sussex TN21 0SN 0435 862053 Map Ref: 3A

Coles Hall, A267, Five Ashes, Mayfield, East Sussex 0825 830274 Map Ref : 3A

Two miles further north along the **A267** Tunbridge Wells road we came to the village of **Five Ashes** where stopped to call in at **Coles Hall**, a simply delightful 16th century former ironmasters house which was at one time a working farm. Today it is the charming home of Michael and Sheila Fausset who provides first class accommodation for their many guests. Set in 17 acres, with five ponds, Coles Hall makes a relaxing holiday base and is beautifully furnished throughout, with lovely antique furniture enhancing the traditional beamed interior. There are four comfortable guest rooms, all well-equipped and some with en-suite facilities. The elegant dining room features a large oak table which provides the setting for Sheila's large breakfast and optional homecooked evening meal.

Two miles to the northeast of Five Ashes, we turned east off the A267 to reach **Mayfield**, an ancient settlement which possesses one the finest main streets in East Sussex. According to local legend, St Dunstan, a skilled blacksmith by trade, paused here in the 10th-century to deliver the people of this remote Wealden community from the clutches of paganism. On this occasion, however, he was confronted by the Devil himself who, disguised as a beautiful woman, attempted to seduce the missionary as he worked at his anvil. However, Dunstan spotted that the feet of his young temptress were in fact cloven and, recognising her as Satan, grabbed her by the nose with a pair of red hot tongs. The Devil gave out an almighty scream and beat a hasty retreat; however, he returned soon after, this time disguised as a traveller in need of new shoes for his horse. Dunstan again saw through the deception and, threatening Satan with his blacksmith's tools, forced him to promise never again to enter a house which had a horseshoe above its door.

St Dunstan went on to become the Archbishop of Canterbury in 959 and some time later, an Archbishops' palace was built in Mayfield, the remains of which include a large mediaeval hall whose roof is supported by a series of colossal stone arches. The site is now occupied by a convent school which is approached through a 15th-century gatehouse in the High Street. Yeomans, a partially remodelled 15th-century 'hall' house stands almost opposite the gatehouse, and a little further along, the Middle House has been converted from an imposing oak-beamed Tudor residence into one of the finest country inns in Sussex.

St Dunstan built a simple timber church in Mayfield which was replaced by a stone structure in the 13th-century; this had to rebuilt after a fire destroyed much of the village in 1389 and again after the building was damaged by lightning in 1621. The present-day St Dunstan's contains a Jacobean pulpit, a font dated 1666 and some impressive 17th- and 18th-century monuments to the Baker family. Argos Hill to the northwest of the village offers some magnificent views over the surrounding landscape. It is also the location of an old post mill which now houses an interesting local museum; opening times displayed on site.

The country lanes to the east of Mayfield led us though the pleasant rural scenery of the Upper Rother valley. After about six miles, we emerged on the **A265** near **Burwash**, an exceptionally pretty village which, like Mayfield, has a High Street lined with delightful period cottages and shops. The village sign testifies to the

Burwash.

fact that this was once an important centre of the Wealden iron industry and for around three centuries, the atmosphere here was very different. Indeed for many years, Burwash had something of a reputation for being a dangerous and unruly place which travellers were advised to avoid at all costs.

Among the exceptional buildings in Burwash High Street is **Rampyndene**, a handsome timber-framed house with a sweeping roof which was built in 1699 by a wealthy local timber merchant. The parish church of St Bartholomew has a broach spire and is believed to date back to the early 12th-century. Set into the wall at the end of the south aisle is a 14th-century iron slab marking the grave of a local iron-founder which is believed to be the earliest example of its kind in the country. Near the door of the church there is a bronze plaque commemorating Rudyard Kipling's only son, John, who was killed at Loos during the First World War.

Kipling moved to Burwash from Rottingdean in 1902, it is said to combat the growing problem of overenthusiastic sightseers, and lived there until his death in 1936. The superb Jacobean house which became his home is located down a steep and narrow lane which runs south from the A265 to the west of the village centre. **Bateman's** was originally constructed for a prosperous local iron-master in 1634 and is set within 33 acres of beautiful grounds which were landscaped by Kipling himself.

Now under the ownership of the National Trust, the house amounts to a fascinating museum of the author's life. The interior is furnished with his portraits, private effects and possessions, and his study remains exactly as it was at the time of his death. Kipling's 1928 Rolls Royce stills sits in the garage, and there is a working water mill in the grounds which he used for grinding corn. One of the oldest working water-driven turbines in the country can be seen nearby; this was originally installed by Kipling to provide power to the house. Open daily (except Thursdays and Fridays), 11am to 5.30pm between April and end-October; admission charge payable (free to National Trust members).

One of Kipling's most famous works, *Puck of Pook's Hill*, was written at Bateman's and is said to refer to the wooded hilltop which can be seen from his study window. This area to the southwest of the house provides some particularly fine walking through the valley of the River Dudwell and up onto Pook's Hill. Access can be gained from the grounds of Bateman's or from the lane which runs between Burwash Weald and Brightling.

Woodlands Farm, Heathfield Road, Burwash, East Sussex
TN19 7LA 0435 882794 Map Ref : 3C

For seclusion and privacy, **Woodlands Farm** in Burwash is hard to beat, lying at the end of a drive 1/3 of a mile long, on the north side of the A265. Run by a charming couple, Liz and John Sirrell, this 16th century working farm is set in 55 acres, home to sheep, cattle and chickens. The house is immaculate and traditionally furnished in keeping with its age and character and the atmosphere here is warm and welcoming. The four guest rooms are all on the ground floor, some with en-suite facilities and the dining room with its large exposed beams and dark oak panelling provides the setting for the hearty farmhouse breakfast, with eggs supplied fresh by the farm's chickens.

The scattered settlement of **Etchingham** is set in the broad lush valley of the Rother, two-and-a-half miles along the A265 to the east of Burwash. The village possesses a 14th-century Decorated church which contains some fine monumental brasses to the Etchyngham family. **Haremere Hall**, to the southeast of the railway station, is an impressive 17th-century house which is now the home of the National Working Horse Trust, a body set up in 1987 to preserve and improve the standard of working horses, and to educate people in their care and use. Open Tuesdays to Sundays, 10.30am to 5pm between mid-April and end-October.

After making our way eastwards to the junction of the A21, we drove north for a mile before turning northwest onto the B2099 Wadhurst road. Our next stop was **Ticehurst**, an ancient village filled with the attractive tile-hung and white weather-boarded buildings which are so characteristic of the settlements along the Kent-Sussex border. There are a surprising number of noteworthy buildings here, including Furze House, a former workhouse, and

Whatman's, an old carpenter's cottage with strangely curving exterior walls. The parish church of St Mary dates from the 14th-century and contains a stained-glass window depicting scenes from the Last Judgment which is made up of fragments of mediaeval glass.

In 1975, the Southern Water Authority dammed the valley of the River Bewl to the north of Ticehurst to create the **Bewl Bridge Reservoir**, the largest area of inland water in southeast England. A great many buildings were drowned in the process; however, one, the 15th-century Dunsters Mill, was taken down brick by brick and moved to its present location above the new high water level. (A couple of timber-framed farm buildings found their way to the Weald and Downland Museum at Singleton in West Sussex.) The reservoir now offers a great many attractions for the visitor, including walking, picnicking, trout fishing and pleasure boat trips.

The sprawling village of **Wadhurst** lies to the west of Bewl Water, four miles northwest of Ticehurst. This was another great centre of the Wealden iron industry in the 17th- and 18th-centuries, and one of the last places in Sussex to hold out against the improved coal-fired smelting techniques which had taken root in the North. The floor of the parish church of St Peter and St Paul is inlaid with a unique collection of around thirty iron tomb slabs which mark the graves of local iron-masters who died between 1617 and 1772. Many are inscribed with curiously-worded messages or elaborate heraldic designs, and resonate strangely to the sound of visitors' footsteps.

Several of Wadhurst's find old buildings date from the heyday of the local iron industry. These include the timber-framed Churchgate House near the churchyard, the Queen Anne vicarage in the High Street, and the tile-hung Hill House next door. With its unusual ironwork, the Gothic-style mid-19th-century railway station to the northwest of the village centre is also worthy of a mention.

Three miles to the west of Wadhurst, **Nap Wood** offers some exceptional walking through 107 acres of National Trust-owned oak woodland. The area is maintained as a nature reserve by the Sussex Wildlife Trust and can be found on the eastern side of the A267 between Mark Cross and Frant. **Frant** is another former iron-founding community which contains an early-19th-century church with some unusual interior features, and a country house, Shernfold Park, which was once the home of the founder of Ottawa in Canada.

Bartley Mill, a restored 13th-century water mill can be found just south of the B2169, one mile east of **Bells Yew Green**. The mill originally belonged to the estate of Bayham Abbey and is now part of a 180-acre organic farm which supplies cereals and other produce to shops and bakeries throughout the locality. Part of the output is

181

ground into flour on the premises, and this and number of other home-produced foods, such as muesli, bread and cakes, are available in the farm shop and tearooms. The grounds also contain a farm trail, picnic area, trout hatchery and falconry centre. Open daily, 10am to 6pm (5pm in winter), all year round.

Our final port of call in Sussex was **Bayham Abbey** itself, a ruined early-13th-century monastery which lies on the Kent-Sussex boundary one-and-a-half miles to the northeast of Bartley Mill. Despite falling into disrepair following the Dissolution of the Monasteries, much of this once powerful and influential monastic house remains. The site is now administered by English Heritage and is open daily between Easter and end-September.

CHAPTER FIVE

Surrey.

*From Farnham and Haslemere to
The River Thames.*

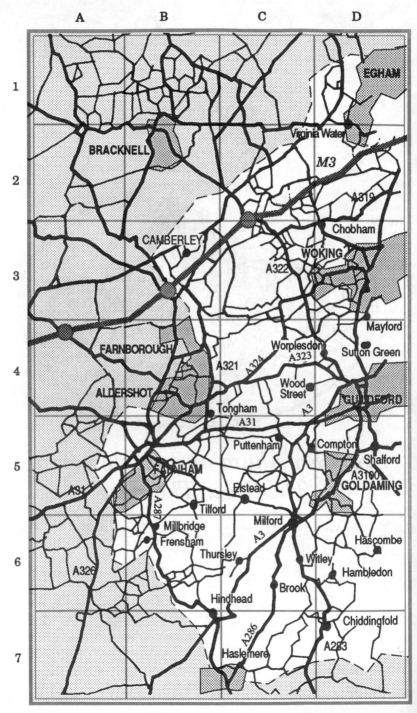

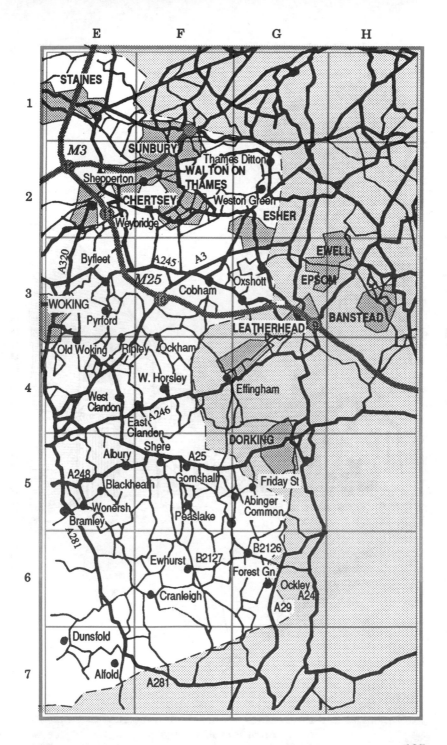

185

Farnham Maltings.

CHAPTER FIVE

Surrey.
From Farnham and Haslemere to The River Thames.

We began our tour of Surrey in the county's most westerly town, **Farnham**. This fine old settlement stands at the point where the old Pilgrims' Way from Winchester to Canterbury crosses the River Wey, and it has long been an important staging post on the busy trading route between Southampton and London. The town first became a residence of the Bishops of Winchester during Saxon times, and following the Norman conquest, the new Norman bishop built himself a castle on a pleasant tree-covered rise above the centre of the town. This impressive structure underwent a number of alterations, most notably in the 15th-century when the decorated brick-built tower was added, and it remained in the hands of the Bishops of Winchester until 1927. (It then became the residence of the Bishops of Guildford until 1956, and is now in use as a training centre.)

Farnham Castle has been visited on a number of occasions by the reigning English monarch and was besieged during the English Civil War. Today, it is approached along Castle Street, a delightful wide thoroughfare of Georgian and neo-Georgian buildings which was laid out to accommodate a traditional street market. The old Norman keep, now owned by English Heritage, is open daily, 10am to 6pm between 1st April and 30th September; admission charge payable (free to EH members). The remainder of the castle, including the Great Hall, can be visited on Wednesdays only between 2pm and 4pm throughout the year; small admission charge payable.

Farnham contains a number of other interesting historic buildings, including row of 17th-century gabled almshouses and **Willmer House** in West Street, a handsome Georgian-fronted structure which now houses the informative Farnham Museum. As well as some fine wood panelling, carvings and period furniture, the museum contains some interesting archeological exhibits and a unique collection of 19th-century glass paperweights. Open Tuesdays to Saturday, 10am to 5pm, all year round; admission free. **Farnham**

Maltings in Bridge Square is a thriving arts and community centre which is housed in a listed early-18th-century commercial building. As well as an excellent café and bar, the centre offers a regular programme of live music, films and exhibitions. Another good place to see a show or enjoy a meal is Farnham's **Redgrave Theatre** in Brightwells.

Just off the **A31** in **Tongham** you will find the Hogs Back Brewery at Manor Farm, where you can discover the brewing history of traditional local ales. Housed within a magnificent old farm building dating back to 1768, the brewery uses the original "Full Mash and Top Fermentation" process with the finest locally grown hops to produce their first class Real Ale.

Locals will often go to the pub and order a pint of TEA (Tongham English Ale) or the popular winter brew, OTT (Old Tongham Tasty)! There are tours of the brewery every Wednesday evening at 6.30pm (bookable), and afterwards you can purchase a memento from the brewery shop's selection of 400 Belgian beers, English wines, farm ciders, traditional cakes, T-shirts, pickles and of course the unique Hogs Back Real Ale. "For that taste of yesteryear.......enjoyed today.

Hogs Back Brewery, Manor Farm, The Street, Tongham, Surrey GU10 1DE 0252 782328 Map Ref : 4B

From Tongham, we retraced our steps back onto the A31 before continuing southwards through the country lanes to reach our next destination, the atmospheric ruins of **Waverley Abbey**. Dating from the 12th-century, this was the first Cistercian abbey to be built in England. The abbey remains are open during daylight hours and are said to have provided the inspiration for Sir Walter Scott's romantic

188

novel, *Waverley*, published in 1814. A lovely two-mile riverside walk leads to **Tilford**, an attractive village which stands at the confluence of the two branches of the River Wey. The monks of Waverley are believed to have been responsible for rebuilding Tilford's two mediaeval bridges following the devastating floods of 1233 during which the abbey itself had to be evacuated.

At the heart of Tilford stands a triangular village green which features a 900-year-old oak tree with a 25-foot girth which is known as the *King's* or *Novel's Oak*; a pleasant early-18th-century inn can be found nearby. Tilford's parish church of All Saints hosts a regular spring festival of early church music. A couple of miles further downstream, the village of **Elstead** is known for its imposing mediaeval bridge, 14th-century church and unusual 18th-century water mill.

In Reeds Road to the southwest of Tilford, the **Rural Life Centre** contains an interesting display of historic agricultural equipment and rural memorabilia, along with working blacksmith's and wheelwright's workshops. Open Wednesdays to Sundays (and Bank Holiday Mondays), 11am to 6pm between April and end-September; admission charge payable. A little further to the southwest, we came to the small community of **Millbridge** where we discovered the first-rate **Mariners Hotel**. Originally built in the 1500s it was on the main route inland from the coast and apparently the large cellars underneath were used to store smuggled goods, hence the hotel's name. There is a welcoming log fire in the bar which offers a selection of six real ales and an excellent range of bar meals, including various Italian dishes. Recommended by Les Routiers and The Good Pub Guide, the hotel provides first class accommodation in 21 beautifully furnished en-suite bedrooms all boasting lovely panoramic views. There are many activities available locally such as shooting and fishing, and on Monday nights you can enjoy live jazz music.

The Mariners Hotel, Millbridge, Frensham, Surrey GU10 3DJ
025 125 2050 Map Ref : 6B

In **Frensham**, one mile to the south of Millbridge, St Mary's Church contains a large mediaeval copper cauldron whose history is surrounded in legend. According to one story, it was lent by the fairies to a human who held onto it for longer than was agreed; when it was finally returned, the fairies refused to accept it, vowing never again lend anything to human beings. Another story tells how the cauldron once belonged to Mother Ludlam, a local witch-like character who inhabited a cave near Waverley Abbey. The A287 to the south of the village runs between Frensham's Great and Little Ponds, two sizable National Trust-owned lakes which provide good bird-watching and recreational facilities. These are now contained with a 1000-acre country park which incorporates four prehistoric bowl barrows and the *Devil's Jumps*, three irregularly-shaped hills whose origin, like many other unusual natural features, is attributed to Satan.

A more spectacular example of this can be found near **Hindhead**, four miles to the southeast of Frensham Great Pond. The **Devil's Punch Bowl** is a steep-sided natural sandstone amphitheatre through which the busy A3 Guildford to Petersfield road passes. Hindhead itself stands near the top of the nearby ridge and at 850ft above sea level, is the highest village in Surrey; perhaps surprisingly, it has only been in existence since the late 19th-century. The National Trust owns 1400 acres of local wood- and heathland which incorporates the Devil's Punch Bowl and nearby **Gibbet Hill**. At almost 900ft, the latter offer spectacular views to the north as far as the Chilterns and to the south across the Weald to the South Downs. In 1786, the hill was the scene a notorious murder, the perpetrators of which were hanged and chained near the Punch Bowl. Today, an inscribed stone commemorates the incident which is also remembered in a series of paintings in the nearby Royal Huts Hotel.

The genteel Surrey town of Haslemere lies a couple of miles to the southeast of Hindhead in the southwesternmost corner of the county. Now a quiet and comfortable home for well-to-do commuters, the central streets are filled with handsome Georgian and Victorian buildings, most of which were constructed following the arrival of the railway in 1859. The building styles, including stucco, redbrick and tile-hung, combine to form an attractive and harmonious architectural mix. Some of Haslemere's finest pre-Victorian structures include the town hall, rebuilt in 1814, the Tolle House almshouses in Petworth Road, Church Hill House, the Town House, and two noteworthy hotels, the Georgian and the **White Horse**.

The White Horse Hotel is situated in the market square. This 300 year old coaching inn is a place full of character with a mahogany bar, lovely brass lamps and a collection of real ale accessories adorning the walls. The excellent restaurant provides an extensive menu of wholesome, homecooked food which includes a good selection of vegetarian dishes, all prepared using fresh local produce. Upstairs, the accommodation comprises seven comfortably furnished guest rooms, all with TV and beverage making facilities. To the rear of the hotel the large beer garden hosts regular summer barbecues, whilst to the front, the wisteria adorning the hotel entrance is a picture during the summer months.

The White Horse Hotel, High Street, Haslemere, Surrey
0428 642103 Map Ref : 7C

Towards the end of the last century, Haslemere became something of a centre for the arts. Alfred Lord Tennyson settled nearby, and a group known as the Haslemere Society of Artists was formed whose number included Birket Foster and the landscape painter, Helen Allingham. At the end of the First World War, the French-born musician and enthusiastic exponent of early music, Arnold Dolmetsch, founded what has become a world-famous musical instrument workshop here. Present-day visitors can make an appointment to view the intricately handcrafted harpsichords, lutes and other authentic early instruments being made. Dolmetsch's family went on to establish the Haslemere Festival of Early Music in 1925 which is still held each year in July.

Another of Haslemere's attractions is the Educational Museum in the High Street, an establishment which was founded in 1888 by local surgeon and Quaker, Sir James Hutchinson, and which now contains an imaginative series of displays on local birds, botany, zoology, geology and history. Open Fridays, 10am to 1pm and Saturdays 10am to 4pm between April and Christmas; admission free. Whilst travelling along the A286 between Haslemere and Milford, you will find the ideal stopping-off point at **The Dog and Pheasant**, a charming country pub covered with Virginia Creeper. Enjoying a pleasant rural location opposite the village playing fields, it was originally a medieval hallhouse dating back to the 17th century, and has a large walk-in inglenook fireplace which adds to the character of the cosy bar, whilst in the cellar there is an original Norman archway. The Dog and Pheasant is renowned locally for its excellent range of homecooked bar food, prepared using fresh local produce. In the summer you can savour your meal in the large beer garden to the rear, which regularly hosts barbecues and boast lovely views up the valley across Whitley Park Estate.

The Dog and Pheasant, Haslemere Road, Brook, Surrey
0428 682763 Map Ref : 6C

Thursley, two miles to the northwest of Brook, is an exceptional village which takes its name from the Viking god *Thor* and the Saxon word for field, or *lea*. The settlement was once an important centre of the Wealden iron industry and number of disused hammer ponds can still be seen to the east. These artificial lakes provided power to drive the mechanical hammers and bellows in the once-bustling iron forges. Today, the village is a tranquil place arranged around a green containing an acacia tree which was planted as a memorial to William Cobbett, the Georgian traveller and writer who is best remembered for his book describing riding tours of England, *Rural Rides*, which was published in 1830. Thursley is also the birthplace of the celebrated architect, Sir Edwin Lutyens, who at the age of only nineteen converted a row of local cottages into a single dwelling now known as the *Corner*.

Thursley's two principal thoroughfares, the Lane and the Street, contain a wide variety of noteworthy domestic buildings. The latter leads to St Michael's Church, a part-Saxon structure which was heavily restored by the Victorians. The spire and belfry are 15th-century and are supported by massive timber posts with tie-beams and arched braces, a good example of late-mediaeval over-engineering. The churchyard contains the grave of the man, a sailor, who was

192

murdered on Hindhead Heath in 1786 by three men he had gone to help. Although the villagers never discovered the victim's name, they gave him a full burial and erected an inscribed stone over his grave. Two interesting old buildings stand near the church, the half-timbered and tile-hung Old Parsonage and the part-timber-framed Hill Farm, both of which date from the 16th-century.

A large proportion of the common to the north of Thursley is a designated nature reserve which is known for its unusually large and varied population of dragonflies. The **Witley Common Information Centre** lies a couple of miles from Thursley Common on the eastern side of the A3. This purpose-built nature centre is managed by the National Trust and is set in woodlands at the edge of a substantial area of Trust-owned heathland. Inside, there is an audio-visual display and an exhibition outlining the history, geology and natural history of the area. Open Tuesdays to Sundays, 11am to 1pm and 2pm to 4pm (weekends 2pm to 5pm only) between 1st April and end-October; admission free.

The historic village of **Witley** lies another mile to the east. This attractive collection of fine tile-hung and half-timbered buildings is loosely arranged around the part-Saxon church of All Saints, a much-altered structure which contains some rare 12th-century frescoes and a delicately-carved 13th-century font, and incorporates a 17th-century tower.

The present village inn, the White Hart, was constructed in Elizabethan times to replace an even earlier hostelry. It is believed to be one of the oldest inns in the country and at one time stood adjacent to a marketplace which hosted a busy Friday market. Witley's Old Manor was visited by a number English monarchs, including Edward I and Richard II, and the village centre contains some delightful 15th- and 16th-century timber-framed houses, many of which are hung with characteristic *fishtail* tiles. These include the Old Cottage, Red Rose Cottage (so-called because the lease granted on Christmas Day 1580 called for an annual rent of one red rose), and Step Cottage, a former rectory which was once the home of Reverend Lawrence Stoughton who died aged 88 after serving the parish for 53 years and outliving five wives.

At one time, Witley was a summer haven for artists and writers, the best known of which is perhaps George Eliot who wrote her last novel, *Daniel Deronda*, here between 1874 and 1876. Her home, the *Heights*, was designed by Sir Henry Cole, the architect of the Royal Albert Hall, and was visited by a series of eminent guests, including the novelist Henry James. Today, the building has been converted into a nursing home and is now known as Roslyn Court.

We continued southwards from Witley along the A283 Petworth road, and after a mile-and-a-half, turned east to reach the scattered village of **Hambledon**. The settlement contains a number of interesting buildings, including the tile-hung Court Farm, which stands near the part-14th-century church, the Old Granary, School Cottage and Malthouse Farm and Cottage. The National Trust own a small timber-framed dwelling in Hambledon known as **Oakhurst Cottage** which has been restored as an old artisan's home. Open by appointment only on Wednesdays, Thursdays, Saturdays, Sundays and Bank Holiday Mondays, 2pm to 5pm between 1st April and end-October; admission charge payable (free to NT members). A memorial to one of the Trust's founders, the social reformer Octavia Hill, stands at the top of nearby **Hydon's Ball**, an unusual conical hill which at 593ft above sea level, offers some fine views over the surrounding landscape.

After returning to the A283 near Wormley, we turned southwards and drove for two miles to our next stopping place, the highly picturesque village of **Chiddingfold**. With its three-sided green, waterlily-filled pond, part-13th-century church, mediaeval pub and handsome collection of Georgian cottages, this attractive settlement contains all the features of a quintessential English village. During the 13th- and 14th-centuries, it was an important centre of the glass-making industry, a once-flourishing trade which utilised local sand as its main ingredient, timber for fuel, and employed skilled craftspeople from across northern Europe. Some fragments of mediaeval Chiddingfold glass can be seen in the small lancet window in St Mary's Church, below which a brass plaque can be seen which is inscribed with the names of several early glass-makers. The church itself was much altered during the 1860s; however, its west tower is 17th-century and contains a peal of eight bells, one of which is believed to be around 500 years old. The churchyard is entered through an exceptionally fine lych gate, a covered gateway with a wide timber slab which was used to shelter coffins awaiting burial.

Of the many handsome buildings standing around Chiddingfold's village green, the Crown Inn is perhaps the most impressive. This is another hostelry which claims to be the oldest in England, its existence having first been recorded in 1383. The structure is half-timbered and incorporates a mediaeval great hall; Edward VI is reported to have stayed here in the 15th-century. Other buildings in the village worthy of note are Chantry House, Manor House and Glebe House, the last two of which have elegant Georgian façades. An 18th-century façade is all that remains of Shillinglee Park, a once-imposing country mansion which stood in the village until the end of the Second World

War. The remainder of the house was destroyed, not by enemy action, but by a party of Canadian service personnel who accidentally set the building on fire during a party to celebrate the allied victory.

One of the nicest bed and breakfast establishments you will find is **Greenaway**, a simply delightful 16th century house, which enjoys a very peaceful location in the heart of Chiddingfold village. A picture both inside and out, its character and charm are preserved and enhanced by the beautiful furnishings throughout. The cosy dining room provides a lovely setting for the homecooked breakfast, whilst upstairs one double room has the added attraction of an en-suite bathroom with original wooden flooring and an old-style free-standing bath. Greenaway is the perfect place to stay for those seeking a quiet break away from it all, set in beautiful gardens featuring a wooden dovecote and boasting fabulous views on all sides.

Greenaway, Pickhurst Road, Chiddingfold, Surrey GU8 4TS
0428 682920 Map Ref : 7D

From Chiddingfold, we made our way eastwards through the country lanes to another settlement with *fold*, a Saxon term meaning 'forest clearing', in its name. **Dunsfold** is a narrow ribbon of a village which lies on either side a long unmanicured green. It contains a number of fine old brick and tile-hung cottages and houses, several of which date from the late 17th-century, and an excellent pub, the **Sun Inn** which stands beside a towering oak tree which is said to have a girth of over 20ft.

The Sun Inn is a lovely, welcoming family pub. Parts of the building date from the 15th century and the bars exude a warm, cosy atmosphere. Here you can choose from five real ales as well as an extensive wine list which includes various New World wines. This popular watering-hole is renowned for its tasty bar meals, a particular favourite being the homemade Steak and Kidney Pie as well as\ other specials including game and fish dishes. On warm Summer days, there is nothing nicer than to sit out on the common or in the rear garden with a refreshing drink, especially when The Sun hosts one of its regular barbecues which always prove popular.

The Sun Inn, The Common, Dunsfold, Surrey GU8 4LE
0483 200242 Map Ref : 7E

Dunsfold's finest feature, however, is situated half-a-mile from the village on top of a raised mound which may once have been the site of a pre-Christian place of worship. The church of St Mary and All Saints dates from around 1280 and apart from the addition of a 15th-century belfry, has remained virtually unchanged since. The structure was much admired by William Morris, the Victorian founder of the Arts and Crafts Movement, who particularly approved of the simple, rough-hewn pews which were built around 1300 by the inhabitants of the surrounding farms. A leafy glade at the foot of the mound is the location of a holy well whose water is reputed to be a cure for eye complaints and blindness. The site of the well is marked by a timber shelter which was erected in the 1930s. To the east of Dunsfold, sections of a disused canal can be made out which was built to connect the basins of the Rivers Wey and Arun.

Another former clearing in the Wealden forest, **Alfold**, lies a couple of miles to the southeast of Dunsfold on the B2133. Like Chiddingfold, this exceptionally attractive village was once an important glass-making centre which reputedly supplied material for the windows of Westminster Abbey. Evidence of the mediaeval glassworks can still be made out in the woods on the edge of the village. The area around the church contains a number of interesting historic features, including an ancient yew tree in the churchyard, a charming Tudor cottage, and an old village whipping post and set of stocks.

The church in the quiet residential town of **Cranleigh**, four miles to the northeast of Alfold, contains a carving of a grinning feline which allegedly provided the inspiration for Lewis Carroll's Cheshire Cat. The town also contains the country's first cottage hospital, opened in the 1850s, and a public school which was founded by local farmers and still incorporates a working farm.

Ewhurst, on the B2127 two miles further east, is a long scattered village containing a sandstone church whose nave and south door are considered to be amongst the finest examples of Norman church architecture in the county. The rest of the structure would have been of a similar age had it not been for an unfortunate attempt to underpin the tower in the 1830s which resulted in the collapse, not only of the tower, but of the chancel and north transept as well. The structure was eventually rebuilt in 'Norman style' with an unusual shingled broach spire. Inside, there is a carved 14th-century font and a Jacobean pulpit, and outside, the churchyard contains a number of mature trees native to North America. The remainder of the village, part of which is set around a small square, contains some fine 18th- and 19th-century residential buildings, including the *Woolpit*, built for the Doulton family in the 1880s. The 843ft **Pitch Hill** is situated a mile to the north and can be easily reached along a pleasant footpath from the village.

An excellent place to stop for a drink or a freshly-prepared meal can be found two-and-a-half miles along the **B2127** to the east of Ewhurst. The delightfully-named **Parrot Inn** at **Forest Green**. The pub tends to be the focal point of the village, with various functions held here throughout the year. Whilst enjoying a drink in the cosy bar area, you will inevitably be tempted by the extensive and varied menu which includes daily specials and has been known to offer Conger Eel for the more discerning customer! The Parrot makes an ideal stopping-off point on any journey and on fine days you can relax outside in the lovely gardens, or watch a local cricket match being played on the green in front of the pub.

The Parrot Inn, Forest Green, Near Dorking, Surrey 0306 70339
Map Ref : 6G

At **Ockley**, two miles to the southeast of Forest Green, there is a village green which, at over 500ft in diameter, is one of the largest in Surrey. In summer, village cricket is played in this classic English setting which is enhanced by a number of handsome period houses and cottages. Ockley has had a long and eventful history: the village once stood on Stane Street, the old Roman road between Chichester and London which is now partially followed by the route of the A29, and in the mid-9th-century, a momentous battle between the forces of King Ethelwulf of the West Saxons and the marauding Vikings reputedly took place near here. Following the Norman invasion, the surrounding woodlands were designated a royal hunting forest and in the 12th-century, the Normans built a fortification half-a-mile to the north of the present village green which has long since disappeared. However, the nearby part-14th-century church remains, although this was extensively remodelled by the Victorians during the 1870s.

Among the many other noteworthy buildings in Ockley are the 18th-century Ockley Court, which stands opposite the church, and the groups of cottages surrounding the green which are built in a variety of styles and materials, including brick, tiling and weatherboarding. An interesting private sculpture and ceramics gallery which incorporates a delightful water garden can be found in Standon Lane. The **Hannah Peschar Gallery-Garden** is open on Fridays to Sundays (and Bank Holiday Mondays), 11am to 6pm (2pm to 5pm Sundays) between mid-May and end-October; admission charge payable. A short distance to the southwest of Ockley, a chapel was built in the 13th-century to serve the population of this once-isolated part of the Weald. Known as the **Okewood Chapel**, it was later endowed by a local nobleman after his son narrowly avoided being savaged by a wild boar when a mystery arrow struck and killed the charging animal.

Two miles to the North of Ockley, the 965ft National Trust-owned **Leith Hill** is the highest point in the southeast of England. In 1766, a 64ft tower was built on the tree-covered summit by Richard Hull, a local squire who lived at nearby Leith Hill Place; he now lies buried beneath his splendid creation. Present-day visitors climbing to the top on a clear day can enjoy a panorama which takes in several counties and reaches as far as the English Channel. Open Wednesdays, Saturdays, Sundays and Bank Holidays, 11am (2pm Wednesdays) to 5pm between 1st April and end-September; small admission charge payable.

The part-17th-, part-18th-century **Leith Hill Place** stands within beautiful rhododendron-filled grounds which are open to public on a limited number of days each year. In its time, the house has been owned by the Wedgwood and Vaughan Williams families, and inside, there is a fine collection of Wedgwood pottery and paintings by such artists as Reynolds and Stubbs. Opening times displayed on site. A recently-opened Edwardian country house designed by Sir Edwin Lutyens can be found on the northern slopes of Leith Hill; **Goddards** on Abinger Common stands within attractive grounds laid out by Gertrude Jekyll and was first opened to visitors in the spring of 1992. Opening times displayed on site.

An excellent pub and eating place can be found on Abinger Common one-and-a-half miles to the north of Leith Hill. The **Stephan Langton Inn** stands beside a pond in **Friday Street**, a simply delightful little hamlet 'hidden' about three miles from Dorking and you will find it signposted off the A25. Apart from a handful of houses, this picturesque place is also home to a superb pub, The Stephan Langton Inn. Named after a 12th century monk who spent his childhood in the village, this charming old pub oozes character and charm, with crackling log fires and exposed beams creating a cosy atmosphere in which to savour the excellent selection of bar snacks and fine ales available. Run by Paul Bancroft and Steve Auckett, the pub's reputation for fine food makes it popular with the many walkers and horse riders in the area.

The Stephan Langton Inn, Friday Street, Abinger Common,
Near Dorking, Surrey RH5 6JR 0306 730775 Map Ref : 5G

The parish of Abinger contains two villages, Abinger itself (or Abinger Common) which lies one mile west of Friday Street at the southern end of the parish, and Abinger Hammer which lies on the A25 Dorking to Guildford road to the north. **Abinger** claims to be one of the oldest settlements in the country having been settled by Middle Stone Age people around 5000 BC. The remains of a Mesolithic pit-dwelling were discovered in a field near Abinger's old Manor House which, when excavated in 1950, revealed over 1000 tools and artefacts which are now on display in an interesting little museum. The Manor House itself dates from the late 1600s but was virtually rebuilt following a fire last century; the remains of a Norman fortification lie within its grounds.

Abinger's parish church of St James is another unlucky building. After having been brutally 'restored' by the Victorians in the 1850s, this part-12th-century structure was largely destroyed by an enemy flying bomb during World War II. It was again rebuilt, this time with greater sensitivity, but was severely damaged in 1964 after being struck by lightning. In the churchyard there is a war memorial designed by Lutyens, and in the corner of the three-side village green, a set of old wooden stocks and a whipping post.

Abinger Hammer, a mile-and-a-half to the northwest, lies in the valley of the River Tillingbourne, a fast-flowing stream which in the 15th- and 16th-centuries was used to power the mechanical metal-working hammers from which the settlement takes its name. At one time, the village was known for the manufacture of cannon balls and a busy blacksmith's workshop can still be found here. Abinger Hammer's industrial past is reflected in the famous 'Jack the Smith' hammer clock which was erected in 1909. This unique clock overhangs the road on the site of an old iron forge and is characterised by the figure of a blacksmith who strikes a bell with his hammer every half hour.

The well-mannered community of **Holmbury St Mary** lies a mile to the southwest of Abinger Common. The settlement was the invention of well-to-do Victorians, one of whom, George Edmund Street, designed and paid for the church in 1879. The village provides a good access point to the 857ft **Holmbury Hill**, an upland with an altogether wilder feel than Leith Hill, its taller neighbour across the valley. A pleasant walk leads to the remains of an eight-acre Iron Age hill fort whose fading earthwork fortifications lie hidden amongst the undergrowth on the hillside.

In the picturesque village of Holmbury St. Mary on the road signposted Leith Hill, stands **Bulmer Farm**, a magnificent 17th century farmhouse set in 30 acres of rolling countryside. Owned and run by Gill and David Hill, this charming establishment offers first class bed and breakfast accommodation within the main house and converted barn bedrooms, plus two self catering units, one of which was specifically designed for the disabled and has a Category 3 Accessibility award. Wherever you stay, you will find every room beautifully furnished, offering every modern facility whilst retaining the age and character of the building. Gill specialises in homemade marmalade which guests can purchase if they wish. A walk through the Victorian walled garden leads to the award-winning conservation lake.

Bulmer Farm, Holmbury St. Mary, Near Dorking, Surrey RH5 6LG
0306 730210 Map Ref : 5F

The picturesque little village of **Peaslake** is situated alongside the Hurtwood, a privately owned forest area, on the A25 Dorking to Guildford road. In the heart of the village stands The Hurtwood Inn Hotel, an impressive country house style establishment built in 1920. Visitors here will find friendly service and an informal atmosphere, whilst the accommodation and food are of the standard one associates with top class city hotels. Of the eighteen very comfortably furnished guest rooms, eight are en-suite family rooms situated on the ground floor with lovely views of the garden. The large oak panelled dining room provides the perfect setting in which to enjoy the mouthwatering a la carte and table d'hote menus as well as the traditional Sunday roast which is sure to complete any weekend away.

Hurtwood Inn Hotel, Walking Bottom, Peaslake, Near Guildford,
Surrey GU5 9RR 0306 730851 Map Ref : 5F

The village of **Gomshall** lies on the A25, two miles to the north of Peaslake and one mile to the west of Abinger Hammer. The once-industrialised community has a Victorian heart and was once an important centre of the tanning and leather-working industries. The old packhorse bridge over the River Tillingbourne dates from the 1500s and the manor house at the southern end of the village from the early 1700s. Gomshall is now known for its fine craft and antique shops, several of which are concentrated in an ancient and beautifully-converted water mill, the **Gomshall Mill and Gallery**.

For a really special day out, a trip to Gomshall Mill is ideal. Set in the delightful Surrey village of the same name, this working water mill dates back to 1086 and now houses attractive and unusual shops, a tea room and a licensed restaurant. Owners Tristan and Brigitte Hole have successfully restored the two water wheels, which you can see in action, and have opened the lovely tea gardens where you can enjoy one of the Mill's famous cream teas. The collection of shops are a browser's paradise with antiques, toys, arts and crafts providing a vast selection of gift ideas, whilst in the evening, this ancient listed building is the perfect venue for that special dinner, with its beautiful candlelit restaurant.

Gomshall Mill, Gomshall, Near Guildford, Surrey GU5 9LB
048641 2433 Map Ref : 5F

Shere, one mile to the west of Gomshall, is one one of the loveliest, and consequently most visited, villages in Surrey. Thankfully now bypassed by the A25, it lies at the foot of the North Downs in the river valley which is particularly known for the growing of watercress, a plant which requires a constantly flowing supply of fresh water. The village church dates from the 12th-century and was tastefully restored in the 1950s. Among its many noteworthy features are the 13th-century Purbeck marble font, the St Nicholas Chapel, and an unusual hermit's cell built in the 14th-century for a local woman who asked to be confined there for life. The churchyard is entered through an impressive lych gate designed by Lutyens and close by stands the White Horse Inn, one of the many fine 16th- and 17th-century buildings to be found in the village. The Shere Museum in the Malt House contains an interesting collection of local artefacts, and the Old Farm behind the church is an open farm which at weekends offers hands-on demonstrations of traditional farming techniques.

Albury, on the A248 one mile to the west, dates largely for the last century and was constructed in fanciful neo-Gothic style as an estate village for nearby **Albury Park**. This large country mansion was built on the site of a Tudor manor house in the early-18th-century and was much altered by Pugin in the 1840s. The most eccentric feature of the house is its collection of chimneys, 63 of them built for only 60 rooms in an amazing variety of shapes and sizes. Although the mansion has now been converted into flats, the estate gardens are open to visitors and are well worth a look. They were laid out by the diarist John Evelyn at the turn of the 18th-century and feature a series of terraced orchards which rise above the house to the north.

A number of interesting communities lie to the southwest of Albury. **Chilworth** is a former munitions and paper-making centre whose church had to be rebuilt in 1850 following an explosion in the nearby gunpowder works; Chilworth Manor was built in the 1600s on the site of a pre-Norman monastic house. **Blackheath** to the south has some fine late-Victorian buildings, including a Franciscan monastery built in neo-Gothic style and a somewhat austere timbered residence, the Hallams. **Wonersh** is a former weaving centre with a fine 16th-century half-timbered inn, the Grantley Arms, and an imposing Elizabethan country mansion, Great Tangley Manor, which is one of the best examples of Elizabethan architecture in the county. Despite being largely Victorian, **Bramley** has some attractive Georgian and Regency residential buildings. It also contains a handsome 16th-century manor house and two homes designed by Lutyens, one of which was built for the landscape gardener, Gertrude Jekyll.

Two miles due south of Guildford, the scattered residential community of **Shalford** contains a fascinating water mill which operated from early 1700s right up to the First World War. Once powered by the waters of the Tillingbourne, this exceptional tile-hung structure retains most of its original machinery. During the 1930s, it was bought and restored by *Ferguson's Gang*, a secretive group of conservationists who hid their identities behind eccentric noms de plume and who eventually donated the building to the National Trust.

Shalford stands near the northern entrance to the **Wey and Arun Junction Canal**, an ambitious inland waterway which was constructed in 1816 to connect the Thames with the English Channel. Conceived during the Napoleonic wars as a way of avoiding attacks on coastal shipping, unfortunately it opened too late to fulfil its function and was soon superseded by the railways. A towpath providing some delightful walks runs along almost two-thirds of the canal's 36-mile length, a significant proportion of which has now be restored by enthusiastic teams of volunteers.

The old market town of **Godalming** lies three miles southwest of Shalford along the former A3, now the A3100. The town was once an important staging post between London and Portsmouth and a number of elegant 17th- and 18th-century shops and coaching inns can still be found in the High Street. A market was established here in 1300 and the town later became a centre for the local wool and textile industries. Perhaps the most interesting building in the old centre is the *Pepperpot*, the former town hall which was built at the western end of the High Street in 1814. Now surrounded on all sides by heavy traffic, this unusual arcaded building once contained an interesting museum of local history which has recently moved to new premises at 109a High Street. Open Tuesdays to Saturdays, 10am to 5pm, all year round; admission free.

Godalming's part-Norman parish church of St Peter and St Paul is built of *Bargate* stone, a locally-quarried hard brown sandstone that was much-loved by the Victorians. This material was also used extensively to build Charterhouse School, the famous public school which moved from London to a hillside site on the northern side of Godalming in 1872. Among its most striking features are the 150ft Founder's Tower and the chapel designed by Giles Gilbert Scott as a memorial to those killed in the First World War. The timber-framed house once belonging to Gertrude Jekyll can be found in dense woodland on the opposite side of town; it was designed for her by Edwin Lutyens in characteristic rural vernacular style and partially constructed of Bargate stone.

Three miles along the B2130 to the southeast of Godalming lies the renowned **Winkworth Arboretum**, a 95-acre area of wooded hillside which was presented to the National Trust in 1952. The grounds contain two lakes and a magnificent collection of rare trees and shrubs, many of them native to other continents. Open daily during daylight hours, all year round; admission charge payable (free to NT members). **Hascombe**, one mile further on, is another characteristic Surrey village with great charm.

From Godalming, we retraced our steps northwards for a couple of miles before turning west onto the B3000. Our next destination was **Loseley Park**, a handsome Elizabethan country estate which lies to the north of the main road, two-and-a-half miles southwest of Guildford. Built in 1562 of Bargate stone, some of which was taken from the ruins of Waverley Abbey, Loseley House is the former home of the Elizabethan statesman, Sir William More. Both Elizabeth I and James I are known to have stayed here, and the interior is decorated with a series of outstanding period features, including hand-painted panelling, woodcarving, delicate plasterwork ceilings, and a unique chimney-piece carved from a massive piece of chalk. The surrounding gardens contain a terrace and a moat walk, and the nearby fields are home to Loseley's famous herd of pedigree cattle. Visitors can take a trailer ride to the dairy farm, which incorporates a rare breeds collection and a farm shop where Loseley's celebrated ice cream and dairy products are on sale. Open Wednesdays to Saturdays, 2pm to 5pm between mid-May and early-October; admission charge payable.

The historic community of **Compton** lies a mile-and-a-half to the west of Loseley Park. Once an important stopping place on the old Pilgrims' Way, the village possesses an exceptional part-Saxon church with some remarkable internal features, including a series of 12th-century murals which were only rediscovered in 1966, an ancient hermit's, or *anchorite's*, cell, and a unique two-storey Romanesque sanctuary which is thought to have once contained an early Christian relic.

The Watts Gallery, Compton, Near Guildford, Surrey GU3 1DQ
0483 810235 Map Ref : 5C

Compton is also renowned for being the home of the 19th-century artist G F Watts, a chiefly self-taught painter and sculptor whose most famous work, *Physical Energy*, stands in London's Kensington Gardens. At the age of 47, Watts married the actress Ellen Terry, but the couple separated a year later; then at the age of 69, he successfully remarried, this time to Mary Fraser-Tytler, a painter and potter 33 years his junior who went on to design Watts' Memorial Gallery,

Loseley House.

which today contains over 200 pieces of the artist's work, along with the Watts Mortuary Chapel, an extraordinary building which was completed in 1904 and is decorated in exuberant Art Nouveau style.

The Watts Gallery is a fascinating place to visit, housing a unique collection of his paintings, drawings and sculptures. It is open daily except Thursdays, from 2pm - 6pm, plus 11am -1pm on Wednesdays and Saturdays, closing at 4pm during the winter period. The nearby memorial chapel is also worth visiting.

The Hog's Back village of **Puttenham**, one mile to the west, lies stretched out along the route of the old Pilgrims' Way. An attractive mixture of building styles, the village contains a restored part-Norman church, several fine 15th- and 16th-century cottages, an 18th-century farm with a number of period outbuildings and oast houses, and an impressive Palladian mansion, Puttenham Priory, which was completed in 1762. The hamlet of **Wanborough** on the northern side of the A31 Hog's Back contains one of the smallest churches in Surrey. Built by the monks of Waverley Abbey, it stands in the shadow a massive monastic tithe barn. The old manor house was constructed between the 15th- and 17th-centuries on the site of pre-Norman manor and was used during World War II to train secret agents.

The Royal Oak, Oak Hill, Woodstreet Village, Guildford,
Surrey GU3 3QQ 0483 235137 Map Ref : 4C

Rather than approach Guildford along the busy A31, we continued northwards from Wanborough and turned east onto the A323; then after two miles, we turned south to reach the village of **Wood Street**, a friendly community which is known for its first-rate pub and eating place, the **Royal Oak**. There has been a pub on this site since the mid-1700s, although the original building was demolished and rebuilt in 1928. Run by Pam and Dave Nicholls, this is a real family pub, with a welcoming atmosphere, an off-licence facility and

207

a lovely beer garden with children's play area. There are very reasonably priced bar snacks available lunchtime and evening, as well as a choice of three Real Ales, and a special bitter called 'Speckled Hen', which was apparently named after the car built in 1927 to celebrate the 50th anniversary of MG in Abingdon.

Two miles to the northeast of Wood Street, on the junction of the A322 and the B380, the village of **Worplesdon** is home to another excellent hostelry, the **Old Malt House**. Part of this lovely old house dates back to the early 1600's and the front area used to be a malt house. Set in three and a half acres, the house enjoys a peaceful location and offers wonderful views of the surrounding countryside, Inside the house, your friendly hostess, Mrs. Millar, provides very comfortable, homely accommodation in three attractively furnished guest rooms, one double, one family and one twin. The garden has a swimming pool and children can run off their energy with various outdoor games and sports.

The Old Malt House, Worplesdon, Guildford, Surrey GU3 3PT
Map Ref : 4D

The route into Guildford from the northwest passes close to **Guildford Cathedral**, one of only two new Anglican cathedrals to have been built in this country since the Reformation (the other is Liverpool). This impressive redbrick building stands on top of Stag Hill, a prominent local landmark which enjoys panoramic views over the surrounding landscape. The building was designed by Sir Edward Maufe with a superb high-arched interior and was begun in 1936. However, work was halted during World War II and members of the local diocese had to wait until 1961 for the new cathedral to be finally consecrated. Guided tours and restaurant facilities are available all year round. In 1968, the **University of Surrey** relocated from London to a site on a hillside to the northwest of the cathedral.

Pleasant and leafy, the campus contains a number of striking buildings including the university library and art gallery.

From the university, we continued southeastwards for a mile to the heart of **Guildford**, the ancient county town of Surrey. Guildford has been the capital of the region since pre-Norman times and in the 10th-century, it even had its own mint. Henry II built a castle here on high ground in the 12th-century which later became the county gaol; today, the castle remains house a renowned brass-rubbing centre and the ruined keep provides a fascinating place from which to view the surrounding area.

Those visiting the town for the first time should make straight for the old High Street, a wonderful cobbled thoroughfare of Georgian and older buildings which rises steeply from the River Wey. Perhaps the most noteworthy of these is the **Guildhall**, a Tudor structure with an elaborately decorated 17th-century frontage which incorporates a bell-tower, balcony and distinctive gilded clock. The timber-framed **Guildford House** is also 17th-century and is known for its carved staircase and ornate painted plasterwork ceilings; **Abbot's Hospital**, a little further along, is an imposing turreted almshouse which was built in 1619 by the Guildford-born Archbishop of Canterbury, George Abbot; at the top of the High Street, the **Royal Grammar School** dates from the early 1500s and was subsequently endowed by Edward VI.

The Angel Hotel, 91 High Street, Guildford, Surrey GU1 3DP
0483 64555 Map Ref : 4D

The **Angel Hotel** situated on the cobbled High Street in Guildford is a superb establishment where 20th century comfort and service blend perfectly with 13th century grandeur. Originally the White Friars Monastery, it became a hotel in 1535 and boasts many famous guests through the centuries. The eleven guest suites are named after some of these former guests and are beautifully furnished

Guildhall Clock, Guildford.

to complement the hotel's age and character, creating a relaxing atmosphere whilst providing every modern facility. Downstairs, the comfortable lounge boasts its own minstrel's gallery and a magnificent oak-beamed Jacobean fireplace, whilst the Oak Room restaurant provides an elegantly intimate setting in which to savour first class English and Continental cuisine.

A number of interesting streets and alleyways run off Guildford High Street, including Quarry Street with its mediaeval St Mary's Church and old Castle Arch. The latter houses the **Guildford Museum**, an informative museum of local history and archeology which also contains an exhibition devoted to Lewis Carroll, the creator of *Alice In Wonderland* who died in the town in 1898. Open Mondays to Saturdays, 11am to 5pm, all year round; admission free. A charming bronze memorial to Lewis Carroll (real name Charles Lutwidge Dodgson) which is composed of a life-sized Alice chasing the White Rabbit into his hole can be found on the far bank of the River Wey, midway between the two footbridges. The famous **Yvonne Arnaud Theatre** stands in a delightful riverside setting at the foot of the castle mound on the town side of the river. As well as offering top quality drama and musical productions, the theatre has an excellent bar, coffee lounge and restaurant which remains open throughout the day. In summer, rowing boats and guided pleasure boat trips are available at the nearby Guildford Boat House.

From Guildford, we drove eastwards along the A25 Leatherhead road and after approximately three miles came to the National Trust-owned property, **Clandon Park**. This magnificent country mansion was designed in the 1730s by Giacomo Leoni, a Venetian architect who combined Palladian, Baroque and European styles to create one of the grandest 18th-century houses in England. The interior is renowned for its magnificent two-storey marble hall, sumptuous decoration and fine Italian plasterwork depicting scenes from mythology. The Gubbay collection of furniture and porcelain is also housed here, along with the Ivo Forde collection of humorous Meissen figures. The surrounding parkland was landscaped by Capability Brown in characteristic style and includes a parterre, grotto and brightly-painted New Zealand Maori house. Open daily (except Thursdays and Fridays), 1.30pm to 5.30pm, between 1st April and end-October; admission charge payable (free to NT members).

The presence of the Onslow family, the owners of Clandon Park, is strongly felt in the nearby village of **West Clandon**. The village inn is known as the Onslow Arms and the Onslow family pew in the part-13th-century village church is an impressive example of 17th-century ecclesiastical furniture. A carved panel in the south porch of the church depicts a hound fighting a dragon, a reference to a local dragon-slaying legend.

East Clandon, on the main A246, contains an interesting old forge, a part-Norman church and a lovely old manor farmhouse dating from the late 17th-century. Another striking National Trust property is located one mile to the northeast; **Hatchlands Park** is a distinctive brick-built house which was designed in the mid-18th-century for Admiral Boscawen after his famous victory in the Battle of Louisburg. Inside, there are some splendid examples of the early work of Robert Adams, some fine period furniture and paintings, and a wonderful assortment of historic keyboard instruments, the Cobbe collection, which was moved here in 1988. The grounds were originally laid out by Repton and have since been remodelled by Gertrude Jekyll; in recent years, they have undergone a process of restoration and been opened up to visitors. Open Sundays and Tuesdays to Thursdays (also Bank Holiday Mondays and Saturdays in August), 2pm to 5.30pm between 1st April and end-October; admission charge payable (free to NT members).

At **West Horsley**, one mile to the east of Hatchlands Park, we discovered a first-class inn, the **King William IV**, where a warm, friendly atmosphere is enhanced by open log fires in the bar. Originally a pair of Georgian cottages, part of The King William dates back to the 1600's. Many alterations over the years include, during the 19th century, a lean-to extension being added on which was used as a brewhouse when the establishment was made into a beer shop. Since then, a more recent extension has provided a comfortable restaurant to the rear where you can sample a wide range of tasty bar snacks or daily blackboard specials, and in the evening choose from the extensive dinner menu.

The King William IV, The Street, West Horsley, Surrey KT24 6BG
0483 282318 Map Ref : 4F

One mile further east at East Horsley, we turned north onto the B2039 and then northeast onto a minor road to reach **Effingham Junction**, a pleasant community centred around the railway station. Our destination was the renowned pub and eating place, the **Lord Howard**, a delightful pub named after the Commander of the English fleet which fought against the Spanish Armada. Run by friendly hosts Alan and Annette Parker, this is a welcoming family pub with a large car park and pleasant rear garden. Inside there is a games room adjoining the main bar area where you can choose from a fine selection of real ales, plus a strong, cask-conditioned cider for the brave at heart! However, what really makes The Lord Howard special is the tasty range of bar snacks and first class restaurant menu, where you can savour a range of mouthwatering dishes at very reasonable prices, accompanied by an extensive wine and champagne list.

The Lord Howard, Forest Road, Effingham Junction,
Near Leatherhead, Surrey KT24 5HE 04328 2572 Map Ref : 4F

On **Chatley Heath**, a mile and a half to the north of Effingham Juction, there is a unique **Semaphore Tower** which was once part of the Royal Navy's signalling system for relaying messages between Portsmouth and the Admiralty in London. Although the semaphore mechanism soon fell into disuse,the structure has remained in good order and is open to the public at weekends. As well as offering outstanding views over the surrounding landscape, the Chatley heath Semaphore Tower house an interesting exhibition and model collection. It can be reached along a pleasant woodland pathway and is open Saturdays, Sundays and Bank Holidays, 12 noon to 5pm between mid-April and end-September; admission charge payable.

Our next stopping p[lace, **Ockham**, lay one and a half miles to the South West. This scattered settlement which once possessed a fine Jacobean mansion, Ockham Park. A serious fire in 1948 destroyed everything except for the orangery, stables, kitchen wing and a solitary Italianate tower. The village church of All Saints still stands within the grounds of the estate; this largely 13th-century building was constructed on the site of a pre-Norman structure and is known for its remarkable east window, a surprising combination of seven tall pointed lancets finished in marble with distinctive carved capitals. The window dates from around 1260 and is thought to have been brought here from nearby **Newark Abbey** following its dissolution in the 16th-century. The church incorporates a brick chapel which contains a robed marble effigy of the first Lord King, the former owner of Ockham Park who died in 1734.

The Royal Horticultural Society's internationally-renowned **Wisley Garden** lies on the opposite side of the A3, one mile to the northwest of Ockham. As well as containing a wide variety of trees, flowering shrubs and ornamental plants, this magnificent 250-acre garden incorporates the Society's experimental beds where scientific trials are conducted into new and existing plant varieties. Wisley also acts as a centre for training horticultural students, and offers a wide range of plants, books, gifts and gardening advice at its first-class plant centre and shop. Open daily (RHS members only on Sundays), 10am to 7pm (or sunset if earlier), all year round; admission charge payable.

A mile or so to the southwest of Wisley, the attractive village of **Ripley** is a former staging post on the old coaching route between London and Portsmouth. The main street contains a number of exceptional brick and half-timbered buildings, including the charming Vintage Cottage with its unusual *crownpost* roof. A walk around the village led us to the **Saddlers Arms**, a delightful establishment which offers an excellent selection of food and drink.

The Saddlers Arms, Sendmarsh Road, Ripley, Near Woking, Surrey 0483 224209 Map Ref : 4E

Originally a saddler's, the licensed premises were next door, but in Kelly's Directory it appears as a beerhouse in 1848 listed as: "James Broomfield - Beer Retailer, Saddler and Blacking Manufacturer of Cooks Green"! Today it is a lively pub with a great atmosphere which oozes old world charm, the low beamed ceilings enhancing the age and character of the building. As well as a fine selection of beers, wines and spirits, the pub has a reputation for the excellent selection of homecooked traditional food served here, which makes The Saddlers a very popular stopping-off point with visitors and local alike.

The B367 to the north of Ripley passes the site of the ruined Newark Priory. In **Pyrford**, a little further on, the largely-Norman church of St Nicholas contains some unusual wall paintings which were painted around 1200 on top of some even earlier murals.

Those wishing to stay in this attractive area of West Surrey should make a point of finding **Weir Cottage** in **Mayford**, a peaceful community which lies near the junction of the A320 and B380 on the southern outskirts of Woking, a charming establishment owned by Ron and Rose Minter which lies within easy reach of many tourist attractions.

Weir Cottage, 120 Westfield Road, Mayford, Woking, Surrey
GU22 9QP 0483 760176 Map Ref : 4D

Ron and Rose enjoy welcoming guests into their lovely home and you will soon find yourself relaxing in the warm, friendly atmosphere. There are four attractively furnished guest rooms available and the cosy dining room is the setting for the incredibly large breakfasts that Ron provides, where guests can choose "anything they want"! Ron's collection of old plates and knickknacks from bygone eras fills the house and forms a popular talking point, as does the fact that Weir Cottage was once the home of actress Mary Pickford, which no doubt adds to the "star" quality of this lovely establishment.

The Fox and Hounds, Sutton Green, Guildford, Surrey
0483 772289 Map Ref : 4D

The village of **Sutton Green** lies midway between Woking and Guildford, one-and-a-half miles to the southeast of Mayford. This is where we discovered the **Fox and Hounds**, an impressive pub and eating place which is well worth making the effort to find. This is an impressive-looking Victorian pub where you can enjoy a good selection of ales in the bright, cheerful atmosphere of the bar, or on warmer days in the large beer garden. The pub also has a fine restaurant which is very popular locally, both at lunchtime and in the evening. Here you can sample a wide selection of traditional English food including Sunday roasts which are a speciality, but booking is advisable for this, as well as for Friday and Saturday evenings, to avoid disappointment.

Woking, to the north, is an unexceptional commuter town which lies on the main railway line to Waterloo. Apart from some good leisure facilities, it has little to offer the casual visitor. The first purpose-built mosque to be founded in Britain can be found in Woking's Oriental Street. The construction of this unusual onion-domed structure was largely financed by the ruler of the Indian state of Bhopal who visited the town in 1889. **Old Woking** is a former market town which is now incorporated into the southeastern suburbs of its more modern neighbour. Its streets contain some noteworthy old buildings, including the 17th-century old Manor House, and the part-Norman parish church of St Peter which has a late-mediaeval west tower.

Enjoying a peaceful location just five minutes drive from Woking town centre, the attractive community of **Chobham** stands at the junction of the A3046 and A319, three miles to the northwest of Woking. The village High Street contains a fine old church and some

216

interesting inns, shops and residential buildings, we also discovered a comfortable and convenient place to stay here, **Oakhill**. Oakhill is the charming home of Clare Hill who provides excellent bed and breakfast accommodation for non-smoking guests. This lovely house is situated at the end of Trotters Lane, off Sandpit Hall Road in Chobham and stands in five acres of grounds, home to various geese and chickens, the source of eggs for the substantial breakfast served each morning. There are several beautifully furnished, well-equipped guest rooms two with private bathroom, and all offering lovely views. Within the grounds there is a floodlit tennis court as well as alternative accommodation in a self-contained cottage. Evening meals are available by prior arrangement and Clare will provide a taxi service within a reasonable distance.

Oakhill, Trotters Lane, Sandpit Hall Road, Chobham, Woking, Surrey GU24 8HA 0276 858021 Map Ref : 3D

Despite containing some pleasant tracts of countryside, the northwestern corner of Surrey contains little to interest to the traveller. Bagshot Heath and Bisley Common together form a stretch of open heathland which was once the domain of outlaws and highwaymen; today, Bisley is better known as a rifle-shooting centre. The substantial town of **Camberley** lies three miles away on the western side of the common. Prior to 1807, when the famous Sandhurst Royal Military Academy was relocated nearby, the town did not exist, and indeed its oldest part, the grid-patterned York Town, was constructed to house the academy's first instructors. (Lying just across the Berkshire border, Sandhurst Academy is set around a group of buildings designed in neoclassical style by James Wyatt.)

From Camberley, we followed the A30 along the northeastern border of the county to **Virginia Water**, a surprising diversion which lies in the heart of the Surrey stockbroker belt. The 'water' referred to is a mile-and-a-half long artificial lake which is set within mature woodland at the southern end of Windsor Great Park; it was created by Paul and Thomas Sandby, two accomplished Georgian landscapers who were also known for their painting. The picturesque ruins standing at the lakeside are genuine remains of a Roman temple which once stood at Leptis Magna in Libya. The Valley Gardens also contain an unusual 100ft totem pole which was erected here in 1958 to mark the centenary of British Columbia. A little further to the north, the **Savill Garden** is renowned as one of the finest woodland gardens in the country. Open daily, 10am to 6pm, all year round; admission charge payable.

The famous Wentworth golf course lies on the opposite side of the A30 on the southern edge of the genteel settlement which takes its name from the Sandbys' lake. At **Egham Hill**, a couple of miles to the north, the Royal Holloway and Bedford New College is housed in an extraordinary Victorian edifice which incorporates a notable gallery of 19th-century paintings and a concert hall which offers regular programmes of music and drama.

A meadow beside the River Thames to the north of Egham is where King John sealed the Magna Carta in 1215. The historic **Runnymede** site and nearby Cooper's Hill are contained within a 300-acre tract of land which is now under the ownership of the National Trust. The area contains three separate memorials: a domed neoclassical temple which was erected by the American Bar Association to commemorate the sealing of the world's first bill of democratic rights, a memorial to John F Kennedy, and the Air Forces Memorial which was erected in memory of the World War II airmen who went missing in action.

From the top of Cooper's Hill there are magnificent views across Windsor Great Park and the Thames Valley. The river below is populated by slow-moving motor cruisers and pleasure craft, and river trips to Windsor, Staines and Hampton Court can be taken from Runnymede, daily between May and October, and at weekends during winter. The nearby Runnymede Pleasure Ground offers a range of children's leisure activities in a pleasant riverside setting.

The ancient town of **Staines** lies on the other side of the M25, two miles to the east. The town stands at the point where the old Roman road from London to the South West crossed the Rivers Thames and Colne, and in the 17th- and 18th-centuries, it became an important staging point on the old coaching routes to the West Country. When walking beside the Thames, look out for the London Stone which was erected in 1285 to mark the boundary of the city's authority over the river. The old part of Staines contains some noteworthy buildings, including the part-17th-century **church of St Mary** and the town hall built in Flemish-style on the **Market Place**.

The M25 to the south of Staines passes close to **Thorpe Park**, a 500-acre leisure park which has been built on an area of reclaimed gravel pits. The park incorporates a shire-horse centre, a series of historic reconstructions of life in ancient Britain, and a permanent theme park containing some of the latest roller coaster rides and fairground attractions. Open daily, mid-March to early-November (weekends only in early and late season); admission charge payable.

Chertsey, a couple of miles to the south, is another ancient riverside town which has altered almost beyond recognition over the centuries. The town once boasted a formidable abbey whose influence stretched over a wide area of southern England; when it was demolished following the Dissolution of the Monasteries, its stone was used to build Hampton Court Palace and later, the River Wey Canal. One of the abbey bells now hangs in the parish church; at one time it was used to sound the evening curfew and it is associated with a local romantic legend concerning a young Chertsey woman who, on hearing that her lover was to be executed at the sound of the curfew bell, climbed into the tower and clung onto the tongue until his pardon arrived.

Thames Court, Shepperton Lock, Shepperton, Surrey TW17 9LJ
0932 221957 Map Ref : 2F

Enjoying a beautiful riverside location in the picturesque village of **Shepperton**, **Thames Court** is a splendid 400 year old country inn, originally built as the Dutch Ambassador's house. There can hardly be a more tranquil setting for a quiet summer drink with friends, than here in the pub gardens beneath willow trees arching gracefully towards the riverbank. Inside, Thames Court has its own character and beauty, with a well-stocked bar providing a wide selection of beers, wines and spirits and offering a superb range of traditional fare. The galleried restaurant above is a picture, with

219

original hand-painted Delft tiles and seafaring pictures all around. Situated on the riverside close to the boatyard, this really is a delightful corner where you can't help but relax as the river flows gently by.

On leaving Shepperton, we re-crossed the Thames and arrived in **Walton-on-Thames**. Perhaps surprisingly, this unassuming London suburb appears in the Domesday Book when it was recorded as having a church, a fishery and two mills. The part-Norman church of St Mary contains a remarkable memorial to Richard Boyle, the Viscount Shannon, which was sculpted by Louis Roubiliac in the mid-18th-century.

Weybridge, two miles to the southwest, is another surprisingly long-established settlement. The town once possessed a palace, Oatlands Park, in which Henry VIII married his fifth wife, Catherine Howard, in 1540; 110 years later, the building was demolished and the stone used in the construction of the Wey Navigation. Weybridge stands at the northern end of this historic inland waterway which was one of the first examples of its kind when it was completed in 1670. It extends for almost twenty miles southwards to Godalming and incorporates large sections of the main river.

In 1907, the world's first purpose-built motor racing track was constructed on the **Brooklands** estate, near Weybridge, and in the years which followed, this legendary banked circuit hosted competitions between some of the most formidable racing cars ever made. With the outbreak of World War I, however, racing came to an end; the track fell into disrepair and Brooklands was never again able to regain its once-preeminent position in British motor racing. For years, the only thing to interrupt the tranquillity of the empty track was the occasional eerie sound of screeching tyres and roaring engines, or the appearance of the goggled ghost of Percy Lambert, who tragically died after his car smashed into the end of the Railway Straight in 1913. In recent years, the circuit has undergone something of a revival with the opening of the **Brooklands Museum**, a fascinating establishment centred around the old Edwardian clubhouse which features a unique collection of historic racing cars, motorcycles and aircraft. Open Saturdays and Sundays, 10am to 5pm, all year round; admission charge payable.

A mile-and-a-half to the southwest of Weybridge, and close to the St George's Hill residential area much-favoured by famous media personalities, lies the remarkable **Whiteley Village**. This unique 200-acre model village was founded on the instructions of the proprietor of a famous Bayswater department store who in 1907, left one million pounds in his will to house his retired staff. The community was designed to be self-contained with its own churches, hospital and shops, and was laid out in an octagonal pattern around a green containing a memorial to the project's benefactor. The site has been planted with a great many trees and flowering shrubs, and is best visited in late-spring and summer.

The well-to-do residential suburb of **Esher** lies three miles to the northeast of Whiteley Village on the old A3, now the A307. The part-16th-century church of St George has an unusual three-tier pulpit and a marble monument to Princess Charlotte of Wales who died at nearby Claremont House in 1817. The part of Surrey nearest to London is well supplied with racecourses: as well as at Kempton Park, near Sunbury, and at the classic course at Epsom, regular meetings are held at Sandown Park on Esher's northern edge.

A little further north, we stopped to call in at the **Greyhound**, an excellent pub and eating place which can be found at **Weston Green**, near Thames Ditton.

The Greyhound is a welcoming family pub with a terrific atmosphere. Run by friendly hosts Rob and Chris Upjohn, the pub is particularly noted for its excellent bar food, which caters for all tastes with dishes ranging from Cottage Pie to Lobster. At the bar you can choose from a selection of five real ales as well as an excellent wine list including a New World and Connoisseur collection and in the Summer there are regular pub barbecues in the large rear garden. However, the latest innovation is 'The Fat Man's Pan', a new concept designed for speed, where a complete meal is served at the table in an enormous frying pan!

The Greyhound, Weston Green, Thames Ditton, Surrey KT7 0JP
081 398 1155 Map Ref : 2G

After returning southwards to Esher, we decided to call in at the beautiful National Trust-owned **Claremont Landscape Garden** which lies on the southern side of the A307 Portsmouth road within a mile of the town centre. Having been laid out in the 1710s, this is

Brooklands Museum.

believed to be one of the earliest surviving examples of an English landscape garden; later in the century, it was remodelled by William Kent whose work was continued by Capability Brown. The grounds have been designed to include a number of striking vistas and contain a grassed amphitheatre, grotto, lake, and an island with a pavilion. Open daily (closed Mondays in winter), 10am to 6pm (or dusk if earlier), all year round; admission charge payable (free to NT members). Nearby Claremont House (not NT) operates as a school and is only occasionally open to visitors. It was designed in the 1700s by Vanbrugh and substantially remodelled in 1772 for Clive of India.

From Claremont House, we continued southwestwards along the A307 to **Cobham,** a busy residential town with some fine period buildings, including the part-15th-century the Cedars and early 18th-century Ham Manor, on its southeastern side. **Stoke D'Abernon** lies on the A245 a mile-or-so to the southeast of Cobham. Like Cobham, the northern part is undistinguished; however, the older southern part, which reaches down to the the River Mole, contains a fine mid-18th-century part-Palladian, part-baroque manor house and an exceptional parish church which is believed to among the oldest in the country.

The south wall of St Mary's Church in Stoke D'Abernon is believed to date back to the days of St Augustine in the 7th-century, and indeed it has been found to contain brickwork and cornices belonging to a Roman structure which once stood on the site. There are also traces of an early Saxon lord's gallery and one of the oldest monumental brasses in Britain, that of Sir John D'Abernon who was buried in 1277. The church, with its wonderful mixture of styles and influences, is certainly worth a look; the north aisle is 12th-century, the rib-vaulted chancel 13th-century, the stained-glass part-mediaeval, and the magnificent walnut pulpit early-17th-century.

The Bear, Leatherhead Road, Oxshott, Surrey 0372 842747
Map Ref : 3G

Travelling along the **A244** to **Oxshott**, you will find a simply delightful pub called The Bear. It really is a picture with its wooden parasoled tables set in the beautiful garden full of flowers, which has twice been awarded first prize by the London Horticultural Society in a pub garden competition. Proprietors Geoff and Christine Young have developed this into a first class establishment and inside, the atmosphere is friendly and welcoming. The restaurant area with its lovely conservatory provides a charming setting in which to enjoy a lunchtime or evening meal and savour popular favourites such as Camembert Surprise, 1/2 pheasant in black cherry sauce, and the delicious sweet, Banoffee Pie, all of which are sure to bring you back again.

On leaving Oxshott, we followed the B280 eastwards to Epsom, the first stop in our next chapter.

Surrey.

From the River Mole to the Kent Border.

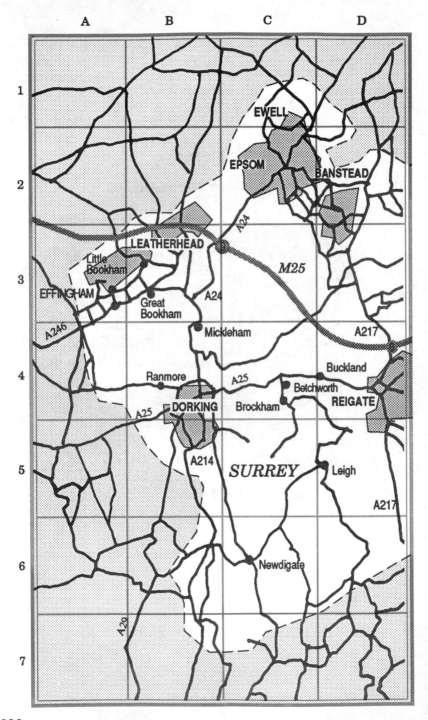

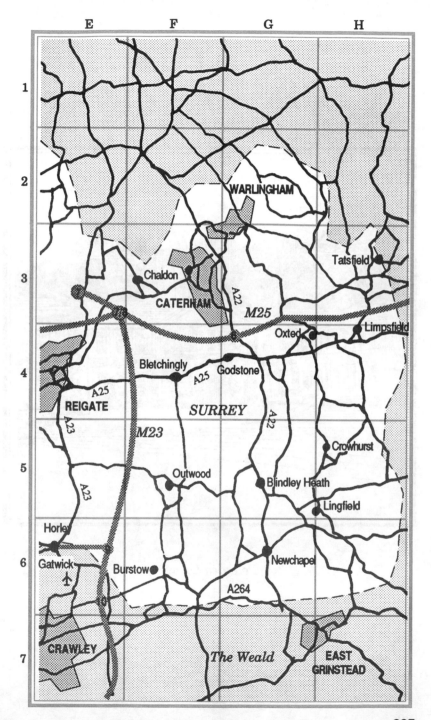

Polesden Lacey.

Surrey.
From the River Mole to the Kent Border.

Our journey around east Surrey began in the old market and spa town of **Epsom**, a prosperous residential centre which lies on the edge of London's southwestern suburbs. In the early 17th-century, it was observed that cattle were refusing to drink from a spring on the common above the town and subsequent tests revealed the water to be high in magnesium sulphate, a mineral believed to have highly beneficial medicinal properties. As the fashion for 'taking the waters' grew towards the end of the century, wealthy people from London came in increasing numbers to sample the benefits of Epsom salts and the settlement grew from a small village to a town with its own street market, a charter for which was granted in 1685.

By the end of the 18th-century, the popularity of Epsom's spa was on the decline, but by this time, the town's pleasant rural location within easy reach of the City of London was already starting to attract well-to-do business people; a number of substantial residential homes were built in and around the town during this period, several of which survive to this day. A lively street market continues to be held every Saturday in Epsom High Street, a wide and impressive thoroughfare which contains some noteworthy old buildings, including a Victorian clock tower and the part-17th-century Waterloo House, formerly the New Tavern.

Epsom's other main claim to fame is as a horse-racing centre. Each year in early June, the downs to the southeast of the town take on a carnival atmosphere as tens of thousands of racing enthusiasts come to experience the annual Classic race meeting and the colourful funfair which accompanies it. Informal horse racing took place on Epsom Downs as long ago as 1683 when Charles II is said to have been in attendance. Racing was formalised in 1779 when a party of aristocratic sportsmen led by Lord Derby established a race for three-year-old fillies which was named after the Derbys' family home at

Banstead, the *Oaks*; this was followed a year later by a race for all three-year-olds, the *Derby*, which was named after the founder himself, although only after he won a toss of a coin with the race's co-founder, Sir Charles Bunbury. (Had Lord Derby lost, the race would have become known as the *Bunbury*.) The Oaks and the Derby were a great success and soon achieved Classic status along with the St Leger at Doncaster, the earliest to be established in 1776, and the 1000 Guineas and 2000 Guineas at Newmarket, established in 1814 and 1809 respectively.

Three miles along the A24 to the southwest of Epsom we came to **Leatherhead**, a pretty Mole Valley town which manages to retain some measure of tranquillity despite being crossed by a number of major trunk routes. Several buildings in the narrow streets of the old town are worthy of note, including the 16th-century Running Horse Inn and the attractive part-12th-century parish church. The grave of Anthony Hope (real name Sir Anthony Hawkins), the author of *The Prisoner Of Zenda*, can be found in the churchyard, and a short distance away in Church Street, the informative Leatherhead Museum of Local History is housed in a charming 17th-century timber-framed cottage with its own small garden. Open Fridays and Saturdays, 10am to 4pm (1pm Saturdays) between April and Christmas; admission free. Built in 1968 in the characteristic style of the period, Leatherhead's celebrated Thorndike Theatre offers a first-rate programme of drama, dance and music theatre; there is also a pleasant coffee shop and bar, and a small studio theatre, the Casson Room, offering a programme of more experimental work.

Fire & Iron Gallery, Rowhurst Forge, Oxshott Road, Leatherhead, Surrey KT22 0EN 0372 375148 Map Ref : 3B

One place that is well worth a visit is the **Fire & Iron Gallery**, which you will find signposted off the **A244** Leatherhead Road. Open throughout the year Monday to Saturday from 9am-5pm, this is a fascinating place where you can marvel at the ancient and beautiful craft of metalworkers and blacksmiths. The site has a special arena where visitors can view demonstrations of the different metalwork techniques and all the work produced is displayed in a large gallery and craft centre, along with work of other blacksmiths and metalworkers. Orders and commissions come from all over the world, ranging from fire-screens to ornate bannister rails. To complete your visit, there is a coffee shop offering refreshments and in the Summer you can relax outside in the beautiful gardens.

Although heavily built up since the Second World War, the residential area to the west of Leatherhead manages to retain something of its historic past. The earliest mention of a settlement in the area dates back to the 660s AD when a manor at *Bocheham* is recorded as belonging to Chertsey Abbey. Present-day **Great Bookham** contains an exceptional parish church, St Nicholas', which has an unusual flint tower with a shingled spire dating back to the Norman era in the 12th-century. A substantial part of the building, including the chancel, is known to have been rebuilt in the 1340s by the Abbot of Chertsey, and the church was again remodelled by the Victorians. Inside, there is some fine 15th-century stained glass and a number of noteworthy monumental brasses and memorials to the local lords of the manor. An early 18th-century owner of the Bookham estate, Dr Hugh Shortrudge, left an endowment in his will to four local churches on condition that an annual sermon was preached on the subject of the martyrdom of Charles I. St Nicholas continues to uphold the tradition of the 'Shortrudge sermon' which is preached each year on the final Sunday in January.

Nearby **Little Bookham** has a small single-roomed church with a wooden belfry which is believed to date from the 12th-century. The adjacent 18th-century manor house now operates as a school. Bookham and Banks Commons to the northwest of Little Bookham provide some welcome relief from the commuter estates and offer some pleasant walking through relatively unspoilt open heathland. The commons are recorded in the Domesday Book as providing *pannage*, the right to graze pigs on acorns, for Chertsey Abbey. Now under the ownership of the National Trust, they are particularly known for their rich and varied birdlife.

Another National Trust-owned property, **Polesden Lacey**, stands on high ground two miles to the south of Great Bookham. The estate was once owned by the writer R B Sheridan who purchased it in 1797 with the intention of restoring its decaying 17th-century manor house; however, a lack of funds prevented him from realising his ambitions, and following his death in 1816, the building was demolished and the estate sold. Then during the 1820s, the architect Thomas Cubitt built a substantial Regency villa in its place which was subsequently remodelled and enlarged by successive owners throughout the 19th-century.

In 1906, the estate was acquired by Captain Ronald Greville and his wife Margaret, the daughter of a Scottish brewing magnate and a celebrated high society hostess. Over the following three decades, they invited a succession of rich and influential guests to Polesden Lacey whose number included Edward VII, and George VI and Queen Elizabeth (now the Queen Mother) who spent part of their honeymoon here in 1923. The Grevilles carried out a number of alterations of their own during this period and the extravagant 'Edwardian-Louis XVI' internal decoration remains as a testimony to Margaret Greville's taste (or, some may say, the lack of it).

Whatever the perspective, the house contains an undeniably fine collection of furniture, paintings, tapestries, porcelain and silver which the Grevilles accumulated over forty years, and Margaret's personal collection of photographs provides a fascinating record of British high society at play during the early part of the century. The surrounding grounds amount to over 1000 acres and incorporate a walled rose garden, open lawns, a YHA youth hostel and a large area of natural woodland; there is also a charming open-air theatre which holds an annual season of events in late-June and early-July. House open Wednesdays to Sundays (and Bank Holiday Mondays), 1.30pm to 5.30pm between 1st April and end-October (also weekends only in March and November); admission charge payable (free to NT members).

The Polesden Lacey estate is bordered to the south by **Ranmore Common**, another area of National Trust-owned upland which is crisscrossed by scenic footpaths and bridleways. This scenic area of the North Downs provides some good walking, and also offers a couple of excellent places to restore oneself afterwards, including the Old Cartlodge Tearooms.

Delicious teas, light meals and homemade cakes and pastries can be enjoyed at the **Old Cartlodge Tearooms** at Dunley Hill Farm. Here you will meet a very friendly lady called Mary Suckling who prepares wonderful homecooked food. You won't find 'chips with everything' here, instead you can choose from a wide range of light snacks and full meals such as mouthwatering steak and kidney pie or a fish dish with yoghurt and asparagus sauce. Soup and a roll takes on a new meaning with the likes of parsnip and apple, whilst homebaked cakes include courgette, mango, and walnut tea loaf, all of which can be enjoyed in the lovely gardens, weather permitting.

The Old Cartlodge Tea Rooms, Dunley Hill Farm, Ranmore Common, Near Dorking, Surrey RH5 6SX 0483 282222 Map Ref:4B

The 563ft **Box Hill** lies a couple of miles from Polesden Lacey on the eastern side of the River Mole. This popular local landmark rises sharply from the valley floor to an impressive tree-covered summit, 400ft above. The hill takes its name from the mature box trees which once grew here in profusion but which were seriously depleted in the 18th-century to supply the needs of London wood-engravers. By then, the site had already been known for over a century as a beauty spot and had been visited by, among others, the diarist John Evelyn.

Today, the National Trust owns over 800 acres of land around Box Hill which has now been designated a country park. The area around the summit incorporates an exhibition centre, a late-19th-century fort and a take-away café, and can be reached either by footpath or by a narrow winding road which leads up from Burford Bridge. The hillside is traversed by a series of nature walks, and there are also several picnic sites which enjoy breathtaking views across the Weald to the South Downs. Car parking charge payable (free to NT members).

The Burford Bridge Hotel stands on the banks of the River Mole at the foot of Box Hill and is connected to it by stepping stones across the river. In the early 19th-century, the establishment was known as the Hare and Hounds and it was here that in 1805, Admiral Nelson said his farewells to Lady Hamilton prior to the Battle of Trafalgar; Keats is also believed to have completed his second volume of poems *Endymion* here in 1818. Chapel Farm at nearby West Humble is an open farm which offers visitors the chance to see a working livestock farm at close quarters. Open daily, 10am to 6pm between 1st March and end-October; admission charge payable. **Mickleham**, to the north, is a highly picturesque village with a good pub, the Running Horses, and a restored Norman church containing a rare Flemish stained-glass window. A little further afield, pleasant open countryside can also be found on Mickleham Down, part of which is known locally as *Little Switzerland*, White Hill and Headley Heath.

The A24 to the south of Box Hill led us to **Dorking**, a long-established settlement which stands at the intersection of Stane Street, the Roman road which once connected London with Chichester, and the ancient Pilgrims' Way east-west ridgeway route which is roughly followed by course of the modern North Downs Way. Despite evidence of Saxon and Viking occupation, present-day Dorking is a congested commuter town which owes most of character to the Victorians. There are a small number of older buildings, most notably the part-15th-century former coaching inn, the White Horse, and the shops and houses in North Street, West Street and at the western end of the High Street; however, the town's two most distinctive architectural features are characteristically 19th-century: the unexpectedly grand parish church with its soaring spire, and the Rose Hill housing development, an assortment of Victorian villas arranged around a green and entered from South Street through an unusual neo-Gothic arch.

Perhaps Dorking's most attractive feature is its close proximity to unspoilt countryside, a testimony to the success of the South East's Green Belt policy. As well as the open spaces in the downs to the north, **Holmwood Common**, two miles along the A24 to the south, is another tract of National Trust-owned land which offers some pleasant waymarked walks through mature oak and birch woodlands.

A couple of miles further south, we turned east off the A24 at Beare Green to reach our next destination, the scattered village of **Newdigate**. This historic settlement contains an interesting parish church, St Peter's, which is believed to have been founded in the 12th-century by the Earl de Warenne as a 'hunters' chapel', a place of worship built to be used by Norman hunting parties during their expeditions in the Wealden forest. The tower, with its shingled spire, was constructed around a massive cross-braced timber frame in the 15th-century, a time when Newdigate was relatively prosperous thanks to its flourishing iron-founding industry. The oak shingles on the spire had to be replaced in the late 1970s after their Victorian predecessors had warped in the hot summer of 1976.

Present-day Newdigate contains a number of exceptional old timber-framed buildings, several of which date back to the 16th-century and before. Some of the finest, including Yew Tree Cottage and the pair known as Old and White Cottages, can be seen near the Six Bells, a building which has been a village pub for as long as records have existed.

Half a mile outside the ancient and picturesque village of Newdigate, on Rusper Road, you will discover Tanhouse farm, a beautiful black and white timbered house typical of the area. Built in 1540, this charming farmhouse has been tastefully refurbished and is full of character with original oak beams throughout. Friendly hostess Mrs. Fries offers first class accommodation for non-smokers in two beautifully furnished guest rooms, with two bathrooms also provided. Tanhouse enjoys an idyllic setting in 30 acres, with a sparkling stream running alongside delightful gardens. Originally the home of a tanner, Mrs. Fries once found a collection of boots and shoes that were 200 years old, and it is also said that smugglers used to stop here to change horses on their way to and from London.

Tanhouse Farm, Rusper Road, Newdigate, Surrey RH5 5BX
0306 631334 Map Ref : 6C

From Newdigate, we followed the country lanes northeastwards for three miles to **Leigh** (pronounced *lye*), a well-kept village which, like at least a dozen others in Britain, takes its name from the Saxon term for *forest clearing*. Like Newdigate and Charlwood to the south, Leigh was an important centre of the Wealden iron-founding industry which prospered from the 14th-century until it was superseded by Northern-based coal-fired smelting in the 18th-century. Indeed, this now-tranquil area was once known as 'Thunderfield-in-the-Forest' because of the number of iron furnaces it contained.

By contrast, present-day Leigh consists of an attractive collection of timber-framed and tile-fronted buildings set around a peaceful and well-manicured triangular green. The Priest's House, a curious row

235

of restored 15th-century cottages, overlooks one side, and the part-15th-century St Bartholomew's Church stands in one corner. This attractive Horsham-stone-covered structure contains several interesting memorials to the Arderne family who lived at Leigh Place, a somewhat crudely-restored 15th-century moated mansion which lies a short distance away to the north.

In the centre of the village of Leigh you will find **The Plough**, a delightful country pub, which is a listed building, with parts of it dating back to the 15th century. There is a "locals" bar, a lovely cosy lounge bar and a separate restaurant area which overlooks the private garden and village green. There is a selection of bar snacks, a restaurant menu and extensive choice on the blackboard, including a variety of fish and vegetarian dishes. Rob serves a selection of beers including three Real Ales and the pub regularly hosts themed events such as Beaujolais Nouveau evenings with an all-French menu, or Australia Day quizzes, all of which adds to the appeal of this popular establishment.

The Plough, Church Road, Leigh, Reigate, Surrey RH2 8NJ
0306 78348 Map Ref : 5D

It is in the centre of Leigh, opposite the ancient church, that you will find Barn Cottage. This delightful conversion of a 16th century barn is home to Pat and Mike Comer who offer first class bed and breakfast accommodation. The cottage features original beams throughout and the two beautifully decorated bedrooms are furnished with antiques as is the charming dining room, retaining the character of the original building. Set in lovely gardens, there is a swimming pool and tennis court for guests to make use of and the local pub, The Plough is just 100 yards away.

Barn Cottage, Church Road, Leigh, Reigate, Surrey RH2 8RF
0306 78347 Map Ref : 5D

The network of country lanes to the northwest of Leigh led us to **Brockham**, a picture-postcard village lying half-a-mile south of the A25 on the banks of the River Mole. Like Leigh, Brockham is set around a quintessential three-sided village green on which cricket is played in summer, a Guy Fawkes' bonfire is lit in autumn, and Christmas carols are sung in winter. The legendary cricketer, W G Grace, is even said to have played here. This delightful tree-lined setting is enhanced by a splendid view of Box Hill, some fine old cottages, and an elegantly-proportioned parish church with a tall spire which was built in the 1840s in uncomplicated Early English style. Other noteworthy buildings in the village include the late-18th-century Brockham Court, which can be seen on the eastern edge of the green, and the part-17th-century Feltons Farm, which lies a short distance away to the southwest. The remains of some 19th-century industrial kilns can be seen on the Downs above the village in the disused Brockham Quarries.

A mile or so upstream, the long rambling village of **Betchworth** was once a much more important settlement than it is today. In the 14th-century, it had its own fortress, Betchworth Castle, which stood beside the River Mole on a site now occupied by the local golf course. This has now virtually disappeared and the only reminder of Betworth's past glory is the parish church of St Michael, a surprisingly imposing structure which incorporates some ancient Saxon masonry, a Norman arch and a succession of more recent architectural modifications. Inside, there is a fascinating map of the local manor dated 1634 showing the vestiges of the feudal field system and a wooden chest which is reputed to have been made before the Norman invasion from a single piece of timber taken from a 1000-year-old oak tree; there is also an unusual font dating from the 1950s. The church is situated at the end of a wide cul-de-sac which also contains an early-18th-century vicarage, an old long barn and a collection of attractive 17th- and 18th-century cottages.

A number of interesting buildings can be seen in other parts of Betchworth, including the 16th-century Old Mill Cottage, the slender Queen Anne 'Old House', and Betchworth House, an impressive part-Georgian manor house which is surrounded by pretty treed parkland. The village also contains an exceptionally welcoming pub and eating place, the **Royal Oak**.

Enjoying a picturesque location overlooking the village green , The Royal Oak is a delightful Grade I listed traditional style village pub. There has been a pub on this site since the 14th century and you will find The Royal Oak retains a lot of its original character with open log fires enhancing the warm, welcoming ambience. Friendly proprietors Mick and Sandra Tames serve a selection of fine ales accompanied by an extensive menu which includes several vegetarian dishes and regularly changing blackboard specials, plus an all-day breakfast. The village of Brockham Green is particularly noted for the excellent bonfire night celebrations hosted here, which in its best year attracted an audience of 20,000.

The Royal Oak, Brockham Green, Betchworth, Surrey RH3 7JS
0737 843241 Map Ref :4C

Alternatively, those looking for top quality farmhouse accommodation in this lovely part of Surrey should make a point of finding **Gadbrook Old Farm**.

Travelling through Betchworth village, if you turn right at the signpost for Brockham, you will discover Gadbrook Old Farm about 1/4 of a mile down on the right hand side. This beautiful early 17th century farmhouse enjoys a tranquil location in lovely rural surroundings and is the home of friendly couple, Jeanette and Derek Bibby. They offer first class accommodation in two lovely guest rooms,

238

whilst downstairs there is a large sitting room with welcoming open fireplace. The adjoining dining room provides a comfortable setting for the hearty breakfast, where guests can have 'whatever they want'! Jeanette will prepare an evening meal by prior arrangement, although there are a number of fine local pubs and restaurants nearby.

Gadbrook Old Farm, Wellhouse Lane, Betchworth, Surrey
RH3 7HH   0737 842183   Map Ref : 4C

On leaving Betchworth, we joined the A25 and drove eastwards towards Reigate, a route which took us through **Buckland**, a pretty settlement which suffers from being sited on the busy main road. The road divides Buckland's tidy rectangular green from its village church, a part-13th-century structure whose interior is worth a look for its 15th-century stained-glass east window and 17th-century pews and oak panelling. The A25 to the east of Buckland passes along the northern edge of **Reigate Heath**; this narrow area of open heathland is the home of the unique **Windmill Church**, the only church in the world to be situated in a windmill.

One mile further east, **Reigate** is a prosperous residential town whose expansion at the hands of postwar developers has done much to conceal its long and distinguished history. The settlement was once an important outpost of the de Warenne family, the assertive Norman rulers whose sphere of influence stretched from the Channel coast to the North Downs. As at Lewes, they built a castle on a rise above the village streets of which nothing remains today except for an arch which was reconstructed in the 1770s from material recovered from the original castle walls. Today, this striking neo-Gothic reproduction stands at the heart of a pleasant public park.

A steep path leads down from the castle mound to the attractive mixture of Victorian, Georgian and older buildings which line Reigate's High Street. The Old Town Hall, a handsome redbrick building constructed in 1729, stands at its eastern end, and a short distance

239

away to the north, the entrance to a disused road tunnel can be seen which was built beneath the castle mound in 1824 to ease the through-flow of traffic on the busy London to Brighton coaching route. Other noteworthy buildings in this part of town include the timber-framed and tile-fronted 'La Trobes' in the High Street, and the 400-year-old Old Sweep's House in the charmingly-named Slipshoe Street.

As well as being effective administrators, the de Warennes were known for their devout religious beliefs, and again as at Lewes, they founded a priory in the town some distance from the centre. After the Dissolution, this became the home of Lord Howard of Effingham, the commander-in-chief of the English navy at the time of the Spanish Armada. The building has been remodelled on a number of occasions since then, in particular during the Georgian era, and now operates as a school. The interior contains some fine period features and an interesting museum which is open from 2pm to 4.30pm on Wednesdays during term time, and from 11am to 4pm on the first Saturday in the month; admission free. Also set away from the town centre, and probably standing on the site of pre-Norman Reigate, is the pale stone-built church of St Mary Magdalene. This contains a number of striking memorials, including one carved by Joseph Rose the Elder around 1730.

Our tour around Reigate led us to the impressive **Cranleigh Hotel**. For genuine hospitality in a friendly, informal atmosphere, The Cranleigh Hotel is very hard to beat. Travelling west towards Dorking, out of this lovely unspoilt town, The Cranleigh Hotel enjoys a prominent roadside position on your left.

The Cranleigh Hotel, 41 West Street, Reigate, Surrey RH2 9BL
0737 223417 Map Ref : 4D

Pino and Carol Bussandri are charming hosts who seem more like friends and who go out of their way to ensure complete comfort for their guests. Eight of the ten beautifully furnished guest rooms are

240

en-suite and all provide first class facilities with lovely views of the well-kept garden and outdoor swimming pool. The intimate Garden Room restaurant with its magnificent conservatory provides the perfect setting for guests and non-residents to enjoy the finest Continental/British cuisine, all served with Pino's Italian flair.

From the centre of Reigate, we continued eastwards along the A25 through **Redhill**, a community which developed around the railway station after the London to Brighton line opened in the 1840s. The parish church of St John has an exceptionally tall and elegant spire, and the Harlequin Theatre in the Warwick Quadrant shopping precinct offers a full programme of drama, film and musical entertainment in addition to having a pleasant bar, restaurant and coffee shop.

Shortly after passing over the M23, three miles further east, we came to the historic community of **Bletchingley**, a highly picturesque village and former 'rotten borough' which once had its own castle and street market. Traces of the Norman fortification thought to have been built by Richard de Tonbridge in the 12th-century can be seen in the grounds of Castle Hill, a private house lying to the south of the A25. Closer to the centre, the old market hall in Middle Row is an exceptionally lovely thoroughfare which, like the nearby High Street, contains some wonderful old timber-framed and tile-hung houses and cottages.

Some fine early buildings can also be found in Church Walk, the lane leading to Bletchingley's Perpendicular church of St Mary. The oldest part of this sizable sandstone structure, the Norman west tower, dates from the end of the 11th-century; it had a spire until a bolt of lightning destroyed it in 1606. Inside, there is a 13th-century hermit's cell, a wonderful assortment of mediaeval gargoyles, a 16th-century monumental brass of a local tanner and his wife, and an extravagant sculpted monument to Sir Robert Clayton, a City money lender and former Lord Mayor of London who died in 1707. The church also contains the sizable tomb of Sir Thomas Cawarden, the former owner of Bletchingley Place, who acquired the manor house from Anne of Cleves after she had won it from Henry VIII in her divorce settlement.

On our travels around Bletchingley led us to a delightful inn, the **Prince Albert**. Situated in the heart of Bletchingley, The Prince Albert provides a super stopping-off point in any journey. Run by Carla and David Lipscombe for the past 17 years, the original character of this traditional 15th century pub is enhanced by oak beams throughout. Here you can sample four Real Ales, accompanied by a wide selection of bar snacks, all of which can be enjoyed in the beautiful rear garden which boasts a fish pond full of Koi Carp. However, the main reason for calling in has to be the excellent, very extensive and varied restaurant menu which includes no less than nine steak dishes, for which The Prince Albert is widely renowned.

The Prince Albert, Outwood Road, Bletchingley, Surrey RH1 4LR
0883 743257 Map Ref:4F

A couple of interesting settlements lie within easy reach of Bletchingley. **Pendell**, three-quarters-of-a-mile to the northwest, contains the striking Jacobean-style Pendell Court, which was built in 1624, and the neoclassical Pendell House, which was built twelve years later on an adjacent site. **Brewer Street**, one mile to the north, contains the remains of Anne of Cleves' manor house; this was remodelled in the 18th-century and is now known as Place Farm.

After returning to the centre of Bletchingley, we joined the country road which leads southwards across the Weald to **Outwood**. Outwood Common, the area of high ground to the east of village, is best known for being the location of one of the oldest working windmills in the country. This was built in 1665 as a 'post' mill, a design which enables the sails to be faced into the wind by rotating the entire timber superstructure around a massive central upright. Another special design feature incorporated around 100 years later allows the angle of the sails to be adjusted to suit different wind conditions using a system of elliptical springs. For over a century, a second 'smock' windmill stood nearby, and the pair were known as the **Cat and Fiddle**; sadly, the Fiddle blew down in a storm in the early 1960s. The Jupp family have milled corn at Outwood for over two centuries and at certain times, they allow visitors inside to see the millstones in operation. The site also contains a small rural museum and children's zoo.

The lanes to the south of Outwood led us through Smallfield to

Burstow, a well-kept village whose church, St Bartholomew's, has a surprisingly well-preserved late-mediaeval timber-framed tower. This hefty 15th-century structure supports a peal of six bells, the largest of which weighs over half-a-ton. The church itself is an attractive mixture of Norman, Perpendicular and Victorian influences; the chancel contains the remains of John Flamsteed, a former rector and the first Astronomer Royal, who is best remembered for his maps of the night skies which were compiled in the late 17th-century as an aid to marine navigation.

A 'hidden place' with a fascinating history and well worth a visit is **The Wiremill Inn** at **Newchapel**. This charming mid-16th century inn is set in an area known as Wiremill Wood, renowned nationally for its splendid display of bluebells in the Spring. Built on three levels, the main bar area enjoys lovely views over a large lake and in the centre of the bar, a coal effect fire has been erected on the grinding stone of the original flour mill. Later the building became a wire mill, and Barbara will readily fill you in on various historic tales about it, but today this is definitely the place to come to enjoy fine ale and excellent pub fare.

The Wiremill Inn, Wiremill Lane, Newchapel, Near Lingfield, Surrey RH7 6HJ 0342 832263 Map Ref :6G

On leaving Newchapel, we continued northeastwards along the B2028 to **Lingfield**, a large and scattered village which is set within delightful wooded countryside in the southeastern corner of the county. Almost large enough to be called a town, 'leafy Lingfield' is perhaps best known to the world at large for its racecourse. However, the settlement has long been an important agricultural centre whose largely Perpendicular church of St Peter and St Paul has been enlarged over the centuries to create what has become known as the 'Westminster Abbey of Surrey'. As well as having a rare double nave and an exceptional collection of monumental brasses, the church also contains a surprising number of memorials to members of the Cobham family, the mediaeval lords of the manor who lived at the now-demolished Starborough Castle, a mile-and-a-half to the east. Each of the first four barons has a sizable tomb showing an effigy of its occupant; these date between 1361 and 1471 and are particularly fascinating to those with an interest in the development of late-mediaeval armour over this period.

The broad thoroughfare leading down from the church is lined with characteristic weatherboarded and tile-fronted buildings, including Pollard Cottage, with its unusual 15th-century shop front, the 16th-century Old Town Stores, and the Star Inn Cottages, built around 1700. The country library on the opposite side of the church is a former farmhouse which was built in the 17th-century on the site of a Carthusian college founded in the 1400s by Sir Reginald Cobham. Elsewhere in Lingfield, a couple of interesting features can be found near the pond in Plaistow Street: the 15th-century village cross and the old lock-up, a small local gaol which was built in 1772 and in use until 1882.

Greathed Manor, to the southeast of Lingfield, is a substantial Victorian manor house built in 1868 for the Spender Clay family. Open Wednesdays and Thursdays, 2pm to 5pm between May and September; admission charge payable. **Haxted Mill**, two miles to the northeast of Lingfield, is a working late-17th-century water mill which also contains an informative mill museum; exhibits include machinery, equipment and artefacts relating to the history of water-power. Open Wednesdays, Saturdays, Sundays and Bank Holiday Mondays, 1pm to 5pm between April and September; admission charge payable.

Crowhurst, three miles to the north of Lingfield, contains a 1000-year-old yew tree whose branches are said to enclose an area over 30ft in diameter; during the 1820s, a covered café was formed by removing some of the central branches and installing tables and chairs. Crowhurst Place, to the southwest, was rebuilt after the First World War on the site of a 15th-century moated manor house.

It would be hard to find a more pleasant setting for a touring base than **Stantons Hall Farm** at **Blindley Heath**. This delightful 250 year old farmhouse enjoys an idyllic location overlooking a duck pond and surrounded by beautiful countryside which belies the fact that Gatwick Airport is only 10 minutes drive away. Run by Vanessa Manwill, this traditional style farmhouse oozes character with oak beams throughout, and provides very comfortable accommodation in six first class guest rooms, some with en-suite facilities. After a refreshing night's sleep, guests can look forward to a hearty breakfast around the table in the large farmhouse kitchen, which sets them up perfectly for a day exploring the surrounding area.

Stantons Hall Farm, Eastbourne Road, Blindley Heath, Surrey RH7 6LG 0342 832401 Map Ref : 5G

From Blindley Heath, we continued north for four miles to the historic settlement of **Godstone**. Although it is now thankfully bypassed by the A22, the A25 east-west route still passes through its heart, making a sharp change in direction as it does so. Fortunately, the village manages to endure the periodic onslaught of traffic and indeed, its Tudor and Elizabethan character has survived relatively intact. Godstone's most distinguished building, the White Hart Inn in the High Street, claims to have been visited by Richard II, Elizabeth I, Queen Victoria and even the Tsar of Russia who broke his journey here in 1815. A series of attractive lanes and alleyways connects the High Street to the village green, a broad open space with a cricket pitch which is surrounded by a wonderful collection of 16th- and 17th-century buildings, including the Tudor-built Hare and Hounds Inn.

Godstone's parish church is situated half-a-mile east of the centre and can be reached from the White Hart along an old thoroughfare known as Bay Path. Although Norman in origin, the building was virtually rebuilt in the 1870s by Sir George Gilbert Scott, a local resident at the time. Inside, there is a marble memorial to a cousin of John Evelyn, the famous 17th-century diarist. The area around the church contains some fine old buildings, including a row of 19th-century almshouses and the 16th-century timber-framed Old Pack House, which lies a short distance away to the south. Bay Path also leads to a former hammer pond, Bay Pond, which is now a designated nature reserve. At one time, its water would have been used to power the mechanical hammers in a nearby iron foundry, an indication of Godstone's lost industrial past which also included the manufacture of gunpowder and leatherware.

Godstone Farm, in Tilburstow Hill Road to the south of the village, is an open farm where children can experience life on the farm at first hand. Open daily, 10am to 6pm between March and October; admission charge payable. The churchyard at **Limpsfield**, three miles to the east of Godstone, contains the grave of the composer, Frederick Delius, who despite having died in France, left instructions that he should be buried in an English country graveyard. **Detillens**, a rare 15th-century 'hall' house, is also located in Limpsfield. This striking building has an unusual 'king-post' roof, and despite having been given a new façade in the 18th-century, is a good example of a house belonging to a Surrey yeoman, a member of the class of small freeholders who cultivated their own land; inside, there is an interesting collection of period furniture, china and militaria.

After returning to Godstone, we rejoined the A22 and drove north across the M25 towards **Caterham**. The route into the town centre from the south passes close to Foster Down, a section of the North Downs Way which incorporates the impressive Tupwood Viewpoint; good views can also be enjoyed from the nearby 778ft Gravelly Hill. Caterham itself is a modern and prosperous residential town which has little to offer the casual visitor. Worthy of note, however, is the East Surrey Museum in Stafford Road which offers an interesting insight into the natural history and archeology of the surrounding area. Open Wednesday, Saturdays and Sundays, 10am (2pm Sundays) to 5pm, all year round; small admission charge payable.

The Old Ship, Westmore Green, Tatsfield, Near Westerham, Kent
TN16 2AG 0959 577315 Map Ref :3G

It is well worth making the detour to **Chaldon**, two-and-a-half miles to the west of Caterham, to have a look at the 11th-century church of St Peter and St Paul which stands within striking distance of the old Pilgrims' Way. Although the exterior of this unassuming

246

flint-built structure has little to commend it (other than, perhaps, its south tower and shingled spire), the interior contains one of the most outstanding mediaeval wall paintings still in existence in Britain. Executed in creamy white on a deep red-ochre background, the mural covers the entire west wall of the church. It is believed to have been painted around 1200, but was covered over during the Reformation and remained undiscovered until 1870. The 'Chaldon Doom' as it has become known, depicts gory scenes from the Last Judgment; a 'Ladder of Salvation' can be seen reaching up to the Kingdom of Heaven from purgatory, a place where horrific punishments are meted out by fork-wielding devils to those guilty of having committed the Seven Deadly Sins.

Our final stopping place in Surrey was **Tatsfield**, a peaceful community which lies between Biggin Hill and Westerham in the northeasternmost corner of the county. Our destination here was the **Old Ship**, a first-class pub and eating place which made a perfect end to this part of our journey.

Set in lovely rural surroundings, this small village pub is full of character, with welcoming log fires for those chillier days. This is a popular stopping-off point with walkers and provides the perfect break in any journey, where you can call in to savour the wide selection of homemade bar snacks and meals, including a blackboard special menu which changes daily. On fine Summer days you can enjoy your drink or a meal in the peaceful setting of the large beer garden at the rear.

And after a stop at The OldShip you will be ready for the wonders of Kent which lies ahead of us.

North and West Kent.

From Westerham to Ashford.

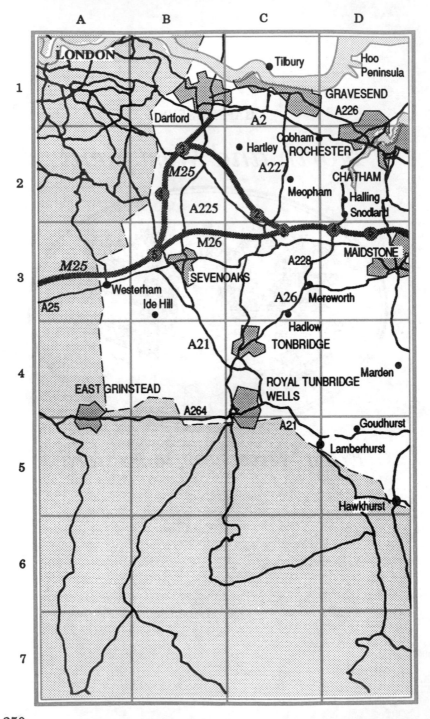

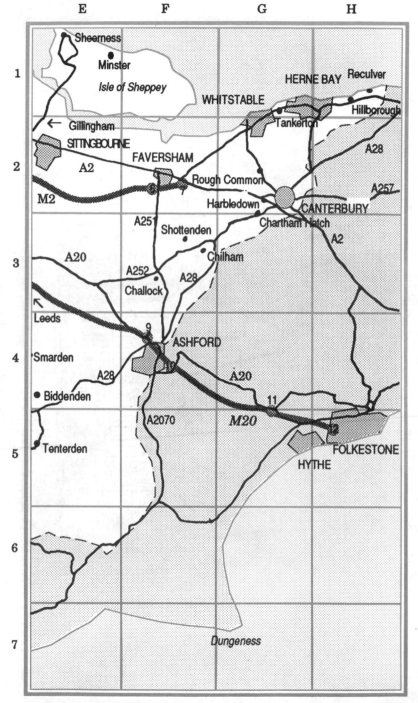

Smarden - Lych Gate.

North and West Kent.

From Westerham to Ashford.

Westerham, the westernmost village in the county, sits right up against the border with Surrey, with the North Downs above and the Greensand Ridge below. How long it can cling to its description as a large village before it officially becomes a small town is open to question, but it is certainly a very attractive place now, and we hope it stays that way.

Westerham's main offering as far as historical buildings is concerned is the Elizabethan house called Quebec House. General James Wolfe lived here during his childhood, and it now houses a museum dedicated to the famous soldier. He was actually born in the Vicarage in 1727, and many houses here seem to have associations with him.

On the village green stands a statue of Wolfe brandishing a sword aloft, portraying him very much as the fighting man who defeated the French at the famous Battle of Quebec. As Westerham is where he was born and bred, it is very much a case of local boy made good. It is worth noting that Churchill's statue on the same green shows him in a hunched position, a rather weary ministerial figure in contrast to the more flamboyant hero nearby.

The other building here which has strong associations with Wolfe is Squerryes Court. In the grounds of the house, a memorial marks the spot where he first received his military orders at the tender age of fourteen. Built in 1681, the house has some fine Dutch Old Masters, together with mementos of Wolfe, who was a regular visitor to the house as a friend of the Warde family. The River Darent rises in the valley of Squerryes Park, and a walk along the river takes you past meadows where the young Wolfe may well have strolled and dreamt of his forthcoming victories.

From Westerham we took the **A25** to take us into **Sevenoaks**. This handsome market town was named after the seven trees which once grew at the southernmost edge of the town. Unfortunately, six of them were toppled in the gales of 1987. Despite all the subsequent jokes to the contrary, no corresponding change of name is planned as far as we are aware. This is probably just as well, as the name 'Oneoak' would be open to all sorts of mispronunciation!

The pride of Sevenoaks is of course **Knole House**, which, standing on a knoll within 1,000 acres of deer park, is one of the largest private houses in the country. Work began on the building in 1456, and it was an Archbishops' residence until Henry VIII took it for himself in 1532. Through the graces of Elizabeth I, the house came into the possession of the Sackville family, and it remains with them to this day. Those areas of the house open to the public are looked after by the National Trust.

Vita Sackville-West was born here in 1892, and no doubt nurtured her dreams of buying Sissinghurst whilst playing in the park. The house contains many treasures, including a virtually unparalleled collection of 17th century furniture. One fact that we found particularly pleasing here is the neat relation between the design of the house and the number of days in a week, the number of weeks in a year, and the number of days in a year. If this sounds confusing, the mystery will be unravelled when you discover that there are seven courtyards, 52 staircases, and 365 bedrooms!

There is a part of Sevenoaks called **The Shambles**. It is a small courtyard area where time stands still. The buildings here have managed to avoid the developer's eye and remain, for the most, unchanged. Recently, the whole courtyard was cleaned up, cars are no longer allowed to park, and the clutter that used to accumulate here has gone. In The Shambles is a very special shop that we were most anxious to visit, Calamus Purveyor of Fine Gifts. It was not just the amazing collection of gifts here that interested us, but also the architecture of the building itself.

In 1984, it was discovered that the building is one of the oldest in The Shambles. It was traced back to the year 1450, when it was constructed from oak beams. The roof, which is a crown post roof, is said to be one of the most perfectly preserved in the town.

Upstairs is devoted to materials of the cloth kind, including hand printed silks from the foothills of the Himalayan mountains. These silks are unique, and are made into romantic flowing dresses which are unparalleled and never copied. Simply cut beaded tops that will flatter any shape are complemented by well cut jersey velvet skirts of the highest quality. One can imagine entering this emporium of silk an ordinary woman, and emerging feeling like a fairytale princess. Even the home is considered here, with colourful hardwearing rugs to throw on the floor, and hand painted picture borders to complement a picture or brighten a dull mirror.

Prilla or Sheena will giftwrap your present for you, expertly and artistically - we can never get the corners tucked away neatly! These two enterprising ladies are used to beautiful things, and the way that they choose and display their wares shows that they have an eye for the unusual. Whether you are browsing or buying, the service that you will receive is friendly and helpful.

Calamus, The Shambles, Sevenoaks, Kent 0732-740603
Map Ref: 3B

Every so often, we like to treat ourselves to dinner in an exceptional restaurant - normally one that we have passed on one of our excursions. Our choice in Sevenoaks was The **Casa D'Or Restaurant** at 115 London Road. The restaurant is owned and run by David and Sheila Watson.

The menu has a Spanish flavour to it, as does the decor of this delightful restaurant which is situated on two floors - upstairs being the more intimate and formal area, with warm colours and attractively laid tables. There are two menus, one for the speedy and varied take-away service, and the other offering a range of dishes that will make your mouth water. Duck and Cranberry soup, a first for us, was followed by one of the house specialities, Paella. It was absolutely delicious; the herbs, spices and fresh fish blended perfectly. It was also extremely filling. We had to award it the prize as the best paella we had tasted since a holiday in Spain some years ago. There are plenty of vegetarian dishes, as well as salads, fish, steaks and chicken. All the dishes are served with fresh vegetables or a side salad. and are very reasonably priced. Our meal was a leisurely one, and we felt that we had made a very good choice for our 'Treat of the Week'.

Casa D'Or Restaurant, 115 London Road, Sevenoak, Kent
0732-458282 Map Ref :3B

A glance at any tourist map of this part of Kent will show an amazing variety of Houses, Manors, Places and Castles. We could not hope to cover them all in the space available, but we will endeavour to point out some of the best of them. At the junction of the **A26** and the **A228** is **Mereworth** . During the 18th century, the village was subjected to one of those eccentric whims of the ego so typical of members of the gentry at that time. John Fane, 7th Earl of Westmorland and owner of the 16th century Mereworth Castle, decided to pull down the original building and replace it with a beautiful Palladian villa.

Finding that the neighbouring houses blocked out the panoramic views of the hills, he then had the entire village transported a little further to the west of its original site. A new church was built here in 1744, with a spectacular steeple that soars above the surrounding trees. The building we see today is very grand, but we felt it would sit more comfortably in a street with similar scale buildings around it. It is just a little too ostentatious for this pastoral setting. The woods around Mereworth are lovely. Gower Hill in particular is worth packing a picnic hamper for, as the National Trust who run it have made it a pleasant place to walk or ride.

Leaving Mereworth on the **A26**, we headed south for **Tonbridge** . When the spring was first discovered, it was originally known as the Tonbridge Wells. As its fame spread and a new resort began to grow up around the site, the 'o' was changed to a 'u' to distinguish it from the older town.

Tonbridge Castle preceded the town by many centuries. There is evidence of a castle on this site as far back as the Iron Age, while the Saxons and Normans added to the earlier building, and

Edward I completed things by constructing the impressive gatehouse. The castle commands fine views standing on its mound overlooking the River Medway, and a personal guided audio tour will teach you everything you need to know about its fascinating history.

Whilst at Tonbridge, make a point of visiting **Uncle Tom's Cabin**. Having enjoyed reading Harriet Beecher-Stowe's most famous novel many years ago, we found it impossible to resist exploring its namesake in Lavender Hill, Tonbridge. After being served a drink in the public bar, which we noticed still retains the original brickwork, we investigated the garden. Here we discovered not only a play area for children with a swing and climbing frame, but a wonderful aviary which, we were told by the owners, Richard and Joan Wilkinson, contains cockatiels, lovebirds, and no less than 27 budgerigars.

Uncle Tom's Cabin, 54 Lavender Hill, Tonbridge, Kent TN9 2AU
0732-365044 Map Ref :4C

Back in the bar, we noted with interest the hop vine above the bar and the map which showed the breweries and real ales which are served in the restaurant. Richard and Joan provide lunches and bar snacks and will even cook dinner for you, provided you supply them with a day's notice. We were very impressed to see that they even provide an optional vegetarian menu. All their food is home cooked, and fresh whenever possible. The restaurant is also available for meetings, and buffets can be provided if required.

If you are lucky enough to come on a Wednesday evening, you may be able to enjoy the added bonus of listening to the folk music which is provided every few weeks.

From Tonbridge the **A26** leads to **Royal Tunbridge Wells**. In 1909, Edward VII decreed that Tunbridge Wells would from that time on be known as Royal Tunbridge Wells . As the name implies, the waters here were considered to be curative, and members of the upper classes came to take advantage of their efficacious properties and to enjoy the pleasant social gatherings. Some 300 years before, Lord North had discovered a chalybeate spring rich in iron in the area where the Pantiles are now situated. After sampling the red-tinged waters his consumptive afflictions were apparently eased, and he enthusiastically spread the word. The future of Tunbridge Wells as a popular spa was thus assured.

The Pantiles is a colonnaded tiled walk which gets its name from the square clay tiles originally laid in the 1700s on the instructions of Queen Anne. At one end of the original walk, a new area has been created which supplies all your shopping needs with many excellent shops to browse in, but the graceful older area is lovelier by far. In the Corn Exchange, visitors are guided through a splendid display known as 'A Day at the Wells'. This is an entertaining presentation of the antics and lifestyle of high society in the 18th century. Here you will experience a day in 1740, seen through the eyes of 'Beau Nash', your Master of Ceremonies!

The Russell Hotel is situated in a beautiful position facing Tunbridge Wells Common. A mere few minutes walk and you are in the centre of Royal Tunbridge Wells. Parking in the private car park to the rear, we were welcomed by Mr and Mrs Wilkinson as we entered the hotel. They ensure that their guests receive the highest quality service at all times, and are very much involved with the daily running of this busy hotel.

Room service is availableand the rooms are all modern and spacious. Subtle colours decorate the walls and carpets, which coordinated nicely with the curtains and bedspreads. A colourful fresh flower arrangement sat atop the table in front of our bay window. Additional features include direct dial telephones, satellite television, hairdryers, and tea and coffee making facilities.

The Russell Hotel, 80 London Road, Tunbridge Wells, Kent
0892-544833 Map Ref :4C

The businessman is certainly not forgotten here. There are telex and fax facilities within the hotel, and breakfast is served from 7.00am to accommodate early risers. A small conference room is available for meetings and private functions. While we were there, a newly married couple were enjoying their reception in the private room. Winding our way downstairs, we went into the bar for a pre-dinner cocktail, and found that the bar area was again resplendent in shades of gold and blue.

The restaurant has covers for 36, and the atmosphere of casual elegance is very much in keeping with the rest of the hotel and a full menu and full English breakfast are available.

At the end of the **A264**, we joined the **A21** and came to **Lamberhurst**. Although Lamberhurst sees its fair share of traffic, the heart of the village is spared by the by-pass and remains unspoilt.

The two pubs, the George and Dragon and the Chequers Inn, comfortably oppose each other on either side of the Teise. Before the reorganisation of county boundaries, the river acted as a border between the two parts of the village. North of the river, the village was in Kent, and the part to the south was in Sussex. Today, all residents can claim to be Kentish if they so desire.

Lamberhurst's former days of industrial glory hark back to the time when the iron furnaces blazed away, and it was here that the ironwork for the balustrades at St Paul's Cathedral was cast. On the far banks of the Teise, a wooded hillside hides Scotney Castle from view. A footpath from the churchyard at Lamberhurst leads you across a footbridge up into the Castle grounds.

A castle has stood on this site for well over 600 years, and the current building's last private owner was Christopher Hussey, the former editor of 'Country Life' magazine, who died in 1970. He lived in the 'new' **Scotney Castle**, the Tudor-style house overlooking the old castle, which was built for his grandfather, Edward Hussey, in the late 1830s. Left to the National Trust, old Scotney is now open to the public from May to August, and its glorious gardens - created by Edward Hussey in the quarry from which the stone was cut to build his house, and now a perfect vision of fine trees surrounded by a blaze of rhododendrons, azaleas, waterlilies and wisteria - can be enjoyed from April to November. There is also an open air theatre, a shop, and a picnic area by the car park.

On a fine summer's day, the beautiful medieval ruins of old Scotney's stone bridge and circular tower are reflected in the still waters of the moat; creating one of the most romantic and memorable scenes you will encounter anywhere in England.

Goudhurst lies to the east, on the junction of the **A262** and

Scotney Castle.

B2079. It is a very pretty place with tile-hung, weatherboarded cottages and its very own duckpond. The village stands proud on the ridge of the High Weald, some 500ft above sea level. If there is any fault to be found with it, it is the intolerable level of traffic that can plague these charming villages during the summer months.

Just two miles west of Goudhurst off the **A262**, we found a real treat. Billed as a 'Living Museum of Music', **Finchcocks** is a Georgian house which is not only beautiful but contains a truly magnificent collection of musical instruments. The noted pianist Richard Burnett purchased the house in 1970, and it is his personal collection of restored keyboard instruments that can be seen on show today. Harpsichords, clavichords, and chamber organs are displayed in rooms with excellent acoustics, and many recitals are performed there by the owner.

After Goudhurst we took the **A262** then the **A229** northwards to **Staplehurst**. There was once a stronghold here, but today all that can be seen is a tree-covered mound, and nobody seems quite certain as to who built the fortification. For those of you who enjoy following an official tour, the Heart of Kent Country Tour is well worth a try. Approximately 50 miles long, the circular route starts at Teston just outside Maidstone, and takes you through some lovely parts of the county, including marvellous views of the Greensand Ridge and the North Downs. All you have to do is look out for the 'Invicta' sign, a prancing white horse on a brown background. The guide is one of several tours that can be picked up from a Tourist Information Centre in any town. We mention it here because one of the places on the list is Staplehurst, and the Brattle Farm Museum. The museum displays all manner of agricultural implements and gives everyone a chance to see a blacksmith, dairyman and craftsman at work.

Tenterden, on the **A28** is very firmly established as the 'Jewel of the Weald'. This is a far cry from its earliest days when it was known as 'Tenet-ware-den', or 'pig-pasture of the men of Thanet'! Despite the fact that pigs flourished here, sheep inevitably became the more profitable animal to farm on these fertile lands, and the wool trade quickly took off. In 1331, the far-sighted Edward III prohibited the export of unwashed wool and encouraged weavers from Flanders to settle here and bring their dyeing and weaving techiniques to the English. The town of Tenterden and some of its neighbouring villages were to become the most important centres for the manufacture of broadcloth.

Once again, it was thanks to that earlier reclamation of the Romney Marsh that the area provided excellent grazing land, and brought about a profitable trade for the Wealden communities. Just outside Tenterden, Smallhythe and Reading Street provided access to the sea. These two small ports were founded as a means of transporting lumber from the Wealden forests, but by the 14th century, Smallhythe was firmly established as a boat-building centre.

The church of **St Mildred** can be found in the heart of Tenterden, and with its unusual twin doors at the western end, it is quite lovely. Near the church we discovered the Town Hall and the delightful Woolpack Inn, a proud reminder of the town's former days as a cloth trading centre.

Tenterden vineyards hit the headlines in the spring of 1991 when they were proud to offer the public their newest product, pink champagne. It has met with approval from many quarters. The French vineyards have suffered badly with the winter frosts, but the vineyards of Kent seem to go from strength to strength.

Biddenden lies at the end of the **A274** at the junction with the **A262**. If we were to hold our breaths every time we came across a lovely Kentish village, we doubt we would be here writing this today! However, we have no option but to refer to Biddenden as yet another beautiful example of rural Kent at its very best.

Quite apart from the physical attractions of its architecture and picturesque High Street - crammed with pubs, restaurants and antique shops housed in fine half-timbered buildings - there is something else here that has assured the village of a permanent place in the history books. For way back around the beginning of the 12th century, two of its most famous residents were born.

One of the finest of Biddenden's houses can be found just to the north of the village green. This is the **Old Cloth Hall**, a superb six-gabled building which was the centre of the local cloth trade in medieval and Tudor times, and housed the workshops of the weavers. As you enter the village, the road takes you past the beautifully maintained churchyard, and it was while we were exploring the church that we were told about Kypp Cottage and its lovely garden. We could not resist going to look at it.

Run by Zena Grant for over 30 years, **Kypp Cottage** dates back to the late 1800s and was originally two workers' cottages. These were lovingly converted into one by Zena's husband, now sadly deceased. At Kypp Cottage there is no television - conversation is encouraged instead. What a pleasant change. The cottage offers bed and breakfast accommodation in two twin bedrooms and one double bedroom, with a bathroom exclusively for guests. Breakfast is served in the aptly named 'cosy room', with its colour scheme of blue and yellow, a wooden bureau against one wall, and a lovely hand-made dresser against another. A very filling, traditional English breakfast is served, although a lighter meal is available at a discount. The other breakfast room, the garden room, has french windows leading into the garden.

Kypp Cottage, Woolpack Corner, Biddenden, Kent 0580-291480
Map Ref: 4E

Intrigued by the glimpses we had seen of the garden, we decided to explore it properly. Secluded, and enclosed in part, the garden leads from a patio to a marvellous variety of shrubs, trees and herbs. We found it hard to believe that when Zena and her husband first came here the garden was a wilderness, and she had to stand guard over the first tree that she planted, a Tamarisk, to protect it from builders' lorries. Nowadays, the garden is part of the National Gardens Scheme Charitable Trust, which benefits several charities - Zena being keen not to keep her treasures all to herself.

Biddenden Vineyards, 'Little Whatmans' Biddenden, Ashford, Kent
0580-291726 Map Ref :4E

Just one and a half miles away from this lovely old Wealden village is **Biddenden Vineyards**. We found it well signposted as we headed south from Biddenden on the **A262**. Richard Barnes is the General Manager here, and he told us that his family established the

263

Vineyard in 1969. At first it was just one third of an acre, but now it extends for 18 acres on a gentle slope in a sheltered valley. Having made us feel welcome, Richard left us to wander wherever we wished and for as long as we liked.

The varieties planted are mainly of German origin and include Muller Thurgau, Ortega, Riechensteiner and Huxelrube, all of which produce fruity, fragrant wines - as we discovered for ourselves when we stopped at the Vineyard's tasting room. Individual wines are made from each variety of vine. Muller Thurgau, which is a widely planted variety both in Germany and in England, produces a crisp and fruity medium dry white wine with a fragrant nose.

Harvesting usually commences on 20th October, when visitors can see the presses in operation in the winery, which is equipped with modern continental wine-making machinery. It is not until March that the bottling takes place. Every effort is made to ensure that the estate wines produced are of the highest quality.

What could be more natural in such a traditional apple growing area than for Biddenden Vineyards to produce a Cider? Made from the juice of freshly pressed Bramley Apples, the strong still Cider is made either Sweet, Medium or Dry, and is an excellent alternative to wine. They also produce something called Monk's Delight, which is made from cider, pure honey and spices, and is ready to mull. It is a marvellous, warming winter drink, and is ideal for parties and barbecues. If you happen to be at the Vineyard at Christmas time, you will be invited to join the Barnes family for Mulled Cider and Mince Pies while you choose your Christmas wines and ciders.

About three miles to the north-east is **Smarden** , whose name comes from a Saxon word meaning 'butter valley and pasture'. Despite the heavy traffic which it is forced to contend with, the main street is one of the finest in the county, with beautiful old houses on either side. At the western end stands a picturesque group of weatherboarded houses with tiled roofs, and the early-14th century church - known as the 'Barn of Kent' due to its scissors-beam roof with intersecting timbers - stands surrounded by trees. Access to the churchyard is beneath a low arch formed by the overhanging first storey of a delightful timbered building called the Pent-house.

The beauty of **Leeds Castle** is renowned far and wide, and it can be found a few miles north of Sutton Valance between the villages of **Leeds** and **Broomfield** . The setting is breathtaking, and you can catch tantalising glimpses of the castle from the road. The castle stands on two islands on a man-made lake that was created by damming the River Len which flows through the surrounding 500 acres of parkland. It is so easy to wax poetical about each and every castle you visit in Kent, but if we had to recommend one and only one, this would probably be our choice.

Although it was first a Norman stronghold, Leeds Castle became the beautiful palace we see today under Henry VIII. The rooms are full of medieval furnishings, tapestries and fine English and French paintings. Among its many obvious attractions, the one that we especially liked was the Secret Grotto. A new maze has been planted, and once you find your way to the middle of it you will discover this underground retreat. With its statues, caves and splashing waters, it is really quite delightful.

Maidstone developed on the site of an important meeting place. The name means 'the people's stone', and it is likely that a stone marked the site of the 'moot'. The River Medway is the ancient boundary which seperated West and East Kent, and Maidstone was once the capital of the former. On the west of the river lived the 'Kentish Men', while to the east lived the 'Men of Kent'. The distinction is still used proudly by many of the inhabitants of the county today, and no doubt the Women of Kent and the Kentish Women would have something to say about it!

Although Maidstone has been extensively developed in recent years, there are several handsome Elizabethan and Georgian buildings to be found hidden away in the High Street and surrounding backstreets. Maidstone's **Museum and Art Gallery** is housed in the beautiful Chillington Manor House, a splendid Tudor residence which we discovered in St Faith's Street. In the Museum is a chair from nearby Allington Castle which bears a fascinating inscription. Henry VIII is said to have first met Anne Boleyn at Allington, and the chair is a fitting testimony to this man who loved women. The motto reads: '.of this (chay)re iss entytled too one salute from everie ladie thott settes downe in itt - Castell Alynton 1530 - Hen. 8 Rex'. Which, loosely translated, means that gallant Henry could demand a kiss from every woman fortunate (or possibly foolhardy) enough to sit on it!

For another unusual glimpse of the past, you should make your way to the Stables of the former **Archbishop's Palace** in Mill Street. Here you will find a wonderful exhibition of horse-drawn carriages. This grand mixture of private and State carriages makes up one of the finest collections of its kind in England.

Approximately half a mile from the centre of Maidstone is **Roslin Villa**. Run by Mr and Mrs Hawes, Roslin Villa is an interesting Edwardian house. Dating back to 1908, the building has lovely large rooms, some with antique furniture which has been beautifully cared for. Here too is the original pine staircase and many other features, all

Leeds Castle.

in excellent condition. The bedrooms, tastefully decorated in subdued colours, are all en-suite.

Roslin Villa, 11 St Michaels Road, Maidstone, Kent 0622-758301
Map Ref: 3D

The Hawes strive to achieve a peaceful, informal atmosphere, and encourage their guests to feel truly at home. We really enjoy a traditional breakfast, and Roslin Villa did not let us down. We had the choice of an English style cooked breakfast or a selection of fresh fruit. The main dining room was very attractive. Large French windows look out onto the secluded walled garden. Beautiful hand crocheted tablecloths covered the mahogany furniture, and there were lots of dried and fresh flower arrangements. Roslin Villa is ideal for a peaceful stay away from home, and could not be more convenient for touring the Kent countryside and surrounding areas.

The **A229** leads to the picturesque village of **Aylesford**. Having travelled these many miles from Pegwell Bay, the Jutish leaders Hengist and Horsa vanquished the ancient Britons at Aylesford in a great battle in 455 AD. This was frankly unsporting of them, having been invited into Britain by the British ruler Vortigern to help him defend the country from his enemies! Horsa died in the battle, leaving Hengist and his son Aesc to establish the kingdom of the Cantware, or 'men of Kent'. For 300 years, the kingdom was ruled by the descendants of Aesc - the dynasty of the Eskings.

In Aylesford's High Street is the splendid medieval **Friary** built by the Carmelites around the middle of the 13th century. We were surprised to find that this was the first Carmelite order to be founded in Europe. Following the Dissolution, it was rebuilt in 1675, but the main part of the house was destroyed by fire in the 1930s. The Carmelites took over the house in 1949 and have successfully restored it to its former glory.

Aylesford exudes history and charm as it sits demurely on the banks of the Medway. As an important river crossing, it has seen a great deal of activity throughout the centuries. A beautiful five-arched medieval bridge spans the river, and the surrounding jumble of timbered and gabled dwellings ensures that many visitors stop to muse for a while.

Countless photographers and painters, both professional and not so professional, have eagerly attempted to capture the tranquil beauty of Aylesford over the years. Make sure that you have some film in your camera when you visit! Alternatively, you can always make your selection from the wide choice of tasteful photo-postcards available in the local shops.

We returned again to the **A229** and on to **Blue Bell Hill**. The views from here are very beautiful, with the full panorama of the Medway Valley spread before you. These chalky lands have their secrets to divulge, and best among them perhaps are **Kits Coty** and **Little Kits Coty**, which are said to be the finest Neolithic monuments in Europe. The larger monolith is Kits Coty, where three upright sarsens support a cap-stone which is said to weigh around ten ton and stands about eight feet tall. The fact that we can see it so clearly is due to soil erosion, either through the passage of time or possibly because of early ploughing methods.

This area was once a vast Neolithic necropolis or cemetery, and the people of that time must have considered the Medway of great importance. The Romans also left many artifacts for us to find. What was first thought to have been a shrine to Mithras was discovered on the banks of the Medway at Burford, but it is more likely to have been a wine vault. We joined the **A227** heading west through **Culverstone Green**, then turned off the main road and arrived at Trottiscliffe. Kent has more than its fair share of oddly pronounced place names, but 'Trosley' (for the latter) must surely take the biscuit! In the village church are the remains of 22 skeletons of those buried in the Neolithic burial chamber at **Coldrum. The Coldrum Stones**, which are around 4,000 years old, can be found by following a footpath east of the church. The impressive chamber which stands at one end of the circle mound is 13ft in length, and has been built from five sandstone slabs.

Meopham (pronounced 'Meppam') lies due west of here on the **A227**. There is a cricket green at the heart of the village, and a fine black weather-board windmill which is open to the public. South of the village is Trosley Country Park, with over 160 acres of woodland and nature trails in which to lose yourself. If you want to avoid doing this literally, you can purchase guides at the information centre! North of the village is Camer Country Park, which offers a more conservative 46 acres and is perhaps more suitable for a stroll than a hike.

From the **A227** you can reach **Gravesend**, which sits opposite the Tilbury Docks site, trying to pretend that the Thames and all her traffic do not flow past its doorstep! Once the plague ships brought the corpses here from Dartford , which might explain the melancholy air which still hangs over the town today. There are, however, a number of delightful places to winkle out, and one of these is the Ship and Lobster, a pub which straddles the sea wall. A very pleasant time can be had here with a tot of rum!

Making our way to the **A226**, we then dropped south through Shorne and Thong and came to **Owletts**. This 17th century red-brick house is owned by the National Trust and can be found just west of the village of **Cobham** . Sir John de Cobham crops up again here as the founder of Cobham College. Sir John was determined that his ancestors would receive masses, and so founded the college in 1362 to ensure the spiritual well-being of his family.

Cobham Hall can be found at the other end of the village, and is a particularly fine Elizabethan dwelling. It was built in red brick and has domed towers and a picture gallery of 130ft in length. The Hall is now a girl's school, although it can be viewed during the school vacation. One of its earlier inhabitants was Frances, the Duchess of Lennox. This lady may be more familiar to you as the original for 'Britannia', who in happier days graced the back of our coins. Cobham wins top marks for being one of the prettiest villages in England, and this distinction also extends to the countryside surrounding it. It is now recognised as an Area of Outstanding Natural Beauty, as officially decreed by the Countryside Commission. We would certainly not argue with this!

Chatham is the 'workhorse' of the three main Medway towns. Its historic dockyards were first established by Henry VIII, but are now sadly feeling the economic pinch of these modern times. Although the yards are closing, visitors are still encouraged to this area - one of the main attractions being the yard where HMS Victory was built. Other famous Trafalgar ships built here include Revenge and Leviathan, and in the past 400 years over 400 Royal Navy ships have started their life at Chatham Docks.

Visitors can wander through eight museum galleries, and discover Drake's world, the magnificent Covered Slips, and the Ropery - which at a quarter of a mile in length is one of Europe's longest brick buildings. Especially popular is the Wooden Walls exhibition, which opened in 1990 and provides all the atmosphere and smells of a docklands scene in 1758. You follow the youngest apprentice William Crockwell on his first day in the yard, and get a real taste of the shipwright's profession. Other attractions of this 80-acre site include rides on a horse-drawn wagon, craftshops, and a cruise on the

'Kingswear Castle', the last coal-fired paddle steamer in this country. All this and more adds up to a great day out.

For anyone with the slightest leaning towards an interest in things of a military nature, a visit to **The Royal Engineers Museum** at Prince Arthur Road in **Gillingham** should come high on your list of priorities when you are in the Medway area. The Museum is large and modern, with collections relating to the character, lives and work of Britain's soldier engineers from 1066 to 1945. The range of the collection is astonishing, and as we wandered from room to room we saw such diverse items as Chinese court robes and a section on Bailey Bridges.

We learnt that 'Sappers' are like no other corps in the British army - and for that reason, their museum is unlike any normal regimental museum you may have seen. The displays include a richly international collection of decorative arts and ethnographic material, together with a fascinating range of technical and scientific equipment, two memorial rooms of medals including 20 Victoria Crosses, and a variety of uniforms, vehicles and weapons.

The new Royal Engineers Museum gives us an insight into the character, life and work of these men and their families, set against the vivid background of Britain's military, political, domestic and social history. There are relics of famous Sappers, like the magnificent collection of Imperial court dress presented to General Charles Gordon by the Dowager Empress of China in 1864.

In the Museum's newest gallery, opened in 1988, we saw the original working models used to demonstrate the Mulberry plan in the War Office before D-day. Heavy construction plant is seen 'at work', and a section of prototype Bailey is in position. We caught the flavour of the tensions of Home Front life as a Sapper's family blacked out their living room and, wandering into a shattered cellar, we found a young Engineer officer at work on a UXB.

The Royal Engineers Museum, Prince Arthur Road, Gillingham, Kent 0634-844555 (ext. 2312) Map Ref :E2

The Medway towns are of course strongly associated with Charles Dickens, and they crop up time and time again in many of his works. His father took up a clerical appointment in Chatham Dockyard and the Dickens family took up residence at 11 Ordnance Terrace, although the street was not called that in the writer's lifetime. To discover more about the characters and settings of a number of his books, you must set your sights on **Rochester**, and be prepared to do some walking around the town. Here in the grounds of the castle mound with its splendid views, Dickens requested that his body be laid to rest. His wishes were not fulfilled, as he now lies in Westminster Abbey, but his spirit lingers on here in the streets that he loved so much.

Rochester Cathedral is easily overlooked if you have already 'done' Canterbury, but it is a handsome building and should not be ignored. King Ethelbert encouraged his Saxon followers to take up the Christian teachings over 1,300 years ago, and he founded a church on this site. Bishop Gundulph established the Cathedral (and the Castle(some 400 years later. The Cathedral is a beauty, with its magnificent Norman nave, and fine arches leading up and up to the oaken roof. We felt that it was not quite so aloof as Canterbury Cathedral. A memorial plate to Charles Dickens can be found here, and the crypts are definitely worth a visit.

We were now near the northern border of Kent, which officially lies along the middle of the River Thames. Above the three towns is the peninsula known as the Hundred of Hoo, and from **Upnor** just north of Rochester, intrepid visitors can walk around the coastline. This peninsula and the Isle of Grain are relatively unexplored; it is not a picturesque area by any means, but visitors with imagination will no doubt find something of merit! Dominating the High Street of Upper Upnor, the Castle was built in 1559 to protect the ships at Chatham dockyards. Its first and only test was a dismal failure. In 1667, the Dutch fleet sailed up the Medway, the English guns blazed away to little effect, and three English ships were burned. Later used as a naval munitions store, the Castle is still in splendid repair today and has altered little since the end of the 17th century.

The **Hoo Peninsula** can be reached by the **A228**. A high ridge of land runs like a backbone along the middle of this strange area of marshland which lies between the Thames and the Medway. The coastal scenery is of mud-flats and marshes, cabbages and cattle. The views from the top of Northwood Hill Nature Reserve - site of Britain's largest heronry - take in the patchwork of fields and farms, and the ever-present ships that sail up the Medway. With England's strong seafaring history, this part of Kent gives you an insight into some of the people and craft that have protected our nation over the centuries.

The days of heavily-laden barges making their way along the River Medway towards the mouth of the Thames. Many of these beautiful Thames barges were built at the boat yards around the town of **Sittingbourne** . There were once as many as 11 boat yards here, but today only Dolphin Yard remains. Situated on the banks of Milton Creek near Crown Quay Lane, it is now a sailing boat museum. Although rather tucked away, this museum is really worth a visit to see the splendid barges with their ornate paintwork. Lovers of these romantic craft can trace their history and inspect several of them at close quarters.

To the north-west of **Sittingbourne**, you can pick up the **A249** and head north to the twin archway of Kingsferry Bridge, which will take you over the narrow tidal channel of the Swale to Sheppey.

Sheppey, the 'Isle of Sheep', can look most romantic when seen from the mainland, but the reality does not really live up to expectations. Much of the southern part of the island consists of low-lying marshland where sheep have grazed for centuries, and here at Elmley Marshes enthusiastic birdwatchers will find an RSPB reserve where thousands of wildfowl and waders winter and breed. To the south-east is the area known as the **Isle of Harty**, which can only be approached by a narrow, winding road off the **B2231**. Harty consists of little more than a handful of farms and houses, the Ferry Inn (now no longer linked to Faversham by the ferry from which it took its name) and **St Thomas' Church**. Still lit by oil lamps and candles, this charming little medieval church is one of Sheppey's few architectural delights, and is surely one of the most remote in England. If you take the two-mile long path that leads north-east from the church, you will come to the National Nature Reserve at Shell Ness, where a variety of habitats support an abundance of birdlife.

North of the marshes the **B2008** leads north-west to the unprepossessing seaside town of **Minster** , as unlikely a spot as you could imagine to find one of the oldest sites of Christianity in England. Nevertheless, it was here on the highest part of Sheppey that Sexburga, the widow of a Saxon king of Kent, founded a nunnery in the latter part of the 7th century. Sacked by the Danes in 855 AD, Minster Abbey was rebuilt around 1130 and re-established as a priory for Benedictine nuns; and in the 13th century, the parish church was built adjoining the old monastic church or 'Nun's Chapel'. And so it was that from the Middle Ages until the time of the Dissolution of the Monasteries, this ancient place served as a 'double church', the church of St Mary and St Sexburga, with the nuns using the northern half of the building and the parishioners worshipping in the southern section. These two distinct parts were joined by an archway that was pierced in the south wall of the earlier Abbey church. To the west of the church is the 15th century abbey gatehouse, which now houses a museum with exhibits on Sheppey's history.

From Minster, a road leads you round the north-western tip of the island to **Sheerness**, where the River Medway meets the Thames. This was once the site of a naval dockyard, the first of them being surveyed in the 17th century by none other than Samuel Pepys, the famous diarist, who held the position of Secretary of the Admiralty during the reign of Charles II. It was here, too, that HMS Victory docked in 1805, bringing Nelson's body back home after the Battle of Trafalgar. In recent years, Sheerness has developed into a busy container and car-ferry port, and most of the island's prosperity is centred here. Current disputes between the management and the workers have, however, put something of a question mark over the future of the harbour, and it remains to be seen what the outcome will be. Most of the town itself is made up of drab Victorian housing for dockyard workers, and if it has a focal point at all it is the rather odd blue clock tower in the High Street.

Faversham came as a complete surprise to us, for as you make the long approach from Sittingbourne along the **A2** past fields and orchards, there is little to suggest just how charming the heart of Faversham will turn out to be. It still functions as a port today, and boats loaded with timber sail up Faversham Creek, a tributary of the River Swale. It was known as the 'King's port' during the reign of Edward I, and had been highly favoured by English monarchs for centuries. Great war ships were built here, and the medieval warehouses still stand today. At various times in its history, Faversham has traded in everything from oysters to gunpowder, and it has not been adverse to indulging in smuggling activities either! King Stephen established the Abbey of the Holy Saviour here, and is said to be buried in an unmarked tomb in the parish church. Sadly, with the Dissolution of the Monasteries, the Abbey virtually disappeared.

The **Market Place** boasts a splendid **Guildhall**, which sits solidly on an arcade that was built around 1574. Market days still play an important part in the life of the town, and are held on Tuesdays, Fridays and Saturdays beneath the Guildhall. Charming pastel-washed cottages blend in quite comfortably with the elegant Georgian dwellings nearby, and this pleasing mixture of styles adds greatly to the character of the town.

Faversham has over 400 listed buildings; a sure indication that this is a prime historic town. Do remember to take your camera with you, as every time you turn a corner you seem to come across a subject more worthy than the last. For full details of Faversham's fascinating heritage, the best of its buildings and guided walks available around the town, we recommend that you stop off at the Fleur de Lis Heritage Centre in Preston Street, pick up some leaflets and spare a few minutes for a chat with the helpful assistants there.

It is a short journey from Faversham to **Whitstable.** As you wander round the busy commercial harbour (originally the port of Canterbury) and down its old-fashioned streets lined with fisherman's cottages and linked by a fascinating maze of narrow alleyways, you soon begin to realise that this is no seaside resort with traditional seaside entertainments, but very much a working town by, and of, the sea. The best way to get the authentic 'flavour' of Whitstable itself is to take a stroll along the beach behind the Royal Native Oyster Stores and the Pearsons Arms, both of which serve an excellent variety of seafood dishes. From here you can head east towards the harbour or west towards Seasalter, and in both directions you will pass the tightly packed rows of traditional black tarred oyster sheds and weatherboarded cottages that give the town so much of its atmosphere. Unlike any other beach we have ever come across, there are always plenty of activities going on, with fishing boats and barges leaving the harbour, the wet-suit brigade energetically indulging in the host of watersports for which Whitstable is renowned, and hordes of seagulls wheeling and screaming over the piles of discarded oyster shells and crabs.

Over the past few years, a lot of effort has been put into recapturing the charm of bygone Whitstable and preserving its heritage, and full marks must go to the Council and the various local organisations (notably the Whitstable Society and the Whitstable Improvement Trust(who have worked so hard together to make this possible. Residential streets have been closed to traffic at one end to reduce congestion, raised flower beds have been planted in many places, and nice little touches like the wonderful carved benches with maritime themes in Harbour Street and on the beach itself all add to the appearance and interest of the town.

Originally a fishing village which developed a notorious reputation for its smuggling activities, **Herne Bay** is one of the main resorts on the North Kent coast. It was a favourite holiday haven for the Victorian middle-classes, and still retains the quiet atmosphere of that particular era - most of the town having been laid out no more than 150 years ago. The town's main landmark is the **Clock Tower** on the promenade; solid, dependable, and just a little preposterous, it stands 80ft high and was erected in 1836 by a wealthy Londoner, Mrs

Anne Thwaytes, to commemorate Queen Victoria's coronation. Some would say that, technically speaking, it is an architect's nightmare, though those who like their edifices built in the classical style will find it charming enough!

Local guidebooks state that all the traditional pleasures of the seaside are on offer here. Until recently, the old sea wall tended to obscure the view along Central Parade, and if you were under four feet tall or travelling by car, you could have been excused for doubting that the sea was just a few feet away!

From the promenade of Herne Bay, and from many other parts of the coast and certain stretches of the Thanet Way, your eyes will be drawn again and again to the distinctive silhouette of **Reculver Towers**, standing proud above the rocky beach at **Reculver** like a pair of giant binoculars. To reach them, follow the signs from Herne Bay through the largely unremarkable suburb of **Beltinge** until you come to **Hillborough** . On your right, a rather charming listed thatched cottage sits on an 'island' opposite the local primary school and seems to shudder visibly as buses edge their bulk around it. A little further on, Reculver Church stands on the brow of the hill which winds down to Reculver.

As a major historic site, Reculver has of course been a happy hunting ground for archaeologists for many years. A grim discovery was made during excavations in the 1960s, when several tiny skeletons were found not far from the Towers. One shudders to dwell on the grisly events which led to their demise some time in Reculver's ancient past, but it is generally believed that these babies were buried alive as human sacrifices. This perhaps lends support to the old legend that local residents are kept awake on stormy nights by the pitiful crying of infants.

To the east of the Towers, you can walk or cycle along the sea wall all the way to **Minnis Bay**, while for the less energetic there is a pleasant walk along the clifftops leading west from Reculver to **Bishopstone Glen**. It was not so long ago that sailing barges could be seen on the horizon, making their passage across the North Sea, and nowadays you will often spot the dark outline of tankers or the impossible bulk of a car-ferry, looking far too large and unwieldy to stay afloat. When you reach the old lifeguard station up on the cliffs (now no longer in use), you can enjoy a spectacular 360-degree view of the landscape. From here, you will see Reculver Towers in the near distance, the towns of Birchington and Margate beyond, the 'pepper pots' of the power station at Richborough, the defunct and sail-less windmill on the hill above Brook Farm, and open fields stretching away to the horizon, broken only by the railway and the silent stream of traffic on the Thanet Way. Ahead of you lies Herne Bay, with the lonely remains of its pier far out at sea.

Bishopstone Glen is a good place to head for if you want to explore the gulley that leads through the cliffs, cut by the little stream which has forced its way through the sand and clay over the years. We well remember visiting this spot as children and sliding down the crumbling sandy cliffs, now dotted with signs warning youngsters against that pleasurable activity! The cliffs continue to change their shape with the passage of time, losing a bit more of their fabric to the elements each year. Just to the west of the lifeguard station, the clifftop path takes you right to the very edge, and if you look carefully you may notice a few odd bricks jutting out from the ground. These are all that now remain of a pair of semi-detached cottages which were used for target practice by the RAF during the war, the remnants of which tumbled down to the beach years ago.

Making our way back to Herne Bay, we then took the coast road heading west to **Swalecliffe** and the quiet resort of **Tankerton**. Tankerton has some fine hotels looking out over the sea, while the steep and grassy Tankerton Slopes roll down to the bathing huts that line the promenade below. From the beach, a favourite haunt for watersports enthusiasts, you can walk along the long shingle bank that juts out into the sea. Known as The Street, more than half a mile of its length is exposed at low tide, and you will find it a rich picking ground for shells and a vast assortment of marine creatures. However, visitors should beware of the dangers of being suddenly cut off by the tide, and on no account should you attempt to swim either off or near The Street, for its unpredictable currents can be deadly.

It is reputed that the artist Turner used to come to Tankerton especially to paint the sunsets. As we stood in the garden of Marine Lodge Guest House , we understood why. The view is breathtaking as the sun sets over Tankerton Downs and the distant Isle of Sheppey, with every colour imaginable being drawn out of land and sea by the sinking sun.

Marine Lodge Guest House, 82 Marine Parade, Tankerton, Kent
CT5 2BA 0227-273707 Map Ref : 1G

Christine Tilley who owns and runs **Marine Lodge** was previously a computer lecturer, and is therefore used to dealing with people and has a natural ability to make her guests feel both welcome and at ease. The guest house has three bedrooms, one of which is en-suite and one with its own shower. Every room has tea and coffee making facilities, colour TV, and the most superb sea views. Downstairs in the heated conservatory, which is also used as the dining room, a vine grows quite profusely.

Christine told us that she has often seen guests sampling the grapes, which are sweet and succulent. Perhaps it had something to do with the close proximity of the sea, but we found that our appetites were excellent. This was just as well, for in addition to being a wonderful hostess, Christine is also a superb cook. So good, in fact, that she gives cookery lessons at nearby Whitstable and Rochester. Dinner was a very pleasant surprise. Every dish was complementary to the next; nicely presented and cooked to perfection. Our only complaint was the size of the portions, which we simply could not manage.

If you carry on along Marine Parade and down Tower Hill, a delightful vista opens up to your right; on a bright summer's day when the sea takes on an uncharacteristic shade of blue, the tree-framed view across Whitstable Bay to the Isle of Sheppey almost puts you in mind of a clifftop setting overlooking a hidden Devon cove. To your left are the gardens of **Whitstable Castle**, otherwise known as Tankerton Tower, originally built as an octagonal 'folly tower' by Charles Pearson in 1792 and added to extensively 28 years later by his son. More recently it housed the old district council offices, and it is currently used as a Community Centre.

Travelling south west out of Whitstable and Herne Bay, past Canterbury brought us to **Harbledown**, once renowned as the last place for pilgrims to rest before making their way into Canterbury. Many of them would have stopped off here to visit **St Nicholas's Hospital for Lepers**, founded by Archbishop Lanfranc in 1084, for the dubious pleasure of kissing its prized relic - one of Thomas Becket's shoes! Below the hospital, now converted into almshouses, there is a spring which is known locally as the Black Prince's Well. Its waters were said to have had great healing properties, and the Prince was apparently so convinced of this that he imbibed a flaskful every day.

The villages of **Chartham** and **Chartham Hatch** lie opposite each other on either side of the A28, mid-way between Chilham and Canterbury. To the south of the road, Chartham sprawls lazily on the well-wooded slopes of Chartham Downs - the road over the Downs providing one of the most scenic routes in the county. The massive church once belonged to the monks of Christ Church, Canterbury, and boasts the oldest set of bells in Kent. In front of the church is the larger of Chartham's two village greens; most of the village houses being centred around the small triangular green behind it. There has been a paper mill by the Stour at Chartham for over 200 years, and today's mill turns out vast quantities of tracing paper.

Heading west from the village on the **A28** you will come to **Chilham** - to our minds one of the most attractive villages in Kent. Unfortunately, the same opinion is shared by the thousands of other tourists who visit the village during the summer, and it can get somewhat overcrowded!

The home of Viscount Massereene and Ferrard, **Chilham Castle** is a red-brick Jacobean mansion which was built in 1616 for Sir Dudley Digges, Master of the Rolls in the reign of James I. Thought to have been designed by Inigo Jones, the house has a most unusual ground plan, forming five sides of a hexagon around a central courtyard. The original medieval castle, built by Henry II and occupying an important defensive position on this hilltop site overlooking a bend in the River Stour, was pulled down for building materials long ago. However, the octagonal keep and inner bailey of this Norman castle still stand and can be found hidden away at the back of the house. Evidence of Saxon defences have also been found here, and some believe that there may even have been a fort on the site before the Roman occupation.

Chilham Castle is perhaps best known for its regular jousting tournaments, and flying displays featuring a fine collection of birds of prey including falcons, eagles, hawks and owls. Other special events throughout the year could include everything from Sealed Knot battles and horse trials, to open air concerts and the Kent Festival of Transport.

Chilham's charming village square is a feast of lovely old Tudor and Jacobean half-timbered houses and inns - the houses for the most part having been converted into tearooms and shops - with the west tower of St Mary's Church rising at one end and completely dominating the scene. If there is a price to pay for living in such a picturesque place, it is the sheer number of people who flock to Chilham looking for a piece of 'olde worlde' charm. The tiny streets become chock-a-block in summer, cars stand bumper-to-bumper in the square, and apart from the publicans and shopkeepers, the residents must breathe a sigh of relief when the autumn months draw near, bringing a slower pace to the village.

Heading east, you will pass through **Sheldwich** on the **A251**.

Chilham Castle.

All lie in a peaceful oasis between the busy M2 and M20 motorways, in an area which has been designated a place of natural beauty.

Some four miles south of Sheldwich on the **A251**, we came to **Challock** (pronounced 'Cholluck') on the crossroads with the **A252**. This village's recorded history dates back to the late 13th century, and its Saxon name means 'an enclosure for calves'. Had we arrived before the coming of the plague, we would have had to look a mile or two further afield, as the village originally grew up around its church, and moved to its present site after that grim visitation.

The **Church of Saints Cosmas and Damian** is not easy to find, but it is certainly worth making the effort to do so. If you continue on the **A251** over the crossroads as if you were heading for Ashford, then turn right at the sign for The Chequers Inn, you will come to Church Lane. Turn left here, and several hundred yards down the lane you will come to Coombs Farm on the right, where you can pick up the key to the church. From the farm we continued along the beautiful tree-lined lane, which drops gradually down a long hill until it eventually comes to a dead end at the bottom. On the left is the church, set in as picturesque a spot as you could wish for.

The real treasure is inside, for here you will find a series of delightful murals which were painted in 1953. Two students of the Royal Academy, Miss Rosemary Aldridge and Miss Doreen Lister, executed the murals in the chapel as part of a competition. They depict scenes from agriculture, fishing and falconry, as well as episodes in the lives of the patron saints and various New Testament scenes.

Ashford, reached by returning to the A28 still boasts some fine Georgian houses, and the earliest parts of the splendid parish church date back to the 15th century. The great central tower rises above the town, each of its four lofty pinnacles crowned by a golden weathervane shaped like an arrow. Ashford's central location makes it one of the most convenient touring centres in the county; and it was in this bustling town that we found a haven for visitors that seems to resist change and gives you the chance to take a breather from your busy schedule in true comfort. It is a convenient spot altogether: you can get to Folkestone within 15 minutes, and Hythe and New Romney in 20 minutes. **Leeds Castle** is also near by, as is **Chatham Historic Dockyards** and **Chilham Castle**.

At Ashford we ended this part of our journey to begin the next and final chapter of our tour of the South East of England.

South and East Kent.

From Canterbury to the Kent Coast.

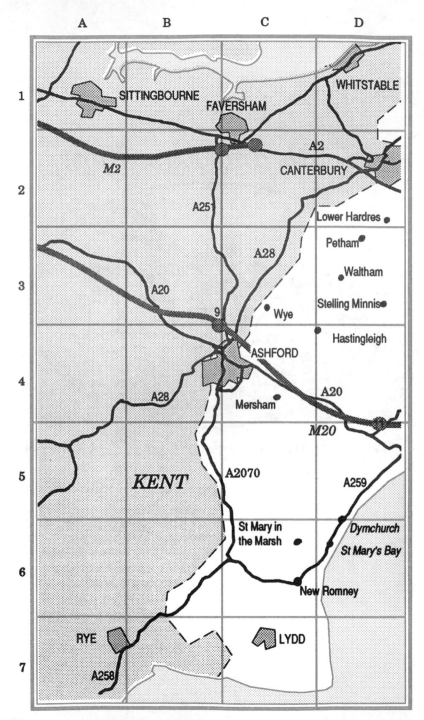

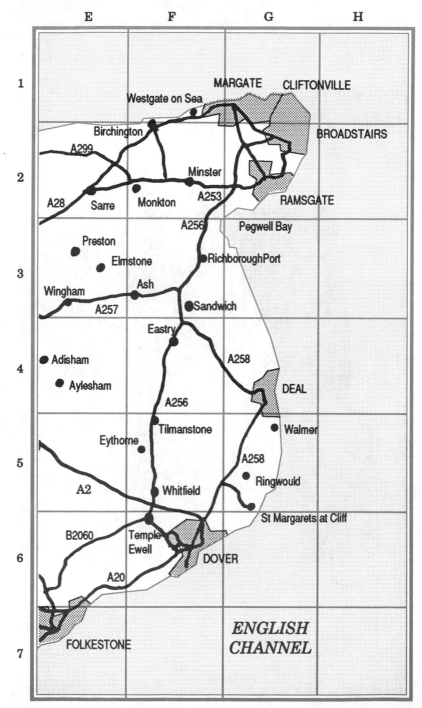

Seven Sisters, Dover.

CHAPTER EIGHT

South and East Kent.

From Canterbury to the Kent Coast.

The final part of our journey begins in **Canterbury**, one of the loveliest of England's Cathedral cities. Above the walled city soars the **Cathedral**. Its highlights include the central Bell Harry Tower designed by William Westall in the late-15th century; Henry Yevele's lofty nave with its magnificent columns; the Trinity Chapel, which houses the splendid tomb of Edward the Black Prince on the south side, and the canopied tomb and alabaster effigies of Henry IV and his queen on the north side; the great north window; and the spectacular Crypt, the largest of any ecclesiastical building in the world.

The Cathedral was founded just after 597 AD by St Augustine after his arrival from Rome. Before his death some seven years later, he had converted large numbers of the native Saxons to Christianity, and Canterbury became the seat of the Mother Church of the Anglicans. Today, the Archbishops of the Cathedral are the Primates of All England, attending all royal functions, and the present incumbent, Dr. George Carey, is the 103rd Archbishop of Canterbury. Nothing now remains of the original, pre-Conquest buildings; the present Cathedral having been constructed between 1071 and 1500.

This is the Cathedral that witnessed the treacherous murder of Archbishop Thomas Becket on its steps, slayed by Henry II's knights. The simple stone marking the spot states that Becket 'died here Tuesday 29th December 1170'. Although the knights apparently 'misinterpreted' the King's wishes, the horror has rung down the centuries, and as you walk through the hushed Cathedral this monstrous act is never far from your mind. A penitent Henry, full of remorse for the death of his former friend, came later as a pilgrim to Becket's shrine. Becket's magnificent tomb was destroyed during the Dissolution of the Monasteries in 1538, but visitors to the Cathedral can still see the Altar of the Swordpoint, commemorating the spot where the sword of one of his assassins shattered on the stone floor.

Canterbury is a compact city, and a short walk in any direction will bring you into contact with some part of its history. As for shopping, there can't be many cities in England that offer greater variety. Specialist shops of every kind stand side by side with all the familiar high street names (many of these can be found in the attractive covered Marlowe Arcade in St Margaret's Street), and surprisingly, neither look out of place in their mediaeval surroundings. However, if you can tear your gaze away from the shop windows every once in a while to look up above street level, you will find just as much to delight the eye there too; for although Canterbury's foremost architectural gems are well marked and easy to spot, many surprises crop up in unexpected places and, like the proverbial two-thirds of the iceberg, will elude the unobservant sightseer altogether. A good example of this is the glorious 'chequer-board' effect above the entrance to the Beaney Institute at the end of the High Street, a splendidly ornate Victorian building which houses the public library, the **Royal Museum and Art Gallery**, and the **Buffs Regimental Museum**.

From the bridge you can see the ducking-stool once used to immerse all manner of miscreants - as the sign implicitly warns: 'Unfaithful Wives beware; Butchers Bakers Brewers Apothecaries and all who give short measure'. The bridge is now a favourite haunt for a motley collection of buskers, who go down well with passing tourists but are not quite so popular with the captive audience of local traders who have become intimately familiar with the repertoire! Opposite The Weavers' you can descend a flight of stone steps below street level to explore the vaults of the 12th century Eastbridge Hospital, founded in 1180 by Edward Fitzodbold as a hostel for poor pilgrims visiting St Thomas' tomb.

The Poor Priests' Hospital in Stour Street dates back to the 14th century and was used as an almshouse for elderly clergy. It now houses the award-winning Canterbury Heritage museum, which tells the story of the city from Roman times to the present day, making effective use of the latest computer, hologram and audio-visual technology. Highlights include an exciting video on the story of Thomas Becket, made by local celebrity and master-pupeteer Oliver Postgate (remember 'Pogles Wood' and 'The Clangers'?); an audio-visual presentation on Canterbury during the Blitz; and displays and memorabilia concerning Mary Tourtel, the creator of Rupert Bear, who was born at 52 Palace Street in 1874.

Those who like their history to be liberally spiced with fun should also make a point of visiting The Canterbury Tales, which is housed in a mediaeval church in St Margaret's Street. Here you can enjoy superb re-creations of scenes from life in the Middle Ages, all based on Chaucer's famous stories. The minute attention to detail which has been lavished on the models and their clothing and utensils is admirable, and the authentic sounds and smells of life in the 14th century abound. There is also a coffee shop and an excellent gift shop, and commentaries in several European languages are available.

Canterbury is also renowned as a centre for the arts, the main event being the annual Canterbury Festival in autumn, when a varied programme of music, drama, dance, film, exhibitions, walks, talks and community events takes place. Among the many places which play host to these events are the Gulbenkian Theatre at the University of Kent (reached by heading west from the city centre along St Dunstan's Street and London Road), and Canterbury's major theatrical venue, the **Marlowe Theatre**, re-located in recent years to The Friars, off St Peter's Street.

This is named after the playwright Christopher Marlowe, who was born in Canterbury in 1564. A contemporary of Shakespeare (who he most probably knew(his works include 'Dr. Faustus' and 'Tamurlane the Great'. He attended the King's School to the north of Mint Yard in the Cathedral precincts (whose Norman staircase is, incidentally, one of the most famous examples of Norman architecture in England), then went up to Benet) now Corpus Christi(College at Cambridge. As a friend of Sir Francis Walsingham, Elizabeth I's Secretary of State, he supplemented his literary career by taking an active role as a spy. At only 29 years of age, he was stabbed to death in Deptford following what was officially referred to as a tavern brawl, but was more likely to have been a deliberately planned assassination. He is buried at the church of St Nicholas, and church records simply state: 'Christopher Marlowe, slain by ffrancis Archer 1 June 1593'.

Alicante Guest House, 4 Roper Road, Canterbury, Kent
0227-766277 Map Ref :2D

Only two minutes walk from the city centre, the **Alicante Guest House** in Roper Road is a pleasant place to stay. It is a late-Victorian house with a garden which is bounded by Roper Wall which belongs to the Roper family whose daughter married Thomas More. The house has six bedrooms, one of which is en-suite, and Mr. and Mrs. Stroud are very happy to have children in the house. Cots are provided and baby sitting is available if you need it. It is a friendly house where superb breakfasts are served, and if you stay there in winter there are some excellent reduced rates.

St Stephens Guest House at 100 St Stephens Road used to be called 'Tudor Cottage', and when you see the beautiful timbered frontage you will know why. There are 10 guest rooms, all of which have been re-decorated and refurbished. Every room is bright and airy. New beds, colour TV and wash hand basins have been installed for extra comfort. A cup of tea or coffee is always available on request, so do please ask because if there is anything that you want, Val or Robin will always endeavour to oblige. Staying here is like staying with old friends. Everyone is instantly on first name terms and you will be made to feel relaxed and welcome the minute you arrive.

Val is an accomplished and imaginative cook and strongly believes in good honest English fare for her guests. The roast lamb and fresh vegetables followed by apple pie and cream were superb. If you have special dietary needs, please let her know in advance so that she can cater for you.

St Stephens Guest House, 100 St Stephens Road, Canterbury, Kent CT2 7JL 0227-462167 Map Ref :2D

As you would expect from such a popular tourist destination, Canterbury is also blessed with an excellent choice of restaurants and pubs. Space does not allow us to feature all those we would like to mention, so we will have to be content with pointing you in the direction of one of each, and leave you to discover alternatives for yourself!

Wandering through the streets to the east of the city, we found ourselves in Church Street, named after Saint Paul's Church, where, opposite the picturesque remains of St Augustine's Abbey (the oldest Anglo-Saxon abbey in England).

This eastern part of the city was much rebuilt after the Second World War, roughly a third of the old city of Canterbury having been destroyed by enemy bombs during the Blitz. Ironically, some good did come of this terrible destruction, for when the rubble was cleared away the ancient foundations of the city were revealed, allowing archaeologists to piece together the history of its people from the Stone Age through to the Roman occupation and mediaeval times.

Before we move on from Canterbury to the surrounding villages, it is worth pointing out one of the most over-looked of all the city's monuments, **Canterbury Castle**.The castle occupies a site to the south of the city near the Wincheap roundabout, and perhaps drivers on the busy Rheims Way ring road could be forgiven for thinking that it is simply a more elaborate part of the ancient City Wall. Nevertheless, a castle it is, and here it has stood for some 900 years. William the Conqueror had the original motte-and-bailey castle built not long after the Battle of Hastings, and the site of this was just to the east of the present castle in what is now the Dane John Gardens. The mound of this Norman 'donjon' survives today within the Dane John mound.

The 'new' castle would have been built sometime between 1080 and 1100, and is first referred to in the Domesday Book of 1086. It would have consisted originally of a three-storied, rectangular keep with 9ft thick walls, surrounded by an outer wall with a tower at each angle and a defensive ditch - the whole enclosure covering an area of some four and a half acres in all. The Castle became the county gaol in the 11th century and served in that capacity for the next 400 years or so. It had fallen into complete ruin by the end of the 18th century, at which time the outer wall was demolished and the ditch filled in. Attempts were made to pull down the keep itself in 1817, but this was only partially successful; the Castle was built of sterner stuff than the demolition crew could handle, and only the top storey would yield to the hammer. The keep was then purchased by the Gas, Light and Coke Company, who used it first to store water-pumping machinery, and ultimately as a glorified coal bin!

Such degradations happily came to an end in 1928, when Canterbury Castle was declared an historic monument and a long-overdue programme of preservation began. If you would like to see the remains of the keep for yourself and discover more about the Castle's history, it can be approached by continuing down Stour Street from Canterbury Heritage, or down St Margaret's Street from the Information Centre and into Castle Street. Alternatively, you can take the footpath walk from the bus station through the Dane John Gardens and see the original castle site at the same time - as well as the Marlowe Memorial, which is also in the Gardens.

Heading out of Canterbury along the **A2**, the countryside around **Adisham** is quite lovely with its rolling wooded hills, and travellers in this area would once have traversed the Pilgrims' Way. Although it was only a track it was nevertheless well trod, and the earliest known church at Adisham was founded in 616 AD. The present church was built in the 13th century, and a large statue of Thomas Becket cast in bronze can be seen outside the west door. We also discovered some beautiful painted woodwork here, which was originally made for Canterbury Cathedral.

An uncommon sight in this part of Kent is that of a colliery works, but at **Aylesham** we had the opportunity to see a 'modern' mining village. Established in the 1920s for the workers of the Snowdown Colliery, it was a fairly successful attempt to 'create' a village which would more or less blend in with its surroundings.

Turnung north on the **B2046**, however, we then discovered **Wingham** , which is by contrast a lovely traditional Kentish village. The character of Wingham is greatly enhanced by the beautiful trees that line its T-shaped High Street. Indeed, the approach is through richly wooded hill country and it was quite a surprise when we suddenly came upon the village, as we were not expecting to see it just there! The through road carries fairly heavy traffic to Sandwich on the coast, but this mediaeval village manages to retain its abundant supply of charm. The old market square has long since gone, but on its site you will find a number of tea rooms and antique shops. The Red Lion Inn, a massive 13th century building, not only provides the locals with entertainment and refreshment, but also served as the local courtroom for many years.

Here you will find that the **Knowlton Court Estate** has much to offer. There are five delightful self-catering cottages available on the estate, each one with its own particular charm. They are extremely well-equipped, with heating and TV. In fact, all you will need to provide is bed linen and towels, and even bed linen can be hired if you would prefer not to bring your own.

The cottages are scattered round the farm, and one thing you can be sure of is that you will have total privacy. If you want some fantastic shops, then Canterbury is no distance at all, and you can combine shopping with visiting some of the wonderful places in this ancient city. Knowlton Court is well-placed for almost anywhere you may want to go in the Kent and Sussex area.

Knowlton Court, Wingham, Kent 0304 617344 Map Ref :3E

Two miles to the north of Wingham is the village of **Preston** , which has an odd legend associated with it. Apparently, buried beneath the pond that lies between Preston Court and the Wingham road is a palace. It was believed to have been the home of one of Kent's wealthiest landowners during the 14th century, Juliana de Leybourne, the 'Infanta of Kent'. Although there are no hard facts to substantiate the theory, lost villages, castles and palaces do tug at the romantic side of our natures, and we had no wish to find any evidence to the contrary. This lovely setting certainly gets its fair share of visitors, perhaps hoping to catch a glimpse of turrets in the waters!

Two miles to the north-east, over the River Stour and just south of the **A253**, we came to the farming village of **Monkton** . This once boasted two churches, but today only one remains, and outside is one of the few surviving village stocks in the county. Traces of Anglo-Saxon settlement have been found here in the form of pottery, glassware and bones, and if you wish to rest your own weary bones.

At the junction of the **A299** and **A253** is the **Monkton Nature Reserve**, where you will find a series of nature trails, an exhibition on local wildlife and an artificial bat cave. The reserve is open daily from 10.00am to 4.00pm throughout the year, and also features a Field Study Centre, a gift shop and a picnic area.

West of here, where the **A253** joins the **A28**, we passed through the small village of **Sarre**. This was once one of the River Wantsum ports, but it is now several miles from the coast. Here, the Wantsum is a watery shadow of its former self and is really not much more than a stream, but we will meet it later on in other chapters and talk more about its 'glory days' then. The Crown Inn at Sarre was frequented by that famous 19th century chronicler, Charles Dickens. Much further back in history, the village was an important site for Anglo-Saxon burials, and excavations in the area have revealed dice, coins, counters and beads, together with other artifacts.

While we were in the town, we were amazed to discover that All Saint's churchyard can claim no less a celebrity than the artist Dante Gabriel Rossetti as one of its 'residents'. He died here in 1882, and a stained glass window in the church is dedicated to the artist. His teacher, Ford Madox Brown, carved the stone which marks his grave.

The shoreline at **Birchington**, four miles north-east of Sarre on the **A28**, (for although we may have neglected to mention it, we are indeed now on the coast!) consists of low chalk cliffs protected from the North Sea by a huge sea wall. Rocky patches of beach are divided by four sandy bays with safe swimming in three of them; the largest is Minnis Bay (from where you can set off on foot or bicycle and walk or ride all the way along the sea wall to Reculver, some four miles to the west) though more attractive and quieter is Epple Bay, accessible by steps or ramp and overlooked by steeper cliffs than its neighbours.

From Birchington, we continued further round the coast on the A28 to neighbouring **Westgate-on-Sea**. We referred to Birchington as a town and we are tempted to call Westgate the same, but strictly speaking, they are both suburbs of **Margate**. Residents of both places will probably take umbrage at this description too, claiming that each has its own individual character. That may well be so, but we will make the excuse that this is not immediately apparent to the tourist who is simply passing through; you probably need to stay there for a day or two to begin to appreciate such distinctions. Perhaps we should offer our apologies and agree to refer to both Birchington and Westgate as resorts, and hope that this doesn't offend anyone!

Besides its two beaches at Westgate Bay and St Mildred's Bay, both with safe bathing areas and family facilities, Westgate is also renowned for its green, open spaces and formal gardens; including a lovely sunken garden on the promontory that separates it from Margate proper.

At the end of the A28 we arrived in **Margate**, a town that fulfills most people's expectations of the typical English seaside resort. Long sweeping stretches of golden sand, promenades, amusement arcades, candyfloss and fun fairs; you either love it or hate it. But Margate undoubtedly exerts a fascination on the young and old alike, and many of the world's most famous writers have had complimentary things to say about it. In bygone days, the resort was a Mecca for the day-tripper from London (greatly assisted by excellent water-transport along the River Thames), and there are still those faithful patrons who come back year after year. The covered bathing machine was invented in Margate in 1753 by a Quaker and glovemaker called Benjamin Beale.

In contrast to more modern attractions, you can also enjoy a number of places of interest of a more historic nature. One of these is the **Tudor House** in King Street, which is thought to be the oldest building of its kind in the county. It was built in the early-16th century during the reign of Henry VIII, and now contains an exhibition on the human occupation of Thanet from earliest times through to the end of the Tudor period. Half a mile inland on Nash Road is the mediaeval Salmestone Grange, originally a grange or farm of St Augustine's Abbey at Canterbury, and arguably the best-preserved example of a monastic grange in England. The chapel, crypt and kitchen are all open to the public. Along St Peter's Footpath, off College Road, you can also visit Drapers Windmill on Sunday afternoons from late-May to mid-September and on Thursday evenings in July and August. This is a black smock windmill built sometime around 1840, now restored to full working order by the Drapers Windmill Trust.

Margate also has two truly 'hidden' treasures, to be found within a few hundred yards of each other at the eastern end of town. Firstly, there are the **Margate Caves** with their entrance in Northdown Road; enormous caverns which were cut from the chalk cliffs over 1,000 years ago. Used variously as a refuge, a mediaeval dungeon and church, and a hiding place for smugglers and their contraband, the Caves are open daily throughout the summer.

Nearby, off Northdown Road on Grotto Hill, you will find the **Shell Grotto**. Do not be misled by the name, which may perhaps conjure up visions of a rather twee collection of shell-studded jewellry boxes, housed in somebody's cellar. In fact, the grotto is thought to have pagan origins, and the underground passages and chamber have been skilfully decorated with literally millions of seashells.

Cliftonville, another suburb of Margate and situated at the eastern end of town, stands high on a plateau above the beach, its buildings centred around a large, rectangular public garden, known somewhat confusingly as The Oval.

Clifton Lodge was originally a handsome, Edwardian semi-detached house, which in 1986 was completely refurbished and brought up to date to become one of the finest guest houses in Cliftonville. The house has two single, two double and two twin-bedded rooms. Each has its own bathroom and colour television, and hair dryers, tea and coffee making facilities and alarm clock/radios are also supplied. An excellent breakfast is served with a variety of dishes, and the evening meal, which is at 7.00pm, is always well-presented and uses as much fresh produce as possible.

The standard at Clifton Lodge is very high and the prices extremely competitive. The house is just 175 yards from the cliff edge, where there are stairs and a lift to the beach below. Just by the house are the excellent St George's Lawns bowling greens and the new David Bryant Bowls Centre, which gives a lot of enjoyment to many people and is open all the year round.

Clifton Lodge, 15 Norfolk Road, Cliftonville, Kent CT9 2HU
0843-226456 Map Ref : 1G

While you are in Cliftonville, also be sure to visit the **Palm Bay Aquarium** with its colourful collection of marine life, tropical and coldwater fish, insects and reptiles. It is possible for walkers to take the clifftop footpaths from Cliftonville all the way around Palm Bay and Foreness Point to neighbouring Kingsgate, where the impressive battlements of the Victorian Kingsgate Castle look out across picturesque Kingsgate Bay. However, if like us you are tied (figuratively speaking) to your car, you will be forced to head almost a mile inland on the **B2052** before you arrive back at the coast, where the road will then lead you through Kingsgate and on to the elegant seaside town of **Broadstairs.**

Broadstairs is probably best known for its associations with Charles Dickens, and those of you who have come in search of Bleak House will find it high up on the cliffs at the northern end of town, overlooking the popular family beach at Viking Bay. The sands of the little harbour here (described by Dickens as 'rare good sands') are partly protected by a small 16th century pier, a replacement for one built during the reign of Henry VIII.

Other famous people associated with the town include Sir Edward Heath, who was born here in 1916, and another famous sailor, Sir Alec Rose, who lived here for many years. Frank Richards, the creator of that now decidedly 'politically incorrect' character, Billy Bunter, also lived in the town, as did John Buchan, whose popular spy

294

thriller, 'The Thirty-Nine Steps', would become an even more popular film. He wrote the story at a house called St Cuby on Cliff Promenade, and the staircase that gave him his inspiration still stands opposite the house, its 78 steps halved by Buchan to make a better title. Another native of Broadstairs was that eminent Victorian railway engineer, Thomas Russell Crampton.

Opposite the railway station you will find the **Crampton Tower**, a railway museum dedicated to his life and work, with exhibits of his blueprints, drawings and photographs. The Broadstairs Stagecoach is also on display, and there is a superb 00 guage model railway for all you enthusiasts to enjoy.

Leaving Broadstairs on the **Ramsgate Road**, we soon discovered a unique place to drop in for a drink and see some unusual sights. Have you ever seen a three-legged pig? No, neither have we, but a lot of people did at **The Brown Jug** near Dumpton , many years ago. Myrna and Jennifer, who have run this popular tavern since 1971, showed us many of the surviving postcards. It seems that the pig was very popular and that people travelled far to see it.

The Brown Jug Inn, Dumpton Park, Ramsgate Road, Nr Broadstairs, Kent 0843-862788 Map Ref :2G

Myrna and Jennifer were offered the unique drinking house on the death of their mother, who had held the license since 1960. It has remained relatively unchanged over the years, as the sisters shun modernisation for the mere sake of change. The quiz team is very high up in the league; the sheer volume of reference books in the bar amazed us and kept us very interested. As you can imagine, judging by the name, there is a collection of jugs here that is second to none. In fact, it grew so large that the sisters had to stop collecting, as there was simply no more space.

Amongst the floral prints, beamed walls and many plants, is a collection of bric-a-brac the like of which never seen before. This includes the clock, an old Cobbs barrel that pours water on the hour and chimes the tune 'Little Brown Jug'. To its credit The Brown Jug is the only pub in England to sell reading glasses!

Along the coast is **Ramsgate**, one of our favourite towns on the south-east coast. Its ancient origins were as a small fishing village, and this it continued to be until the harbour was built in 1749. In 1822 George IV landed here (the obelisk on the East Pier commemorates this historic event), and since that time it has adopted the title of 'Royal Harbour'. By the end of the 19th century, its fishing fleet had grown to become the largest of any port on the south coast of England, and even though the fishing industry fell into decline at the beginning of the First World War and the future of the harbour began to look uncertain, it was soon to enjoy a brief moment of glory that would earn it a permanent place in the history books. This was in 1940, when over 40,000 British troops evacuated from Dunkirk were landed here, snatched from the jaws of death by the brave armada of 'Little Ships'. The parish church of St George commemorates this important episode in Ramsgate's and England's history with a special stained glass window.

West of the harbour, in the old **West Cliff Hall** above the Sally Line ferry terminal, you will find the **Motor Museum**, where a fascinating range of veteran and vintage cars and motorcycles from Edwardian times to the 1950s are on display. Many famous marques are represented, and there are well over 100 exhibits to enjoy.

As for evening entertainment, you will find that Ramsgate has a wide selection of pubs, clubs and restaurants to choose from, and quality shows can be enjoyed at the Granville Theatre.

Heading south from **Ramsgate** on the **A256** coast road takes you round the great curve of Pegwell Bay, a broad, sheltered bay at the mouth of the Stour, its sand dunes and mudflats home to many species of wading birds and migrating butterflies. Above the old hovercraft terminal you will pass the unlikely sight of a full-sized replica Viking longship called the Hugin, complete with dragon's head prow, coloured shields and oars. This striking vessel was sailed across the Channel in 1949 by a crew of 20th century Danish 'warriors' (they actually landed at Viking Bay at Broadstairs), to commemorate the 1,500th anniversary of an even more historic event.

If you follow the lanes inland from here across the marshes you will come to **Minster** , one of the earliest centres of Christianity in Kent, where St Mary's Church occupies the site of a nunnery founded in 669 AD by Domneva. By 741 AD, the growth of the community necessitated a move to more spacious accommodation, and the new Abbey was built on its present site with St Mildred, Domneva's daughter, as Abbess. From then on, the history of the Abbey is a turbulent one: it was sacked by the Danes at the end of the 10th century, then became a part of St Augustine's Abbey in Canterbury and was rebuilt; in 1085 it was partly destroyed again by the Normans, and after the Dissolution of the Monasteries in 1538 it fell into complete decay. Its fortunes changed once more in 1937, when a group of Benedictine nuns returned to the Abbey and re-established it; the order is still there today and has opened its doors to the public.

Back on the **A256**, we continued heading south along the coast, past the massive cooling towers of Richborough power station, and on to **Richborough   Port** . Here in 1916, at the 'neck' of a great horeshoe-shaped bend in the River Stour, a modern port was built to ship men and munitions to France during the First World War. It was used again during the Second World War to construct a section of the Mulberry dock, which, when completed, was then towed across the Channel to Normandy.

It was about 285 AD that the Romans built the present Richborough Castle, close to the point where the **A256** now crosses the Stour, and the ruins of the massive outer wall are among the most impressive Roman remains left standing in Britain today. Within the wall stood an enormous triumphal arch which was built some 200 years earlier; only the foundations remain to indicate its great size, but it would once have been visible many miles out to sea.

Sandwich is one of the ancient Cinque Ports and is a town full of historical interest. It is not a big place, and one of the best ways of seeing it is to follow the Sandwich Town Trail. Your starting point is the **Guildhall**, built in 1579 and enlarged in 1912 and in 1973, when the New Hall and offices were added. It is the third Guildhall, the previous one being sited on what is now St Peter's churchyard, and the original having almost certainly stood between King Street and The Chain, in the area behind the Old Parsonage.

It is well worth taking the time to seek out some of the fascinating historical pieces here in the Guildhall. One of these is the Moot Horn, which is brass and 'of great antiquity', and has been used to summon the people of Sandwich to hear important announcements from as far back as the 12th century. Today, it is still used to announce the death of a sovereign and the accession of the new. Then there is the Hog Mace, which, as the name implies, was used to round up straying animals after the Goose Bell had rung from St Peter's Church at 4.00am. All such animals, if not re-possessed by their owners on payment of a fine, passed to the Brothers and Sisters of St John's Hospital. The evening curfew at 8.00pm is still rung every day, continuing a tradition going back some 800 years.

As you explore the narrow mediaeval streets, you will pass many buildings of historic importance; indeed, the entire town centre has been declared a conservation area. Guarding the northern entrance to the town is the Barbican Gate, a turreted 16th century gatehouse on the quayside. Sandwich is now almost two miles from the sea, and although its days as a major port have long since passed, it continues to be used as an inland berth by a colourful array of yachts and cruisers. Places that you should make a point of seeing include the Guildhall, the Dutch House in King Street, Strand Street with its fine timbered houses, Sandwich's three mediaeval churches, and St Bartholomew's Hospital at the far end of New Street, originally founded in the 12th century and consisting of a quadrangle of almshouses grouped around the old chapel.

Yes, the sandwich was 'invented' here! John Montagu, the 4th Earl of Sandwich. Dissolute and corrupt, perhaps the only worthwhile thing that Montagu did in his life was to order a slice of beef between two pieces of bread as a substitute for a more conventional meal - a snack he could eat without having to leave the gambling table. Thus the Great British Sandwich was born!

As we explore this particular part of the Kentish coast, it would be an appropriate time to mention the **Cinque Ports** once more; the collective name for the ports of Romney, Hythe, Dover, Sandwich and Hastings. These five ports were given a number of special privileges under royal sanction, in return for providing armed ships and men at the monarch's request.

Henry III bestowed a Royal Charter on the towns in 1260, and towards the end of the 13th century, during the reign of Edward I, they achieved their full commercial potential. A downturn in trade and traffic was apparent by the middle of the 14th century, and the ports suffered heavily as a result of French looting in the 1370s. However, with Britain's love of the traditional and occasionally superfluous, the office of Lord Warden of the Cinque Ports still exists today. The official residence of the Warden was at Walmer Castle.

The charming fishing town of **Deal** has altered very little in character since the 18th century. The fact that its beach is of shingle rather than sand meant that it escaped Victorian development into a full-blown seaside resort of the 'bucket and spade' variety. The fishing trade has always played a major role along this coastline, and the roots of the industry are still very much in evidence today.

The seafront is one of the most picturesque to be found anywhere on the South-East coast, and with its quiet alleyways, traditional cottages and houses (many of them colour-washed), and shingle beach festooned with fishing boats, Deal is a delightful place to explore.

The quiet waters just off the coast are known as The Downs, and they create a safe natural anchorage for shipping that may otherwise run aground on the treacherous Goodwin Sands. The Sands have been the setting for hundreds of tragic shipwrecks throughout the centuries, and the sad sight of 'drowned' ships with their masts poking above the water is still in evidence at low tide, serving as a permanent reminder of the darker side of the sea. As many as 50,000 men may have perished on these Sands, and there are many tales of 'ghost ships' having been sighted here.

A good way of learning more about these aspects of the town's past is to take the time to visit its various museums. In St George's Road, in stables once used to house army mules, is the **Maritime and Local History Museum**, where a large collection of models, pictures and other memorabilia relate the maritime history of the town. Also on display are a number of original boats constructed by local boat builders up until the turn of the century. The Costume and Accessories Museum, a personal collection of original costumes and accessories put together by Doris Salter, can be found in a private house at 18 Gladstone Road; while in the Town Hall is the Victoriana Museum, its displays of toys, dolls, china, ornaments and jewellery from the Victorian and Edwardian eras illustrating the growth of the 19th century souvenir trade.

You should also look out for the distinctive **Timeball Tower** near the (landward) end of the pier. Built in 1795 to give time signals to ships in the Channel, the four-storey tower had a curious device whereby a black copper ball was dropped down its central shaft to register 1.00pm Greenwich Mean Time each day - so sailors would always know when it was lunchtime! The original timeball was replaced by the modern radio time signal, but a replica ball now drops down the shaft on the hour. On the fourth floor of the building there is a museum devoted to time and telegraphy, including working models.

Close to the Timeball Tower is **Deal Castle** with its distinctive 'lily-pad' shape (you may have to take an aerial trip to fully appreciate this description!), which was built by Henry VIII during the early 1540s. The castle was actually designed to resemble a Tudor Rose, and was the largest in a chain of five coastal defences built along the south-east coast against possible French invasion. The ruins of another of these, Sandown Castle, can be seen at the northern end of town; its few remaining buttresses holding out valiantly against the encroaching sea. Deal Castle was built very specifically as a war bastion, and with

119 guns trained across the sea, it must have been a formidable sight. A permanent exhibition here describes Henry VIII's various castles and their defensive role throughout history.

Just three minutes away from the Castle is **The Canongate Guest House** in Gilford Road. The house was built at the beginning of the century on the site of the old harbour. At that time it was a private residence, but is now a comfortable, unpretentious family guest house where Ena Beer has five guest rooms, one of which is en-suite.

Ena runs the house and does all the cooking, making sure that she keeps everyone happy. She is an excellent cook and will provide evening meals if requested. Whenever possible, Ena uses fresh produce when preparing her meals. The bedrooms are all well furnished and have television and tea and coffee making facilities. Children are very welcome and you can also bring your dog with you, providing it is well behaved.

The Canongate Guest House, 2 8 Gilford Road, Deal, Kent
0304-375238 Map Ref :4G

Just to the south of the Castle, Deal merges almost imperceptibly into neighbouring **Walmer**, and we thought it would be interesting to compare the castle here with its larger 'sister'. **Walmer Castle** was another of Henry VIII's five coastal defences - the other two being Sandgate and Camber (the latter just over the border into East Sussex), which, like Sandown, are both in ruins.

From Walmer the **A258** led us gradually inland to the village of **Ringwould**. The land here runs along a ridge that gave us splendid views of the rolling Downlands. Ringwould's village church was built around 1628 and has a distinctive 'onion'-capped roof; a type more usually seen in the county of Lincolnshire. Just off the road in a dramatic wooded setting is the ruined Oxney Court, and several gravestones to the La Coste family who lived here can be found in the wooded edge.

The Five Bells, run by Mr. and Mrs. Glasson in Front Street is about 300 years old and has low ceilings and open fires; just the place to enjoy a drink and, as we discovered later, an excellent meal. The pub was once a farm dwelling, brewing its own ales, and it was also a toll house.

All the food is home-cooked, with fish being the speciality of the house. If you have a particular favourite, you will find that you can choose from cod, rock salmon, prawns or plaice; some caught locally.

The two cottages only have one bedroom each, they will both sleep four with the aid of a bed settee in the lounge. They are fully equipped, with particularly nice kitchens. They have in fact been converted from a barn and still retain the stable doors; this has been done most effectively. Here you will have everything you need for a super holiday; including, of course, the close proximity of The Five Bells to Kingsdown Golf Course which is just a mile away. There are also some lovely walks; try ambling along the white cliffs or Freedown, both of which are within easy reach of the village.

The Five Bells, Front Street, Ringwould, Near Deal, Kent
0304-373489 Map Ref :5G

About a mile and a half to the south of Ringwould, leaving the **A258** and heading back towards the coast once more to discover the lovely hidden cove of **St Margaret's Bay** . Although the cliffs at Dover are meant to be the stuff of poetry and patriotic songs, to our minds those at St Margaret's seem higher, whiter, lonelier, and more impressive in every way; perhaps it is simply that they are less well-known and that you have more space to appreciate them. This is England's nearest point to France - some 21 miles away - and has been used as the starting and finishing place for many of those brave souls who have taken it into their heads to swim the Channel.

301

A steep road takes you down to the bay from the clifftop village, **St Margaret's-at-Cliffe** . On the day of our visit, the sun shone, the sea was almost turquoise, and the sudden glimpse of water through the trees looked as beautiful as any picture postcard.

Back on the A258, it is now just a short drive into the ancient town of **Dover**, our major cross-Channel port. Known as the 'Gateway to England' to those coming in, it is also one of the major routes to Europe for those going out. From here you can take a jetfoil, hovercraft or ferry to Calais, Boulogne, Zeebrugge or Ostend, and your choice of transport will soon be extended to include the new giant catamarans - although for our part, we were more than happy to stay in Dover a while!

Dating back to 1180, the massive Dover Castle sits astride a high hill above the clifftops, dominating the town from almost every angle. It was here on the site of an Iron Age fort that the Normans built this impressive stronghold during the last years of Henry II's reign at the then colossal cost of nearly £7,000, and today it ranks among the greatest fortresses in Western Europe.

Apart from an impressive 19th century scale model of the Battle of Waterloo which is displayed in one of the first floor rooms, the chambers and passageways are relatively bare - yet the Castle exerts a forceful presence and it is not hard to visualise it as a busy working garrison, teeming with life. It is the sort of place where you are sorely tempted to run around like an excited child from room to room, playing at knights, totally oblivious to the reproachful stares of your fellow visitors!

Of course, Dover has many other attractions besides its castle. One of the most popular of these, **The Roman Painted House**, can be found in New Street in the centre of the town. The main features of this Roman town house are a complex system of underfloor heating and the most beautifully preserved painted walls. First discovered in 1970, the house has won various awards for the way in which it has been preserved, and excavation is currently still in progress. One of the team, Wendy Williams, has put together a very special display using the features of those who once lived here. Working on the skulls excavated at the site, she has painstakingly built up their features to produce an uncanny group of extremely lifelike faces. We look forward to visiting the site again sometime to see what other Roman artifacts are unearthed here.

At first sight, the **Victorian Town Hall** in the High Street may not look as though it warrants any special attention, but if you step inside you will find that it incorporates the magnificent Maison Dieu, a hostel for Canterbury pilgrims which was originally founded in

Roman Lighthouse, Dover.

1203. Beneath the building lie the cells of Dover Old Town Gaol, now open to the public throughout the year. Starting in the Court Room, your tour will take you back in time to the horrors of prison life during the Victorian era, including a visit to the exercise yard, washroom and cells. The prisoners and gaolers themselves relate their stories to you, courtesy of 'hi-tech' talking heads and the very latest animation and audio-visual techniques.

While you are in the town centre, you can hardly fail to notice the modern glass and chrome building facing the Market Square, which houses Dover's exciting visitor attraction. It is called **The White Cliffs Experience**. Here you will find yourself being drawn into 'live' action here. You can chat to a centurion, encounter the warring Cantiacii tribe who greeted the Roman invaders, experience life as a galley slave, and wander through the rubble of a typical Dover street after it has endured the horrors of a World War II air raid attack.

All this and more takes place in the 'Historium', and in addition there is a Museum with three floors full of displays on the history of Dover from its earliest beginnings to the present day; the Archaeological 'Gardens' featuring the remains of the Norman church of St Martin-le-Grand and those of the 'Classis Brittanica', the headquarters of the Roman fleet in England; together with a cinema, a themed restaurant and coffee shop, a top-floor research centre which is open to visitors, an educational resource centre and a gift shop. All in all, this is a stimulating and unforgettable experience which all members of the family will enjoy - and you will need to set aside several hours of the day to fully appreciate all that the attraction has to offer.

The best way to enjoy Dover's premier attractions is to purchase a 'Passport to Dover' from the Tourist Information Centre at the White Cliffs Experience. You will find this both convenient and kind to your pocket, for the enclosed vouchers will give you access to the 'Experience' itself, Dover Museum, the Roman Painted House, the Old Town Gaol and Dover Castle. The savings are quite substantial, and don't worry - you won't have to rush round all these attractions in a day as the vouchers can be used whenever you wish, subject to the time limit indicated at the time of purchase.

Heading north, just off the **A2** is **Denton**, a charming village with a green surrounded by pretty half-timbered cottages. The handsome 18th century Denton Court can be found next to the church. Set in some 200 acres, this Victorian mansion was frequently stayed in by the poet Thomas Gray, of 'Elegy' fame.

Exploring the country roads to the west of the **A2** was a delight, as the charming cottages surrounded by pleasant green hedgerows and trees is a tonic to the city dweller. Some of the prettier villages we passed through were Barham , and the hamlets of Bishopsbourne and Lower Hardres. Bishopsbourne boasts a particularly fine Queen Anne residence, and a rectory which was once home to the writer Joseph Conrad.

The Hardres family gave their name to the villages of Upper and **Lower Hardres** (pronounced 'Hards'), and were landowners here for 700 years following the Norman Conquest. The Domesday Book mentions Robert de Hardres, and later in Henry VIII's reign, Thomas Hardres assisted the king in the seige of Boulogne. With the falling of the city, Hardres brought back the city gates as a souvenir!

Giles and Phillipa Hilton run **The Granville Inn** at Lower Hardres. It is an attractive place; the front part of the building dates back to 1780 and inside, the old oak beams reflect the age. For those of you who enjoy real ale, you will discover that the Master Brew bitter from the privately owned Shepherd Neame Faversham Brewery will tempt you into more than one pint - that is if you are not driving, of course.

The restaurant, which is only open in the evenings from 7.15pm Monday to Saturday with last orders at 9.15pm, has room for 54 covers. The menu is extensive, and if you had dinner there every evening for a month or more, you would still not get bored. Exciting starters like Stilton and Spinach Pancakes set the scene for the main course, which could for example be Duck with Ginger and Pineapple or Honey and Chestnut Sauce. The sweets are equally tempting, with perhaps a Strawberry and Coffee Roulade.

The Granville Inn, Street End, Lower Hardres, Nr Canterbury, Kent CT4 2HY 0227 70402 Map Ref :2D

Petham lies south-west of Lower Hardres on the other side of the Roman road called Stone Street, or the **B2068** to give it its somewhat less evocative modern name. The countryside hereabouts is really lovely, and with the views of the hills glimpsed through the trees, you know you are truly in the heart of rural Kent. Close to the village Upper Ansdore Farmhouse is a particularly pleasant place to stay.

Upper Ansdore Farmhouse dates from the 14th century and has recently been converted to provide accommodation on the first floor. From here you can witness the fine views of the valley. The house once belonged to Sir William Cockaine, a former Lord Mayor of London in 1619, and was mentioned in Hasted's History of Kent. The house overlooks a Kent trust for nature, which enhances the already idyllic situation. Roger and Susan Linch have two en-suite guest rooms and offer bed and breakfast to those fortunate enough to stay here. One room is twin bedded whilst the other offers double bed with an extra single bed. Facilities include an open plan sitting and dining room with a modern kitchen with built in oven and hob as well as bathroom and shower. Upper Ansdore is a non-smoking establishment. In addition to this Mr. and Mrs. Linch offer a self-catering barn. They are open from Easter to October. To find Upper Ansdore from Canterbury, take the B2068 and after approximately three and a half miles turn right at the signpost to Petham. In the village, take the left-hand fork by the telephone box, and one and a half miles along this lane, take the first turning on the right where you come to a no-through road. Upper Ansdore is the last house. Within easy reach of the golf course at Canterbury and 30 minutes from Dover and with two local village pubs and restaurant Upper Ansdore Farmhouse is an ideal touring base for your holiday.

Upper Ansdore Farmhouse, Duckpit Lane, Petham, Kent CT4 5QB
0227-700672 Map Ref : 3D

Two miles south-west of here is **Waltham**. This village is situated on fairly high ground, and is yet another place which has close associations with the ancient order of the Knights Templar. In fact, the village was originally known as Temple Waltham.

Heading south-east from here through North Leigh, we crossed Stone Street once more and came to **Stelling Minnis**. The name 'Minnis' (which crops up several times in this part of Kent) indicates that the land is rough common or moorland, and indeed the surrounding countryside is a rough terrain of grass, bracken and gorse. If you park your car in the village you can wander down the dirt track to see the tarred weatherboarded smock windmill that was built here in 1866. Operational until 1970, it is now open to the public on Sundays and Bank Holiday Saturdays and Mondays in the afternoon, from April to September. From here, the Forestry Commission trails lead you into the dark pine woods of Lyminge Forest. Whether you appreciate the merits of pine forests or not, the paths are well set out and give the walker or horse-rider several miles of traffic-free pleasure.

If, however, you prefer more open spaces to ramble in, then one of the most glorious parts of the county is close at hand. West of Stone Street and the Forest, the lanes lead you through the delightfully remote villages of **Elmsted** and **Hastingleigh** , and on to Wye at the foot of the downs. Wye nestles under the North Downs in the valley of the Great Stour, which flows through lovely countryside from Ashford to Canterbury and on to the sea at Sandwich. Here you will find yourself in a true walker's paradise.

Wye Downs are composed of a series of chalk hills, and the panoramic views over the surrounding countryside are truly spectacular. The trail we chose to follow led us around a rim shaped like a horseshoe. Buffeted by the wind, we looked down into a small hidden valley that seemed impossible to get to as the sides were so steep. A convenient series of steps have in fact been cut into the hill to make this achievable, but as all casual strollers learn to their cost - it's a lot easier going down than coming up!

Wye itself is an attractive market town which can be found by turning off the **A28** Ashford to Canterbury Road, three miles out of Ashford. It is steeped in history and is a delightful place to stay for a while, absorbing everything around you and perhaps taking time to visit the Romney, Hythe and Dymchurch Railway and the Romney Marshes, Dover Castle or historic Rye, all of which are no great distance away.

Wye is also the home of the famous Agricultural College, which is affiliated to the Universty of London. The beautiful College buildings were built by John Kempe, who was born in the town in 1380 and went on to become Archbishop of Canterbury.

At Spring Grove Farm Charles and Liz Amos have carried out the sympathetic conversion (with assistance from the English Tourist Board) of an old oast house to top quality holiday homes on their 100-acre farm, which is within walking distance of Wye. The conversion offers six luxurious and spacious properties, designed to give maximum comfort with splendid views of the surrounding countryside, whilst maintaining the fine character of a traditional building. There are one and a half acres of landscaped gardens, an all-weather tennis court, a heated outdoor swimming pool, a games room with table tennis and darts, and laundry facilities.

The needs of wildlife have been taken into account in the management of this farm, and four acres have been set aside by the river as a wetland conservation area, where wading birds, as well as geese, swans and ducks may be seen during migration periods. Visitors are encouraged to take an interest in the farm and may walk anywhere they like. It really is a splendid area; you can walk the North Downs Way and the Wye circular walk, both of which cross the farm, and a farm trail will take you on an exploration through the fields. You can fish on the private bank of the River Stour, and riding can be arranged with a local stable. Clay pigeon shooting, or rough or game shooting in season, are also available. You can visit the Wye and Crundale National Nature Reserve, which as we mentioned above is famous for its orchids and overlooks Wye on the top of the Downs. Or you can simply relax by the swimming pool.

Did You Know...

There is a full list of
Tourist Information Centres
at the back of the book?

You will find that Wye is right in the heart of Kent, just 60 miles from London, with Ashford four miles away and the splendid cathedral city of Canterbury 12 miles away. Access to the M2 and M20 is simple, and Wye has a railway station with a direct service to London.

Heading south-east from Wye, we purposefully avoided the relative ease of the M20 in favour of the more interesting minor roads to the north of the motorway. These led us through such villages as Brabourne, Stowting, Etchinghill and Paddlesworth with its tiny church.

Our final stop was at **Folkestone**, the second busiest cross-Channel port on the south coast. What is most unusual about this particular seaside resort is that it does not have a recognizable seafront as such; instead, it has The Leas, a series of delightful clifftop lawns and flower gardens with a distinctly Mediterranean feel to them, which run for a mile and a half from the centre of town towards Sandgate to the west. A water-driven lift takes residents from the clifftop hotels to the beach below, and the warm south-facing aspect makes this a very pleasant area to explore.

Much of Folkestone's history is conveniently 'condensed' into an area known as 'The Lanterns' on the Sandgate Road. The attractions centred in this part of town are many and varied. The Bayle was once the site of an ancient fort, and the lovely 13th century church of St Mary and St Eanswythe (the oldest building in Folkestone) stands nearby. The bones of the latter patron saint are buried here.

Church Street, formerly called Mercery Lane, was home to the traders of silk and cloth, and William Harvey, one of England's most famous physicians, was born here in 1578. Perhaps Harvey's greatest gift to medicine was his discovery of the circulation of the blood; his statue can be seen near the centre of The Leas, appropriately clutching a human heart in his hand. It would seem, however, that all of Harvey's skills in the world of medicine came to naught when it came to his own fate, for he is reputed to have committed suicide in 1657 after discovering that he was going blind.

Westbourne Gardens is a quiet road tucked behind The Leas and it was here that, once again on recommendation, we came to **The Horseshoe Hotel.** Mrs Newman, our hostess, is friendly and helpful and chatted to us about all the special breaks arranged. One that particularly appealed to us was two nights bed and breakfast with dinner upon arrival, and a full day in France with a tour to and from the harbour.

The Horseshoe Hotel, 29 Westbourne Gardens, Folkestone
CT20 2HY 0303 43433 Map Ref : 7E

309

All of the 10 bedrooms have colour television, tea and coffe
making facilities and wash hand basins. In addition, two of the room
are en-suite. The hotel is also centrally heated, so it is ideal for a
winter break. There are special terms available for people over 65 wh
wish to stay for two days or more, and not just in winter. This specia
facility is available any time except over Christmas.Meals are serve
in the spacious dining room from an ever changing menu of goo
English cooking. Mrs Newman insists on using only fresh seasona
produce, so delicious dishes are the norm at the Horseshoe.

One of Folkestone's most popular tourist attractions is th
Eurotunnel Exhibition Centre, which can be found to the north o
the town just off Junction 12 of the M20. A special viewing towe
overlooks the Channel Tunnel terminal site here, and the exhibitio
includes a superb model railway, an interactive map of Europe, a
tunnel boring machine and many other items used during th
construction, and a full size shuttle wagon to walk round.

Everything in the main hall is designed to give you the experienc
of actually going through the system - and no doubt cynics woul
advise you to make the most of it just in case the real thing is neve
completed! The exhibition also explains the various historical attempt
that have been made to forge a channel link with our Europea
neighbours. Napoleon himself thought it would be an excellent idea
although Henry VIII was obviously not quite so keen!

From Folkestone it a short journey to **Hythe**. The recorde
history of Hythe goes back to 732 AD, when Ethelred, king of th
Saxons, first granted it a charter. Its name means 'landing place', an
the town once played an important role as one of the five Cinqe Ports
Its decline in this respect came with the silting up of its harbou
which left it completely high and dry - it is now over half a mile fron
the sea and no trace of the harbour remains.

A mile to the north of Hythe is **Saltwood Castle**, whicl
although not open to the public can be seen from a nearby bridleway
It was once the residence of the Archbishop of Canterbury, and it wa
here that Becket's murderers stayed the night on their way fron
France to do the evil deed. More recently it was the home of the lat
Lord Clark, the famous art historian and presenter of the pioneerin
television series, 'Civilisation'. His son, Alan Clark MP, still lives her
today.

From Hythe heading along the **A259** and you can make you
way down the coast towards **Dymchurch** . At various points alon
the road, you will notice those decidedly odd and not especiall
attractive buildings, the **Martello Towers**. Looking more like th
truncated cooling towers of a modern power station than the pride o

Britain's defence against Napoleon, there were at one time 74 of these massive 'pepper pots' positioned along the coast. Their name derives from the fact that they were constructed along the lines of a tower at Cape Mortella in Corsica; an ironic choice of model bearing in mind that Napoleon himself was born on that particular island!

At one time a quiet, secluded village, Dymchurch has now been transformed into a busy seaside resort. Amusement arcades, gift shops and cafes line the road, and you need to park the car and clamber over the formidable Dymchurch Wall before you can even catch a glimpse of the reason why everybody comes here! The sea-wall is the only thing that prevents the sea from flooding both town and marsh - Dymchurch lies about seven and a half feet below high-tide level - and a barrier of one sort or another has existed here since the Romans came to Kent.

The next village along the coast road from Dymchurch is **St Mary's Bay** , which is largely given over to holiday homes, seaside amusements and a holiday camp, and is famous for its sandy beach. About two miles inland to the west is the small hamlet of **St Mary-in-the-Marsh** , where we came across two more literary connections.

The locals love **The Star Inn** and guard its traditions zealously. Darts, crib, chess, shove ha'penny and pub quizzes keep them well occupied whilst they enjoy the well kept ale or perhaps a glass of very good 'own label' house wine. Food is high on the priority list, with some first rate dishes on offer. Try the Asparagus Mornay; the sauce is creamy and beautifully flavoured, or perhaps the Bubble and Squeak, which is a very popular house speciality.

The Star Inn, St Mary-in-the-Marsh, New Romney, Kent
0679-62139 Map Ref : 6C

Staying at The Star Inn is a real pleasure. There are five letting rooms, three of which are en-suite, and each is delightfully decorated and very comfortable. With a super breakfast as part of the price, you

311

will find rates for both single and double en-suite rooms very good value for money. Such reasonable terms will enable you to enjoy some very convivial, well-fed evenings and days of sheer pleasure spent wandering along the many footpaths, exploring the Martello towers, and perhaps taking a drive into Folkestone or Hythe, just nine miles and six miles away respectively.

Back on the **A259** and still heading south, we came to the peaceful little town of **New Romney** ; 'capital' of the Marsh, one of the five original Cinque Ports, and headquarters of the Romney, Hythe & Dymchurch Railway. We spent some time in the station here - which you will find roughly midway between the town and the seafront - looking at the workshops and the various engines in their sheds. If you are keen on even smaller scale models, then you will also find the Romney Toy & Model Museum here. Vintage models, toys and photographs are on display, and there are two working model railways to enjoy.

A great storm in 1287 diverted the course of the River Rother and choked it with shingle, causing it to flow into the sea at Rye and leaving the port of Romney without a harbour. To see just how high the flood waters rose, you have only to visit the splendid Norman church of St Nicholas, where the floodmarks can be seen high up on the pillars inside. This disaster was a severe blow to the town's former days of glory as one of the most important of the Cinque Ports.

New Romney was to be our last stop on our journey of the South East. The Kent countryside still thrives, bravely coping with those of us who come armed with maps and guides to see the county at its best - and in many places it is still outstandingly beautiful. But change is inevitable, despite even the most energetic efforts of those who fight for preservation and conservation. We hope, therefore, that this personal tour of ours may in some small way inspire you to go out there and see it now, before yet another part of it is lost forever.

Tourist Information Centres

ARUNDEL, High Street 0903 882268
ASHFORD, 18 The Churchyard 0233 629165

BATTLE, 88 High Street 0424 773721
BEXHILL-ON-SEA, De La Warr Pavillion, Marina 0424 212023
BOGNOR REGIS, Belmont Street 0243 823140
BOSHIP, Boship Roundabout (A22), Hailsham 0323 442667
BRIGHTON, 10 Bartholomew Square 0273 323755
BROADSTAIRS, 67 High Street 0843 862242

CANTERBURY, 34 St Margaret's Street 0227 766567
CHERITON, Eurotunnel Exhibition Centre, St Martins Plain,
Cherton High Street 0303 270547
CHICHESTER, St Peter's Market, West Street 0243 775888
CRANBROOK, Vestry Hall, Stone Street 0580 712538

DARTFORD, The Clocktower, Suffolk Road 0322 343243
DEAL, Town Hall, High Street 0304 369576
DOVER, Townwall Street, 0304 205108

EASTBOURNE, Cornfield Road, 0323 411400

FARNHAM, Vernon St, 28 West Street 0252 715109
FARTHING CORNER SERVICES, M2 Motorway, Gillingham
0634 360323
FAVERSHAM, Fleur de Lis Heritage Centre, 13 Preston Street
0795 534542
FOLKESTONE, Harbour Street 0303 258594
FONTWELL, Little Chef Complex 0243 543269

GATWICK, International Arrivals Concours, South Terminal
0293 560108
GRAVESEND, 10 Parrock Street 0474 337600
GUILDFORD, The Undercroft, 72 High St, 0483 444007

HAILSHAM, The Library, Western Road 0323 840604
HASTINGS, 4 Robertson Terrace, 0424 718888
HERNE BAY, Central Bandstand, Central Parade 0227 361911
HORSHAM, 9 Causeway 0403 211661
HOVE, King Alfred Leisure Centre, Kingway 0273 746100

HOVE, Norton Road 0273 778087
HYTHE, Prospect Road Car Park, 0303 267799

LEWES, Lewes House, High Street 0273 483448
LITTLEHAMPTON, Windmill Complex, Coastguard Road
0903 713480

MAIDSTONE, The Gatehouse, The Old Palace Gates
0622 673581
MARGATE, 22 High Street, 0843 220241

NEW ROMNEY, Light Railway Car Park, 2 Littlestone Road
0679 64044

PEACEHAVEN, Meridian Centre, Roderick Avenue
0273 582668
PEVENSEY, Pevensey Castle, High Street 0323 761444

RAMSGATE, Argyle Centre, Queen Street 0843 591086
RYE, The Heritage Centre, Strand Quay 0797 226696

SANDWICH, The Guildhall, Cattle Market 0304 613565
SEAFORD, Station Approach 0323 897426
SEVENOAKS, Buckhurst Lane 0732 450305
SHEERNESS, Bridge Road Car Park 0795 665324

TENTERDEN, Town Hall, High St 0580 63572
TONBRIDGE, Tonbridge Castle, Castle Street 0732 770929
TUNBRIDGE WELLS, Monson House, Monson Way
0892 515675

WHITSTABLE, The Horsebridge,0227 275482
WORTHING, Chapel Road 0903 210022

Town Index

THE HIDDEN PLACES

If you would like to have any of the titles currently available in this series, please complete this coupon and send to:

M & M Publishing Ltd
Tryfan House, Warwick Drive,
Hale, Altrincham, Cheshire, WA15 9EA

	Each	Qty
Somerset, Avon and Dorset	£ 5.90	......
Yorkshire and Humberside	£ 5.90	......
Devon and Cornwall	£ 5.90	......
North Yorkshire	£ 5.90	......
The Lake District	£ 5.90	......
Southern and Central Scotland	£ 5.90	......
Hampshire and the Isle of Wight	£ 5.90	......
The Cotswolds (Gloucestershire & Wiltshire)	£ 5.90	......
Thames and Chilterns	£ 5.90	......
East Anglia (Norfolk & Suffolk)	£ 5.90	......
Lancashire & Cheshire	£ 5.90	......
Hereford & Worcester	£ 5.90	......
Northumberland & Durham	£ 5.90	......
North Wales	£ 5.90	......
South Wales	£ 5.90	......
Set of any Five	£20.00	
	Total £	

Price includes Postage and Packing

NAME..

ADDRESS..

....

................................POST CODE....................................

Please make cheques payable to: M & M Publishing Ltd

NOTES.

NOTES.

NOTES.

NOTES.

NOTES.